Praise for *Women and the War*

'This is a significant book on Boko ...., ...,..... ... role or women and girls in the insurgency in north-east Nigeria, and the gendered impacts of the enormous humanitarian crisis which the conflict has produced.'
Adam Higazi, University of Amsterdam

'An original, innovative, and much-needed addition to the growing literatures on both women and conflict in Africa and the Boko Haram insurgency.'
Brandon Kendhammer, Ohio University

'Provides an important corrective to the general reporting on women associated with Boko Haram. As Matfess persuasively argues, improving the position of women and increasing gender equality in north-eastern Nigeria will surely support efforts to bring peace to the region.'
Elisha Renne, University of Michigan (Emerita)

Theodore Trefon, *Congo's Environmental Paradox: Potential and Predation in a Land of Plenty*

Paul Richards, *Ebola: How a People's Science Helped End an Epidemic*

Louisa Lombard, *State of Rebellion: Violence and Intervention in the Central African Republic*

Kris Berwouts, *Congo's Violent Peace: Conflict and Struggle Since the Great African War*

Forthcoming titles

Odd-Helge Fjelstad, Wilson Prichard and Mick Moore, *Taxing Africa*

Celeste Hicks, *The Trial of Hissène Habré*

Ebenezer Obadare, *Religion and Politics in Nigeria*

Published by Zed Books and the IAI with the support of the following organizations:

The principal aim of the **International African Institute** is to promote scholarly understanding of Africa, notably its changing societies, cultures and languages. Founded in 1926 and based in London, it supports a range of seminars and publications including the journal *Africa*.
www.internationalafricaninstitute.org

Now more than a hundred years old, the **Royal African Society** today is Britain's leading organization promoting Africa's cause. Through its journal, *African Affairs*, and by organizing meetings, discussions and other activities, the society strengthens links between Africa and Britain and encourages understanding of Africa and its relations with the rest of the world.
www.royalafricansociety.org

The **World Peace Foundation**, founded in 1910, is located at the Fletcher School, Tufts University. The Foundation's mission is to promote innovative research and teaching, believing that these are critical to the challenges of making peace around the world, and should go hand in hand with advocacy and practical engagement with the toughest issues. Its central theme is 'reinventing peace' for the twenty-first century.
www.worldpeacefoundation.org

About the author

Hilary Matfess is a research analyst, working on issues of governance, security and gender. She is a PhD candidate at Yale University in the Political Science Department and a contributor to the Nigeria Social Violence Project at the Johns Hopkins University School of Advanced International Studies, and has previously worked as a Senior Program Officer at the Center for Democracy and Development in Nigeria. Her work has been featured in *International Security, Foreign Affairs, Newsweek* and *The Washington Post*.

WOMEN AND THE WAR ON BOKO HARAM

WIVES, WEAPONS, WITNESSES

HILARY MATFESS

In association with
International African Institute
Royal African Society
World Peace Foundation

ZED

Women and the War on Boko Haram: Wives, Weapons, Witnesses was first published in 2017 by Zed Books Ltd, The Foundry, 17 Oval Way, London SE11 5RR, UK.

www.zedbooks.net

Typeset in Haarlemmer by seagulls.net
Index by Rohan Bolton
Cover design by Jonathan Pelham
Cover photo © Chris de Bode/Panos

A catalogue record for this book is available from the British Library

ISBN 978-1-78699-146-1 hb
ISBN 978-1-78699-145-4 pb
ISBN 978-1-78699-147-8 pdf
ISBN 978-1-78699-148-5 epub
ISBN 978-1-78699-149-2 mobi

MIX
Paper from
responsible sources
FSC® C013604
www.fsc.org

Printed and bound by CPI Group (UK) Ltd, Croydon, CR0 4YY

To my parents, who always say 'yes, and ...'
rather than 'no, but ...' BBKF.

CONTENTS

GLOSSARY AND LIST OF ACRONYMS

Almajirai   a term for Qur'anic students in northern Nigeria who are sent away from their homes to study with imams, often in urban centres – they are the subject of much debate and concern

APC   All Progressives Congress

Aqidah   the beliefs of Islam; also a religious term meaning 'creed'

AQIM   Al-Qaeda in the Maghreb

AUN   American University of Nigeria

Bayat   an Islamic term for allegiance

CEDAW   Convention on the Elimination of All Forms of Discrimination against Women

CJTF   Civilian Joint Task Force

DDR   disarmament, demobilisation and reintegration, a process through which combatants are brought back into society at the end of conflict

DFID   Department for International Development

DRC   Democratic Republic of the Congo

FARC   Revolutionary Armed Forces of Colombia

FOMWAN   Federation of Muslim Women's Associations in Nigeria

GEP   gender equality programming

Hijab   a head covering that many Muslim women wear

ICVA   International Council of Voluntary Agencies

Iddah	the period of waiting that women observe after a divorce before they can take a new husband
IDP	internally displaced person
ISIL	the Islamic State in Iraq and the Levant, also known as IS (the Islamic State)
JAS	an alternative name for Boko Haram, Jamā'at Ahl as-Sunnah lid-da'wa wal-Jihād
Jihad	a 'struggle or fight against the enemies of Islam'
LRA	Lord's Resistance Army, a long-running insurgency in Uganda
Malam	a Hausa term, taken from Arabic, to refer to a man or teacher well versed in the Qur'an
MSF	Médecins Sans Frontières, an 'international, independent, medical humanitarian organisation' that provides care in conflict zones
NEMA	National Emergency Management Agency
NGO	non-governmental organisation
Niqab	a veil for the face that leaves only the eyes uncovered
NPC	National Population Commission
NPF	Nigerian Police Force
NPR	National Public Radio
NSVP	Nigeria Social Violence Project
OCHA	UN Office for the Coordination of Humanitarian Affairs
PDP	People's Democratic Party
Purdah	the practice of female seclusion
RUF	Revolutionary United Front, a rebel army that fought in Sierra Leone from roughly 1991 to 2002
SEMA	State Emergency Management Agency
SGBV	sexual and gender-based violence
UN	United Nations
UNDP	United Nations Development Programme
UNHCR	United Nations High Commissioner for Refugees
VSF	Victims Support Fund

ACKNOWLEDGEMENTS

I would like to extend my sincere thanks to everyone who has helped me develop this fledgling idea into a book. I owe a great deal of thanks to the Hodson Trust, whose generous scholarship programme allowed me to pursue an education at the Johns Hopkins University. Had I not been selected as a recipient, I would have never attended the Homewood campus, nor enrolled in the five-year bachelor's/master's programme that took me to the Washington DC campus for my graduate studies. While pursuing my graduate degree, I benefited from the wonderful academic community at the Johns Hopkins University School of Advanced International Studies. Without the support of those at SAIS – especially Dr Peter Lewis – I would never have joined the Nigeria Social Violence Project or started studying events in Nigeria.

I would also like to thank the incredible community of Africa scholars and practitioners who have helped me along my way. Matthew Page has not only been an infinite source of knowledge of Nigerian facts, anecdotes and political networks, but is also a reservoir of humour and kindness that I am lucky to be able to draw upon. The support of Lesley Warner, who has acted as a mentor, advocate and friend, is an invaluable resource in helping to conduct fieldwork. The kind folks at the Center for Complex Operations at the National Defense University, especially Michael Miklaucic, are owed thanks for their support for my time abroad and for their patience in listening to my (often rambling) thoughts on security and governance in sub-Saharan Africa. I am indebted to Ambassador Reuben Brigety, whose guidance and encouragement is a constant source of motivation. Stephanie Burchard has acted not only as a sounding board for my ideas, but also as a role model. Brandon Kendhammer, Alexander Thurson and Nate D. F. Allen's feedback on early drafts of this book and related projects was invaluable. Similarly, not only was I inspired by the scholarship of Valerie Hudson, Mia Bloom and Marie E. Berry, but also so grateful for their encouragement of my research agenda.

Those who accompanied me on my fieldwork trips, and those who I met along the way, are owed a great deal of thanks. Joe Read, Michael Baca, Graeme Blair, Adam Higazi, Dionne Searcy and Jane Han provided wonderful insights and good company over drinks, during car rides, and in the sweltering Sahelian sun. Chitra Nagarajan and Chika Oduah were incredible sources of support, encouragement, information and company during my time in Maiduguri.

I am genuinely blessed to have come across such insightful and amiable people – and I am thrilled to call them friends.

The hospitality that I was extended during my visits to the region is difficult to convey. I am so appreciative of the assistance that the Wali of Adamawa State extended to me and to the help I received from Madinah mosque, because of the kindness of Khalifa Abulfathi. Similarly, I am grateful to all those who shared their time with me for interviews during my trips to the region. In particular, my interviews with Governor Kashim Shettima and Governor Bindo Jibrilla were extraordinarily enlightening. I also extend my thanks to the humanitarian workers and civil society advocates who spoke with me anonymously for their insights and time.

I am humbled to have been entrusted with the stories of so many northern Nigerians. In my conversations with those in host communities, in official camps and in transit, I was struck by their resilience and the incredible fortitude of the human spirit. I am deeply grateful that they confided in me; I hope that this text does justice to the complexity of the crisis that they have faced and to the magnitude of bravery of the communities across the region.

The editorial team at Zed Books was a genuine delight to work with; I am deeply grateful to Ken Barlow and Stephanie Kitchen of the International African Institute who oversaw this project from the beginning. The reviewers deepened my analysis and greatly improved the quality of my work and I want to extend my thanks to them for their time.

On a personal note, I want to thank those who helped me identify and pursue my passion. Without Tracy Roden, I would not have emerged from high school with such a clear sense of what course of study I wanted to pursue in college. Emma Backe has been a continuous source of support, affection and feminist inspiration. Finally, my parents have been the greatest source of support and unconditional love that I could ever have asked for.

It is important to note that I have chosen to use the first-person translation of my conversations with displaced people, community members, vigilantes and former insurgents. In using the English translation of their speech (often in Kanuri or Hausa), some fidelity is lost. However, I believe that this choice conveys individuals' experiences most effectively. I am deeply indebted to my translators, some of whom requested anonymity, for their assistance, not just in translating the conversations that I had, but also in contextualising them.

While it has not always been possible to include precise details of every encounter contributing to the book, fieldwork interviews have been referenced as accurately as possible as far as documentation has allowed.

All errors and shortcomings in the text remain the fault of the author.

INTRODUCTION

'They would tell the girls, "In heaven there is a special house for you made of glass," and that is how they got them to blow themselves up,' a Civilian Joint Task Force (CJTF) commander translated excitedly for me. I was interviewing a group of vigilantes to understand how Boko Haram managed to engage in so many female suicide bombings, recalling stories of adolescent and even prepubescent girls transformed into weapons in the markets and bus stations of Nigeria's north-east. The response to my question came from a boy who could not have been older than 15. The baby blue football jersey he was wearing and his shyness around strangers like me accentuated his youthfulness. Over the course of our interview, he revealed that he had been abducted by Boko Haram and had served as a driver for two years before he was able to escape. He made his way to Maiduguri, the capital of Borno State, where he joined the CJTF – a vigilante group that has fought alongside the Nigerian military in the state – as an informant.

Sitting across from me at an off-kilter plastic table under an unrelenting sun, he and the other vigilantes relayed what life was like on the front lines of the Boko Haram insurgency. Amid the stories of the insurgency's brutality, one striking feature of the conflict became evident: women and girls were central to understanding the crisis that was tearing apart the Lake Chad Basin. They fulfil a number of roles, serving as wives of the insurgents, weapons in the war, powerful symbols of both state and insurgent power, and witnesses to the violence and post-conflict rebuilding processes.

Other conversations I had during my visits to north-east Nigeria, with non-governmental organisation (NGO) workers, politicians and internally displaced persons (IDPs), highlighted a devastating feature of the north-east's social structure: by and large, women are excluded from influencing government policies and programmes. Their marginalisation became clear to me in the trips that I took to the country's seats of power, in government offices in the capital city of Abuja and in Governors' mansions in Adamawa and Borno, and in the makeshift shelters that have blossomed in the secure urban centres as the crisis has dragged on.

This project originated in work that I did to record incidences of lethal violence in Nigeria as part of the Nigeria Social Violence Project (NSVP) at the Johns Hopkins University School of Advanced International Studies. Culling newspaper reports from Nigeria and news outlets around the world for information relating to political, religious, state-led and communal violence in Nigeria since 1999 sparked an interest in understanding the motivations of those who joined the groups. Subsequent research in the field, as well as the media attention devoted to the Chibok abductions and the stunning rise in the use of female suicide bombers by Boko Haram, inspired me to examine the insurgency through the experiences of women.

The research for this book draws from the data I collected with NSVP, a desk review of relevant literature, and interviews conducted during multiple trips to the region between 2015 and 2016 and whilst living in Nigeria for the first half of 2017. Much of the desk review was based on NGO reports and 'grey literature', as the academic literature on Boko Haram is limited. While NGOs have their obvious biases and do not always adopt the best methodological practices, groups such as Mercy Corps, Human Rights Watch and Amnesty International have all gained reputations for probing and sound research. I have relied on these organisations, as well as on reports funded by USAID and the UK's Department for International Development (DFID), for significant portions of my research and to help inform the questions that I asked while conducting fieldwork.

I conducted interviews with IDPs living in informal settlements and government-run displacement camps in a number of cities, including Yola, Mubi, Damaturu, Abuja and Maiduguri. In the course of the project, I interviewed more than 50 women; some of these were cursory interviews, others were extensive, in-depth interviews that lasted several hours and were conducted over several days. I also interviewed 'host families' and 'host organisations' to better understand the strain that caring for IDPs can cause. The interviews were conducted one on one when conditions allowed, but were mostly with small groups of women, often from the same community, sharing their experiences. The most comprehensive interviews that I conducted were at a camp run by Governor Kashim Shettima in Maiduguri, which held more than 20 women who had joined the sect voluntarily and who maintained their loyalty even after being 'liberated' from insurgent control. Over the course of four days at this 'Safe House', I conducted interviews with more than six of these women. The small size of the camp often allowed for these interviews to be held individually.

In addition to these interviews with displaced people (generally women), I also interviewed a number of vigilantes in Yola and Maiduguri. These men (and some women) had fought alongside the Nigerian military and were able to provide insight into the ways in which the insurgency functions and the conditions in liberated areas. Again, a mixture of group and one-to-one interviews were conducted; in total, I spoke to roughly 30 vigilantes, and approximately six of these interviews were in-depth.

In Maiduguri, I travelled to the razed plot where Mohammed Yusuf's mosque once stood and interviewed members of the community who remembered what the area had been like before the state crackdown in 2009. I was also able to speak with members of the northern political elite, including the Governors of Borno and Adamawa States, as well as with a smattering of their staff. In addition to these politicians, I also spoke with members of groups such as the Borno Elders' Forum and the Victims' Support Fund. In planning and conducting my visits to IDP camps, I also interviewed humanitarian aid workers at both the managerial and implementation level responsible for providing care to IDPs. These NGO workers included both Nigerians and international staff. I also spoke with a number of advocacy NGO workers, and particularly with humanitarian aid workers. These workers are in short supply throughout the north but provided great insights about the condition of the women arriving at the camps.

Through these interviews, I found that women's exclusion from policy planning in the region is a result of the scarcity of female-focused civil society groups, as well as being influenced by the characteristics of some Nigerian politicians and international groups. While the contentious relationship between the #BringBackOurGirls movement and the administration of former President Goodluck Jonathan (whose wife tried to have some of the family members of abducted Chibok girls arrested for protesting outside government buildings in Abuja, the capital) was the most visible manifestation of the disconnect between the needs of women and the government, so-called 'women's issues' have been widely ignored by politicians throughout the country. Sprawling across the couch in the foyer of his residence in Yola, the otherwise charming Governor of Adamawa State told me that 'my wife is working on that problem [of women and girls]', with a wave of his hand. He then returned with gusto to describing the intricacies of the cattle market in his state. This attitude is shared by many who consider women's empowerment to be a luxury that they cannot afford when responding to the crisis in northern Nigeria.

It is important to note that, even when women's needs are recognised as important, policy programming to that end faces a number of challenges. The Governor of Borno State, Kashim Shettima, has identified that investments in women and girls are critical to overcoming the impacts of the insurgency; he asserted proudly that 'a deliberate policy of gender empowerment' guides his initiatives.[1] Shettima's emphasis on empowering women was not mere rhetoric

– it was incorporated during the planning of the 2016 Ramadan feeding scheme in Borno State, when 1,000 families in each of the state's 28 wards were targeted to receive food assistance. Given that the average family unit identified by the scheme contained 20 people, this was no small endeavour. The Governor was at pains to emphasise that the women in the household would be the ones to receive the assistance; yet every day the crowd collecting the bags of rice was overwhelmingly male.[2] Some days it seemed as if the entire population of able-bodied males in the city was queuing outside the Governor's palace, shifting uncomfortably in the sun and hoping that they would be among the lucky few to hoist bags of rice onto their shoulders and make their way home. The Ramadan feeding scheme illustrates that targeting women alone is insufficient – they must be incorporated into the decision-making process.

The results of the simultaneous centrality of women to the insurgency and their marginalisation in society are evident across northern Nigeria. Camps and informal settlements for the internally displaced are swollen with those who were abducted by Boko Haram and fled the group to live in these settlements; most had lost a family member to the insurgency, and nearly all were without a means of earning an income or a sense of their future.

Toma,[3] a remarkable 20-year-old woman living in the grounds of Madina mosque in Maiduguri, the capital of Borno State, had lost her husband, father and siblings to the insurgency. After her town had been held by Boko Haram for more than two months, she managed to flee to the city and now cared for four children of her own and her ten nieces and nephews, who were orphaned by the violence. Not providing for these children was never an option for Toma, who stated simply: 'They are my family – the children of my dead brothers and sisters. How can I not care for them?' Although Toma had the dedication to provide for the 14 children who depend on her, she lacked the resources. 'We all go on the streets and beg, from the sunrise until the sunset,' she told me. It was the only way to get enough to eat. Her story was not remarkable in the Madina settlement; nearly every hand-constructed shelter housed a woman who shouldered the burden of extended family members and who had overcome incredible risks to reach safety.[4]

Although the temptation is great to cast all women's experiences in relation to the insurgency as victimising and traumatising, it would be dishonest to do so. From the group's inception, Boko Haram's ideology provided opportunities for women to advance their own agendas. In a revealing exchange, the wife of a Boko Haram member asserted that the group had been successful in overrunning territory as a result of Divine will. She explained with a discomforting pride: 'Allah gave us the power to hold this place.'[5] The power to assert oneself, to claim a place in a movement and in society generally, is a powerful factor in explaining female participation in Boko Haram's activities. The group's radical return to scriptural interpretations and practices (which include the 'proper' practice of bride price, access to Qur'anic education, and prohibitions against women farming) and their advocacy of the adoption of sharia law have a number of gender-progressive implications, giving women an opportunity to assert their place, as difficult as it is to believe that such a thing is possible. Many women married willingly into the group, followed spouses or accompanied sons because the lives they were promised under the rule of Boko Haram were tangibly better than their lives as Nigerian citizens. The discrimination, misogyny and structural violence that women face in Nigeria make it difficult to draw clear distinctions between actions that are coerced, voluntary or merely coping mechanisms.

This book seeks to debunk the conventional wisdom surrounding both Boko Haram and women, which portrays the group as an inherently violent, transnational jihadist movement and depicts women universally, as victims lacking autonomy. Discussions about the role of gender in the crisis have been reduced to merely recalling the horror of the Chibok abductions and celebrating the corresponding advocacy movement #BringBackOurGirls. Despite this oversight, it is clear that gender has been used strategically throughout the crisis by both Boko Haram and in the Nigerian military's response to the insurgents. Boko Haram has roots in the political debate over the implementation of sharia law in Borno State, a debate in which a number of actors (both Muslim and not) across civil society and the government contested the role of women. While not the only factor in enabling Boko Haram's rise and continued relevance, gender politics are one of the least understood aspects of the region and the insurgency. The role of women and girls in the affected communities is also relevant, as the brunt of the process of rebuilding and reconciling the north-east will be borne by them.

There is a pressing need to improve our understanding of Boko Haram's operations. At the time of writing, the Boko Haram insurgency is one of the most lethal contemporary terrorist groups in the world and the greatest security challenge that Nigeria has faced since the country's brutal civil war in the 1960s.[6] The group's violence has spilled across borders, attracting recruits and taking lives in Chad, Niger and Cameroon, establishing it as a regional crisis. Amid the din of high-level political and military agreements, the stories of women like Toma are often lost. This is not only a humanitarian travesty and a continuation of patriarchal gendered discrimination, but also counterproductive to establishing stability in the area. If we overlook women's position in the roots and operations of Boko Haram, we miss an opportunity to understand the internal dynamics of the insurgency and to cultivate more effective counter-insurgency strategies; ignoring the role of women in the post-conflict rebuilding process sets the stage for continued instability in the region by affirming the discriminatory institutions that prime an area for rebellion and violence.

Chapter 1

UNDERSTANDING BOKO HARAM

Should the uprooted, deprived and repressed urban masses ever unite around a charismatic leader with a coherent ideology and an organization capable of mobilizing the excluded, then the anti-institutional energy expressed by the 'Yan Tatsine may generate a radically different outcome than self-destructive millenarian protest.

Paul Lubeck[1]

Which Boko Haram?

In a video released by Boko Haram in 2014, members of the insurgency are 'seen waving Kalashnikovs in the air as a tank performs a donut in the middle of the street' in an unidentified town while crowds on the streets cheer.[2] As towns were liberated by the Nigerian military following a renewed effort against the insurgency in 2015, more images emerged, including aerial surveillance showing 'ghost towns' and photographs showing burned-out homes and razed villages. From the footage, it is difficult to imagine that just five years earlier the group was a ragtag militia with unsophisticated weapons. The testimony of those displaced by the violence was even more disturbing; life under the insurgents was strictly regulated according to the group's idiosyncratic interpretation of the Qur'an. It is even more difficult to grasp how such a brutal insurgency, which once controlled a significant swathe of northern Nigeria, emerged out of the largely peaceful, dissident sect that had been founded by Mohammed Yusuf in 2002.

Jama'atu Ahlis Sunna Lidda'awati wal-Jihad (referred to as Boko Haram throughout this book) has been described in a number of ways by analysts. To some, most notably the Jamestown Foundation's Jacob Zenn, the group is deeply entwined with global Salafi-Jihadist groups. This purported relationship is thought to have started with joint training with fighters of Al Qaeda in the Maghreb (AQIM) in 2009–10. Others, such as scholar Murray Last and journalist Andrew Walker, consider the group a continuation of the long-standing patterns of dissent in northern Nigeria. The name 'Boko Haram', which means 'Western education is forbidden and deceitful', was given to the group by the community from which it emerged and reflects the organisation's roots in local political debates. Although each of these definitions illuminates an aspect of Boko Haram, they fail to capture the nuances and evolution of the organisation.

Fundamentally, the group 'is an Islamic sect that believes politics in northern Nigeria has been seized by a group of corrupt, false Muslims', according to Andrew Walker. Boko Haram wants to 'wage a war' against the government and these false Muslims in order 'to create a "pure" Islamic state ruled by sharia law'.[3] This characterisation of the intent of the insurgency is largely correct. While this objective has remained a constant, the scope of Boko Haram's grievances and the tactics it has adopted to achieve these objectives have varied. The aim of this book is to discuss what prompted these changes and to illustrate the important roles that women have played throughout the course of the organisation's evolution.

In discussing such a contentious phenomenon, it is helpful to establish some of the uncontroversial aspects of the sect and to discuss the general arc of the group's evolution. Mohammed Yusuf, a Salafi preacher, founded Boko Haram in 2002. With help from his father-in-law, he established a dissident religious community near the railway station in Maiduguri, the capital of Borno State in north-eastern Nigeria. The centre was named Ibn Taymiyyah Masjid, in honour of the medieval Islamic scholar credited with influencing modern Wahhabi, Salafi and Jihadi movements. Ibn Taymiyyah's community engaged in a number of self-help and social organising activities, including offering assistance with building homes, providing welfare services, and arranging affordable weddings. Under Yusuf, the group not only denounced Western education, as has been widely reported in the press, but also considered working with the Nigerian government to be *haram*. Yusuf's condemnation of 'corrupting Western influences' and the inadequacy of the Nigerian government helped him gain support for his movement among the city's economically marginalised. Although many of its members were socially and economically marginalised, Yusuf's religious community included some of the city's elite. Andrew Walker explains the group's position relative to both modernity and the local political economy of the north-east, observing that:

> Boko Haram, as a group, clearly does not utterly reject the modern world out of hand. The group's use of mobile phones, video cameras, DVDs, YouTube, chemical explosives, automatic weapons, and cars shows it is more than prepared to use the fruits of Western education when it suits them. Boko Haram is, however, against those in northern Nigeria known as 'yan boko.' Yan boko is literally translated as 'child of the book.' It refers to the elite created by the policy of indirect rule used by the British to colonize Nigeria – the people who have had their heads turned away from Allah by easy money and corrupting Western values. To be yan boko is to be spiritually and morally corrupt, lacking in religious piety, and guilty of criminally enriching oneself rather than dedicating oneself to the Muslim umma (community).[4]

As the group gained more support, it also attracted criticism, especially from local religious leaders. The response was often targeted violence towards these critics – and in some cases their assassination. Boko Haram became increasingly isolated from the northern Islamic establishment and became a progressively more frustrating thorn in the side of the government and the security sector. The violence (which is detailed later in this chapter) escalated until it came to a breaking point in 2009, when the Nigerian police and military raided Ibn Taymiyyah and the surrounding community, killing an estimated 700 people, including Yusuf. After a brief 'regrouping' period, the insurgency re-emerged under the leadership of Abubakar Shekau, with more sophisticated tactics deployed against softer targets. Between its re-emergence at the end of 2010 and the declaration of a state of emergency in the three north-eastern states of Borno, Yobe and Adamawa, the group was responsible for the deaths of more than 2,500 people. The state of emergency marked another turning point in the course of the insurgency, and the formation of the CJTF forced Boko Haram out of the city of Maiduguri and prompted the insurgents to adopt a more rural strategy, in which they abducted civilians, raided villages and held territory. The Buhari administration's more aggressive military offensive against the insurgency shifted the conflict again, resulting in an increased reliance on urban attacks. Despite regular proclamations that the insurgency has been defeated – or is at least on the back foot – Boko Haram has shown remarkable resilience.

It is worth noting that geo-political, religious and ethnic differences in Nigeria have prompted many outside the north-east of the country to write the crisis off as a 'northern problem' rather than a Nigerian issue.

The rise of Mohammed Yusuf

The 'sharia debate' that emerged in the late 1990s and early 2000s, about the legality and desirability of the adoption of sharia law at the state level, was not a singular event. There was a series of debates at the state and local level, each taking on the characteristics of that area's political economy and religious landscape. These debates were largely conducted in a similar way to other sensitive domestic policy debates in Nigeria – through the mobilisation of patronage networks and the use of quasi-state-sponsored militias to promote through force any notions that failed to gain traction through logical, political or emotional appeals. In the early 2000s, the debate over sharia law in Borno State gave rise to a number of groups scrambling to benefit from patronage opportunities that came with the democratic transition. The 'Yan Izala, well represented by the Alhaji Ndimi mosque in Maiduguri, was well positioned to influence this debate over sharia. Mohammed Yusuf, a former *almajiri* himself, was the leader of the youth wing of the Ndimi mosque and a 'favourite student' of the popular Sheik Ja'far Adam.[5]

Sheik Adam was a rising star within the Izala movement. He had risen to prominence in the late 1990s within the Salafi community, where his charisma, coupled with his political connections and his Islamic education at the Islamic University in Madina, lent him significant influence.[6] Working within the system, Adam was the spokesman for 'Izala B', a Salafi subset that was mostly in line with Izala orthodoxy but that promoted the interests and inclusion of younger, well-educated members. Izala B gained traction as young preachers returned from their sophisticated overseas Islamic universities and were disappointed when they struggled to gain influence and find employment.

Yusuf and Adam first met when Yusuf was studying in Kano, in north-west Nigeria. It did not take long for Adam to take the young man under his wing. Yusuf was born in Yobe State but his family had left when the 'state was in crisis' to settle in Maiduguri; Yusuf travelled to various cities pursuing his religious education.[7] Yusuf's father was an accomplished Tijaniyya scholar,[8] a surprising lineage considering the enthusiasm with which Yusuf, as a Salafi preacher, would later condemn the 'innovations' of this popular and influential Sufi order.

A childhood friend, who still lives around the corner from the rubble of Yusuf's mosque in Maiduguri, recalled that 'even as a child he was very harsh. He was hot tempered and he did not tolerate nonsense'; from a young age, he focused primarily on his Qur'anic studies.[9] At times, the young Yusuf took breaks from his studies and sold kerosene and worked his father's land as a farmer. He left these occupations behind when he found success as a preacher. His studies led him away from his father's Sufism to Shi'ism for a period of time, before he finally settled into the Izala movement under Adam's tutelage. Their partnership was mutually beneficial, as Yusuf needed a patron and Adam's profile benefited from bringing in such a charismatic young preacher as his mentee. Another former friend of Yusuf, who watched his childhood playmate turn away from Ndimi mosque, start his own community, and then be captured and killed by the Nigerian police, noted that 'he was always very brilliant in persuading people. He realised that Nigeria is oil rich but people suffer', and that Yusuf 'saw that the youth are stranded and he capitalised on it'.[10]

Although they were close associates at Ndimi mosque, Yusuf eventually fell out with Adam. Their theological disagreements revolved around two of Yusuf's radical contentions: that 'modern Western education was religiously forbidden to Muslims, and [that] employment in the government of Nigeria was also religiously forbidden'.[11] The former belief led to Yusuf's group being given the nickname 'Boko Haram' by locals, translating roughly as 'Western education is forbidden'. Although some have dismissed the group's anti-modernisation ethos as a religious Ludditism, Yusuf's activism against Western education and employment in the civil service served two strategic purposes. The first, detailed in Eli Berman's book *Radical, Religious, and Violent*,[12] was that it weeded out those likely to defect. This process of sacrifice to prove commitment is common to self-help groups *cum* terrorist organisations around the world. Giving up Western education closed off some of the most profitable avenues of employment available (although, realistically, these positions were not particularly easy to come by – especially for those lacking a powerful patron). Rejecting employment with the government was also a clear sacrifice in a region where government employment is one of the few alternatives to farming and petty trade. Berman has written extensively on how mutual aid and membership sacrifices help leaders screen 'cheaters and shirkers out of their mutual aid operations'.[13] Demanding public, difficult sacrifices is thus a way of making collective action easier. This heuristic for dedication is particularly valuable for terrorist groups and insurgencies.

The second strategic implication of Yusuf's ideological innovation was its more obvious populist appeal. As Johannes Harnischfeger, a professor at the University of Frankfurt notes, the Izala 'apology of appropriating secular education and accepting jobs in an un-Islamic government appeals to those who have found employment, especially if they are young and better educated. But it is less attractive to the millions of jobless youths.'[14] Yusuf's rejection of Western education and government employment spoke to these frustrations and humiliations. Without showing photographs of the residences of 'average' citizens in Maiduguri side by side with illustrations of the opulence of government employees' homes, it is difficult to convey the gaping inequality. Suffice to say that the squat, unpainted concrete homes of the majority of the population leave much to be desired, particularly when they are flanked by gated mini-mansions with intricate wrought iron gates, generators to provide reliable light, and storage tanks brimming with clean water. Even more damningly, the government appears to care more about the houses of its civil servants than about the living conditions of its average citizens. This unfortunately continues to be the case. As of winter 2017, the Legacy Estate Housing Project in Maiduguri is a very visible example of poor government planning and the favourable treatment received by civil servants. The project, which comprises 40 blocks of six-unit, three-bedroom apartments, was supposed to house civil servants; however, they complained that the units did not meet their standards and the buildings remained empty in 2017 – neither drawing rent from private citizens renting rooms nor providing shelter to IDPs.[15] The rejection of employment in the civil service was thus not only a means of weeding out likely defectors or those who would be insufficiently committed to the cause; it was also good politics in a highly inequitable political economy.

By 2003–04, the break between Adam and Yusuf was public and growing more contentious by the day, with Adam speaking out against his errant protégé's beliefs and condemning his followers. Following his return from a trip to Saudi Arabia, described as a pilgrimage by his supporters and as an expulsion by his detractors, Yusuf started to organise a new religious community.[16] He founded the Ibn Taymiyyah mosque near the railway station in Maiduguri, using money and land lent by his father-in-law, and established a farm in Bauchi to facilitate the group's self-help ethos.[17] According to Andrew Walker, the central location of the mosque was instrumental in forming the group's early membership profile. Walker recalls that 'urbanization and desertification across the state had led to a population boom in Maiduguri, thus by embedding themselves in the town rather than the wilderness, the group had many more avenues for recruitment and funding'.[18] In addition to leveraging the lack of economic opportunity for the youth demographic to recruit members, reports suggest that Boko Haram also encouraged the city's wealthy to 'atone' for their success and their sins through donations to the group.[19] This allowed Yusuf to criticise the corruption of the system, while still benefiting from its largesse.

As well as having a strategically placed mosque, Yusuf travelled to surrounding communities and more remote villages in Borno to spread his message and cultivate his reputation as a preacher.[20] Young people in the villages would enthusiastically record his preaching; a girl from Banki who was so convinced by Yusuf that she joined Boko Haram reported that, after he preached in her town, 'my friends would have me listen to his sermons on my phone'. Yusuf attracted crowds, according to this young woman, because 'the Islamic teaching with Yusuf was really very excellent'.[21] For many in the rural areas, this was one of the few opportunities they had to pursue 'quality' education.

Despite Boko Haram's virulent anti-state rhetoric and violence, the growth of the sect is believed to be tied to the patronage of the Governor of Borno State at the time, Ali Modu Sheriff.[22] Sheriff was one of the northern politicians who followed in the footsteps of the Governor of Zamfara State, Ahmad Yerima, supporting sharia law to garner political favour, despite the reservations of the state's small Christian population. He cultivated a symbiotic relationship with Yusuf, in which Boko Haram would deliver votes through endorsement, persuasion or force, in exchange for influencing the terms and implementation of sharia. Under the terms of this agreement, a Boko Haram member, Buji Foi, was given the post of Minister of Religious Affairs, and Ali Modu Sheriff became the first Governor of Borno State to serve two consecutive terms, from 2003 to 2011.[23] As a result of the combination of high-level patronage and grassroots popularity, Walker recalls that:

> By the end of 2008, the group was operating like a state within a state; it had its own institutions, including a shura council to make decisions and a religious police force to enforce discipline. It had a rudimentary welfare system, offered jobs working the land it had acquired in Bauchi and even gave microfinance loans to members to start their own projects. Many used the money to buy motorcycles and worked as [motorcycle taxi] drivers. The group also arranged marriages between members, which many of the poorest could not afford in normal life.[24]

The influence of the group quickly expanded beyond Maiduguri and into the surrounding communities. Clearly, Boko Haram successfully leveraged a threatened sense of self and general lack of opportunity to mobilise support among young men.[25]

Local religious leaders – particularly those in the Izala movement, from which Yusuf had defected – and some politicians greeted the rise of Boko Haram with condemnation. As Yusuf was building his social services infrastructure and community, he was also responding to his critics through limited and targeted violence. Ja'far Adam was one of the victims of this campaign; following his public denunciation of Yusuf's ideology, Adam was assassinated by Boko Haram followers in 2007. In his final speech, Adam questioned the motives of Boko Haram's leaders:

> There are certain things it's not time to disclose yet, but their time will come. When you still have hope that somebody will correct himself, you must give him time to correct his behavior, for the essence of preaching is to correct the behavior of people. But when the evil of a man starts clearly overriding his good, you must say publicly everything that you know about him. But I swear: I have no doubt that most of the youth who have been dragged into this matter are, for the most part, in good faith, and are only acting according to their own understanding of religion. But as for the very people who are dragging them into this matter, they have a hidden agenda of their own.[26]

The intra-religious violence and low-level criminality eventually escalated into violence between Yusuf's adherents and the state, prompting outcries from local imams and residents. Alexander Thurston, a scholar of Islam in West Africa, documents the criticism from 'mainstream Salafis' of Boko Haram, observing that, 'in Nigeria and elsewhere, mainstream Salafis have worked to sustain an oppositional religious politics that advocates for Salafi views of public morality and for the perceived interests of Muslims, but they have also sought to distinguish themselves from violent Salafis'.[27]

In response to the mainstream Salafi disapproval of their activities, Boko Haram targeted critics with both overt physical violence and implied threats; despite many media outlets suggesting that the insurgents targeted its political critics and Christians in the region, more substantive evidence points to the group being more intentionally brutal to critical Islamic groups – especially in the early years of the insurgency.[28] This eventually attracted the government's attention.

The residents of the neighbourhood explained that Yusuf was frequently 'called [in] for questioning', when the government would 'admonish him, but allow him to continue'.[29] The increasing popularity of Ibn Taymiyyah mosque emboldened Yusuf, and a member of the Railway neighbourhood remarked to me that: 'He started agitating the government after he got momentum.' The growing animosity between Yusuf's followers and the state, however, called into question the long-term viability of his political relationships.

The year 2009 marked a turning point in the history of the group, moving it towards jihadism and more widespread violence. On 20 February, a group of Boko Haram members were travelling to a funeral by motorbike when they were stopped by police officers for failing to wear their helmets. It is unclear who instigated the violence, but the result was that a number of those in the funeral party were wounded and killed by the police as part of this fairly routine stop.[30] This appears to be the straw that broke the camel's back. Until then, Operation Flush, the federal government's security response aimed at stymying the group, had been a nuisance to Mohammed Yusuf and was mentioned in his speeches, but it had not been a major topic in his propaganda. Following the assault on the funeral party, however, Yusuf began to campaign against this harassment. Those who lived in the Railway neighbourhood at the time remembered that Yusuf 'turned more harshly against the government after the funeral incident. He said the government is after us and we must fight back.'[31] A man who lived near the mosque at the time asserted that Yusuf 'felt like they broke their agreement, that he would preach without interference and not cause trouble'.[32] According to Walker, he 'made a series of speeches, circulated widely on tapes and DVDs and over Bluetooth connections, calling on Muslims to prepare to "come to Jihad"'. This media blitz encouraged members to engage in 'preparation such as learning shooting, buying rifles and bombs, as well as training the Islamic Soldiers to fight the infidels' and to be prepared to 'sacrifice your souls, your homes, your cars and your motorcycles for the sake of Allah'.[33]

The Nigerian government responded by giving Yusuf an ultimatum: they demanded that he report to Abuja for questioning or face the consequences. According to a resident of Railway I spoke to, Yusuf 'consulted with his *shura*, and they all agreed to resist all government action'.[34] Gesturing to the unpaved stretch of road that stood in front of us, now dotted with errant grazing goats, he continued: 'By Sunday at 8pm, his followers were walking down this very street with guns. We had never seen them with weapons before.' The government's response was swift: 'The police came with their Hilux trucks and started firing warning shots.'[35] Boko Haram made use of their newly acquired weapons, engaging the Nigerian security forces in a firefight that lasted until 3 or 4am. The significance of this as a turning point in the sect's relationship with the state became clearer by the hour; a resident of Railway neighbourhood recalls that, 'following that firefight, they launched attacks on government buildings', including an election centre, prisons and a police station – although Railway residents were quick to emphasise that, 'at that time, they were not attacking any civilians'.[36] That Monday and Tuesday, the neighbourhood was put under lockdown: 'We were told to clear the area by Wednesday,' a resident recalled.[37]

According to these residents, Wednesday's activities commenced with a door-to-door raid targeting Boko Haram members.[38] An estimated 700-plus people were killed in extrajudicial, indiscriminate state violence.[39] Yusuf himself was captured, interrogated, and finally killed by the Nigerian police. The house in which Yusuf was seized is an unremarkable, unpainted brown home a few hundred yards from his mosque. It is currently rented out to a number of families, who apparently are capable of ignoring their neighbours' distaste for the property in light of what followed Yusuf's capture. In an act of almost unimaginable folly, the police recorded the interrogation on video; inevitably, this was circulated widely and helped ensure that Mohammed Yusuf was considered a martyr. One particularly telling portion of the interaction went as follows:

Officer: We went to your house yesterday and we saw a lot of animals, syringes and materials used for making bombs, what were you keeping all that for?

Yusuf: Like I told you, to protect myself …

Officer: [Interrupts] … to protect yourself how? Isn't there the authorities, the law enforcement agencies?

Yusuf: The authorities, the law enforcement agents are the same people fighting me …

Officer: What did you do?

Yusuf: I don't know what I did … I am only propagating my religion, Islam.

According to the BBC, 'his bullet-ridden body was shown to journalists hours after police announced they had captured him alive'.[40] The graphic image was circulated widely across the north, provoking fear and mistrust of the government.

The raid appeared, at first, to have been successful. The violence stalled and Ibn Taymiyyah mosque was bulldozed. It seemed that the excessive force had shattered the sect, as it had done to the 'Yan Tatsine decades earlier. However, Boko Haram proved to be more resilient than previous groups.

It takes two to tango: the destructive state–insurgency relationship and the reflexive evolution of Boko Haram

Boko Haram poisons rivers, puts dead bodies into the wells, fill the wells with cement … They wage war on every living thing, even the vegetation.

Dr Bulama Gubio[41]

The remaining members of Boko Haram regrouped and expanded their membership roles, 'going underground' for a little over a year as they reconstituted and refocused their efforts. Leadership of the sect transferred from Yusuf to his number two, Abubakar Shekau. Little is known about Shekau's background; it is believed that he was born in Yobe State, in north-east Nigeria. From his videos and public statements, it is clear that he is fluent in Kanuri, Arabic and Hausa, and has at least a cursory knowledge of English. He has a reputation for being well-versed in theology and for relishing violence.[42] Although Shekau changed the scope and intensity of the group's violence, by and large the group's demographic profile remained the same. Mercy Corps found that the group maintained the diversity that initially characterised it, noting in 2016 that 'there is no demographic profile of a Boko Haram member ... some had jobs, and others did not. Some had attended secular school, others Islamic school, and others had dropped out.' The group is, in fact, a constellation of cells united under the banner of 'Boko Haram', resulting in diverse recruitment methods and member profiles. Hence, the discussions about the group's fragmentation in the late summer of 2016 might have been the result of the media's misinterpretation of longer-standing organisational characteristics.

Because of this diffuse structure, Boko Haram relies on social networks for voluntary recruitment. Mercy Corps noted that 'almost all former members cited a friend, family member, or business colleague as a factor in their joining Boko Haram'.[43] Despite Shekau's reputation for propagating wanton violence, under his tenure Boko Haram maintained its emphasis on mutual aid and bolstering the identity and self-perception of members that Yusuf had cultivated. Mercy Corps found that 'many youth described either accepting loans prior to joining or joining with the hope of receiving loans or capital for their mostly small, informal businesses'.[44] Shekau also maintained the sect's gender politics, continuing to preach men's responsibilities to care for their wives.[45]

The radical changes that did occur under Shekau included a shift away from precise violence against local targets towards more indiscriminate violence against symbols of the state and the adoption of more technically sophisticated tactics. Indeed, Shekau's leadership is considered by many to be a critical factor in widening the scope of the insurgency.[46] Under his leadership, the group moved beyond the somewhat crude gunmen tactics of the Yusuf era and experimented with explosives and territorial control, and even began using landmines.[47] Some reports have emerged that, when Shekau was second in command, he and Yusuf came into conflict because Shekau considered the group's founder too moderate.

Whether or not Shekau always planned to expand the scope and scale of the insurgency before Yusuf's death, or whether the group's shift in grievances and targets was in response to heavy-handed state repression, is ultimately a moot point. What is evident is that under Shekau's guidance, Boko Haram declared war on the Nigerian state. Shekau tried to portray the sect as the vanguard of Nigerian Muslims, which he considered to be targeted by the government. Shekau released a statement clarifying the group's new set of targets in 2011, in which he reminded his audience:

Nobody is persecuting us [Muslims] like this government … nobody is persecuting our religion and our Prophet like it. They use their soldiers, their police, their system of unbelief and their collaborators … We are being persecuted … in a village in Kaduna State Muslims were pushed into a dug out hole and petrol was poured on them before they were set ablaze. What did your government do about this? … We are aware of how they are persecuting the ordinary people in the city.[48]

In this statement, and countless others like it, Boko Haram portrays the Nigerian government as illegitimate and abusive. Part of the reason why Boko Haram was able to regroup under Shekau is because the government's security presence receded to pre-2009 levels when it believed the group had been destroyed. Under Shekau, the group's successful new campaign of attacks against police stations, beer halls and military outposts was allowed to continue without much government resistance until May 2013. It was only then that the Goodluck Jonathan administration classified Boko Haram as a terrorist organisation, declared a state of emergency across the three states of the north-east (Borno, Yobe and Adamawa), and deployed a joint task force to urban areas to quell the insurgency. Demonstrating the tactical and operational flexibility that continues to frustrate the Nigerian military effort against the group, Boko Haram shifted from an urban guerrilla movement to a rural insurgency capable of holding territory. The slowness of the security sector's response may be woven into the Nigerian government's DNA, as the 1999 constitution makes the police a federal force, rather than a state-level one.[49]

When Boko Haram fighters took control of a village during this period, they would implement their version of sharia law on those trapped there. The claims that Boko Haram was not engaged in a state-building process may be inaccurate, as a number of members of the sect living under government surveillance told me that, once an area was entirely under Boko Haram's control (part of a *daula*, Hausa for 'state'), Qur'anic schools were established, marriage ceremonies continued, and food was provided to all residents.[50] One girl, who had joined Boko Haram of her own volition, was then 'rescued' by the government, and is now held in a government-run small camp, explained that when Boko Haram invaded a village, people were given the chance to convert (or to 'submit') to the group. Submitting to the group meant that you 'support the ideology and submit to the will of Boko Haram but are not a part of the *jihad*'.[51] Those who converted were considered members of the 'Yan Uwa, a term that Boko Haram members use to describe their community.[52] Members of the Boko Haram, according to former members, were well-provided for by the insurgents. Others report that those who did not 'submit' were killed.

Given the lack of attention paid to the community-building endeavours within Boko Haram, the extent of physical and social support is surprising. Even those who described themselves as Boko Haram's 'slaves' reported that the group provided such support. One woman who lived for a year and a half under the group explained: 'They would sometimes give us 1,000 naira because we were among them. They would give you rice and food if you needed it.'[53] This support came with an ideological agenda, propagated through their schools, preaching, and other social services.

According to Boko Haram's ideology, as summarised by Zainab, a wife of a Boko Haram member, the ''Yan Uwa and their submissives are the only real Muslims'; the group was therefore justified in killing *kafir* Muslims who did not abide by Boko Haram's tenets.[54] Even Aisha, an IDP living in the grounds of Madina mosque in Maiduguri, who expressed nothing but hatred for the group, recounted that during the invasion the insurgents gave residents the option of 'conversion' (even though the majority were already Muslim). She was told before she fled the town of Marte in 2014 that 'if you want to follow our ideology, you should come with us or leave'.[55] Any men who refused to convert 'were killed instantly', along with some non-believing women.[56]

Life in Boko Haram is discussed at greater length in Chapter 5; however, it is worth noting here that the media portrayals of the sect and its governance patterns are frequently incomplete. Reports of a process of cajoling recruitment directed at those living under Boko Haram's rule were common and have spawned a series of occult explanations for the group's success.[57] Broader social support systems were complemented by gifts of food and clothes. In particular, rumours abound throughout the northeast of Boko Haram 'putting things' in the food and tea given to potential members. Shettima, a 55-year-old man whose son joined the group and then helped to orchestrate the kidnapping of two of his younger siblings, blames his son's actions on the food he was given as a gift, with a simple 'once you eat their food, you will follow them'.[58] This belief is pervasive. Elder, a top commander in the CJTF, says that when the men under his control discover Boko Haram's food stores, 'you have no choice but to burn them, because if you eat their food or drink, it will change your mind. It is dangerous.'[59] Even a social worker at an IDP camp, Fatima, believed that 'if they take you and give you tea and you eat their food, they can control your mind'.[60] It is easier to deploy occult explanations than to grapple with the implications of government absence and politicised religiosity.

Despite the sect's radical reputation, many former members residing at Safe House, a special camp for women who joined Boko Haram voluntarily, asserted that day-to-day life with the insurgents was not radically different from life outside Boko Haram – it was just simpler. Zainab was adamant that she and her husband 'were living a normal life, doing normal chores' while living under Boko Haram in a village called Walasah. She recalled that 'the men would leave and we [the wives] wouldn't ask them what they did and anyway they weren't keen to talk about it even with the wives'. The most noteworthy changes for Zainab were that her husband treated her more kindly and that she was expected to cover herself entirely, using a *niqab* and socks.[61] Others agreed with Zainab's description of relative normalcy, and a number of wives of Boko Haram members asserted that 'the Qur'an that they taught us is the same we learn here [in the government camp]'.[62]

Another important difference was the restriction on farming that came with life under Boko Haram. Female farming is banned according to Boko Haram's Qur'anic interpretation, but this ban sometimes extended to everyone living under Boko Haram control. Zainab explained that 'even in the bush ... nobody was allowed to farm under Boko Haram. They said it was too tedious.'[63] This is particularly striking given that the vast majority of the population across the north-east relies on farming to survive. In order to feed its ranks, the insurgents raid other communities, compounding the devastation wrought by the group.

Following the 2013 declaration of a state of emergency, the insurgency seems to have shifted from being an almost entirely volunteer force towards kidnapping to complement their manpower. The most infamous of these kidnapping was the Chibok abductions in April 2014, although this event is merely the tip of the iceberg. Amnesty International estimated in 2015 that Boko Haram had abducted more than 2,000 women, to say nothing of the scores of young men and boys taken forcibly.[64] In August 2014, the group took control of a significant amount of territory and declared an Islamic state. According to Professor Kyari Mohammed, a historian at Modibbo Adama University of Technology in Yola, Adamawa State, this was the era in which Boko Haram fragmented into a number of cells, led by various emirs. According to Kyari, these 'emirs have very little relationship to one another – they all act completely independently', giving rise to heterogeneity within the movement. Kyari Mohammed observes that the cells south of Maiduguri are more ideological, whereas cells on the shores of Lake Chad are more commercially oriented. For the latter, 'it is mostly about power and access to women. You can take anyone's woman and she is yours; they also control the fish and pepper trade.'[65] Fatalities in this period reached new heights, especially as Boko Haram began attacking soft targets (such as schools, markets and bus depots) with abandon. During this period, Boko Haram also began deploying female suicide bombers, a phenomenon that I discuss later.

Preparations for the 2015 elections again saw a redoubling of military efforts against Boko Haram; the election of Muhammadu Buhari, a former military dictator and a Muslim from the north, was due in large part to his promise to eradicate Boko Haram. Despite Buhari's commitment to restoring stability in the north-east, the increased military presence has not reduced the insurgency. Instead, the group has become a transnational phenomenon, spilling over the (porous) borders of the Lake Chad Basin and destabilising communities in Chad, Niger and Cameroon. Even the towns that have been reported as being 'cleared' of Boko Haram are not secured by the Nigerian police or military. The result is that the military often goes in, burns villages to the ground (ostensibly to prevent looting), harasses any residents who did not (or could not) flee from Boko Haram's rule, and then retreats – allowing the insurgents to filter back into the destroyed villages. This pattern only seems to validate Boko Haram's refrain that the military is persecuting them and their followers and that 'the military will kill you' if you try to leave or if the Nigerian security sector is successful in entering areas under Boko Haram's control.[66]

The persistent lack of security outside urban centres has prevented displaced populations from returning to their homes safely. A displaced family I spoke with outside Mubi, a town in Adamawa State, looked mournfully at a bundle of household goods wrapped in a mattress in the courtyard of the compound in which they were staying. A woman in the compound was considering returning to Madagali, the northern Adamawa town from which they had fled, but had to abandon her plans because of news that returnees were being slaughtered. The woman I spoke with, an elegant figure with three happily curious children playing with bags of water by her feet, told me simply: 'We cannot return now to Madagali. We know women who returned and were killed. We know many who were killed after returning.'[67]

The government's lack of success in the fight against Boko Haram can be traced to the security sector's rampant misconduct and lack of professionalism. The military's actions throughout the crisis underline long-standing grievances in the region and the general mistrust of the government in the north-east. As Mercy Corps noted, 'broad frustrations with government created initial community acceptance of Boko Haram ... About half of former members said their communities at some time generally supported the group, hoping it would bring a change in government.'[68] Heavy-handed tactics, extrajudicial violence and illegal detention have characterised the state of emergency and the response of the Nigerian security sector to Boko Haram. According to Marc-Antoine Pérouse de Montclos, 'the repression, continued massacres, extra-judicial killings and arrests without trial' that have typified the state of emergency 'have widened the gap between communities and the armed forces, to the point where some civilians have sought the protection of Boko Haram, even if they did not initially sympathize with, support or subscribe to the actions and doctrine of the movement'.[69]

The abuses have not been sporadic; it is clear from reports from groups such as Amnesty International and Human Rights Watch that there are systemic and widespread human rights abuses committed by the Nigerian police, military, special units and pro-government vigilante groups. A recent report from Amnesty International on the activities of the Nigerian military units sent to counter Boko Haram estimated that as many as 7,000 Nigerians died in detention as a result of mistreatment; an additional 1,200 civilians were summarily executed; and perhaps 20,000 were arbitrarily detained during military campaigns. These round-ups were often conducted following insurgent attacks, subjecting communities to even more harassment. This abuse is made all the more horrifying in light of recent research that suggests that communities that hold 'pro-counter-insurgency attitudes' (which means that they are sympathetic to the government) are more likely to be targeted by the insurgents.[70] Applying this to those affected by Boko Haram, the very communities that would have been the most willing to cooperate with the government are disproportionately targeted by state security forces.

In September 2016, it was confirmed by the Nigerian military that some of its officers had sold arms and ammunition to Boko Haram insurgents – confirming long-standing suspicions that some in the military were contributing to the crisis and further eroding trust in the security sector.[71]

This state violence has prompted some to accept Boko Haram's assertion that it is a vanguard of Muslim communities. Zainab, though living in a government centre and learning English, still asserted that 'Boko Haram would be just and pure leaders', and earnestly said that 'Boko Haram is better at governance than the

Nigerian government. They respond to people's needs better.'[72] Umi, just 11 years old, stated: 'Shekau is like a Governor … he provides for his people and is a leader.'[73] Perhaps this sense of responsiveness and concern explains why Zainab (and other women) 'supported the violence against the *kafirs*' and 'wanted all of Nigeria to be a *daula*'.[74] An anonymous UNICEF employee reported that it was not just the wives of the insurgents who maintain an affinity with the group, explaining that 'there are those among the IDPs who do not sympathise with the soldiers'.[75] These IDPs believe that Boko Haram 'only did bad things to the soldiers because of the military's abuse of Muslims and that if the soldiers had not been killing, things would not have escalated'.[76]

It is worth noting that this state violence has also been gendered. Another UNICEF employee who requested anonymity also relayed stories from northern Adamawa, where it was reported that, in March 2016, 'soldiers were killing local men and taking their wives'.[77] There is also evidence to suggest that the gendered violence of the state encouraged Boko Haram to explicitly target women and girls. In 2012 and 2013, following the detention of Abubakar Shekau's wives and the wives of other suspected Boko Haram members, Shekau released statements complaining of this abuse and threatening to kidnap the wives and daughters of Nigerian officials. Shekau accused the security forces of sexual abuse against the detained women. In 2012, he asserted that 'they have continued capturing our women … In fact, they are even having sex with one of them. Allah, Allah, see us and what we are going through', and he promised retaliation along the same lines.[78] He threatened: 'Since you are now holding our women, [laughs] just wait and see what will happen to your own women … to your own wives.'[79] Jacob Zenn and Elizabeth Pearson, researchers who documented the role that gender played in the tactical versatility of the insurgency, noted that 'these events demonstrate an established cycle of government detentions of women related to Boko Haram, and the group's retaliatory abduction of Christian women'.[80] Emerging reports of sexual abuse against women and girls in IDP camps throughout the north by Nigerian police, soldiers and vigilante groups (who are tasked with the management of these settlements) are distressing both for their humanitarian implications and for the value of such abuse in propaganda efforts.

As Boko Haram began attacking soft targets and engaging in indiscriminate violence, support for the group waned among local communities, according to locals and NGOs operating in the area. Ultimately, however, the population remained stuck between a rock and a hard place, with abuses escalating on both sides. This brief summary brings us to the present situation: a virtual stalemate in the country's north-east, with an abusive security sector taking on humanitarian responsibilities that it lacks the capacity to perform well, seeking to stamp out a relentlessly flexible, transnational insurgency. In the war against Boko Haram, women have taken sides, borne the brunt of the humanitarian crisis, and been caught in the middle. The question of how they will rebuild the country remains – and the obstacles to their ability to exercise their autonomy grow all the more entrenched by the day.

Chapter 2

PRECURSORS TO THE INSURGENCY AND THE SHARIA DEBATES

Politics and religion in a 'mere geographical expression': the Nigerian Fourth Republic

Understanding Boko Haram requires at least a cursory under-standing of the Nigerian political landscape since the country's return to constitutional democracy in 1999, marking the beginning of its 'Fourth Republic' (see Table 2.1).[1] After years of vacillating between military misrule and inept civilian administration, the 'Giant of Africa' seemed to be on the path to sustainable democracy in 1999.

Managing Nigeria's size and heterogeneity has been a challenge since the territorial state was declared. Under British colonial policies, which spanned from 1885 until Nigerian independence in 1960, the multitude of ethnic groups and religious divisions in the country problematised the governance of Nigeria as a single geographic unit. The British solution was to divide the country into two geographic chunks – north and south – and to adapt their governance patterns as local practices dictated.[2] Following independence, the country struggled to assert civilian control over the military; as a result, the country suffered from a series of coups and counter-coups.

Table 2.1 Nigerian Republics and years

First Republic	1963–66
Second Republic	1979–83
Third Republic	1993
Fourth Republic	1999–present

Despite the optimism during the 1999 transition, it clearly brought to the fore issues of ethnic, religious and regional balance that the country is still struggling to manage. With a population estimated to be more than 170 million people, divided nearly evenly along religious lines between Islam and Christianity, spread across 36 states (themselves organised into six geopolitical blocks) competing for representation and their share of the federal budget, even taking a headcount is a formidable task – it is a deeply political process. The census in Nigeria determines the allocation of patronage and state resources and is thus frequently contested. As recently as 2013, the chairman of the National Population Commission (NPC), Chief Festus Odimegwu, admitted that: 'We do not really know our population … all the census ever conducted in this country ended in controversy.' He went on to argue that, although the NPC endeavours to present accurate statistics, 'politicians interfere and at the end, you do not really know what population or census figures are'.[3] If something as mundane as a census causes such political controversy, it is unsurprising that the selection of the executive is also a process mired in ethno-regional politics.

The election of Olusegun Obasanjo, a Christian from the country's south, to the office of the presidency in 1999 was perceived by some as marginalising Muslims in the north; some Christians and southerners, on the other hand, saw the election of Obasanjo as a necessary corrective following a long history of northern representation throughout military rule. Ultimately, Obasanjo's election was the result of an elite pact that depended on the rotation of power from north to south. Unsurprisingly, almost immediately after the 1999 constitution was adopted, it was tested by sub-national differences, crass political opportunism, and persistent citizen frustration with the corruption of the Nigerian government. The 'sharia debate', which re-emerged with the return to democracy, was a microcosm of all of these aspects of Nigerian politics at the end of the twentieth century.

Democracy and sharia in northern Nigeria

Under the country's federal system, Nigeria's 36 states are afforded certain rights and liberties with respect to the central, federal government. Governors in the country's largely Muslim north asserted that the adoption of sharia law at the state level was one of these rights. This charge was led by then-Governor of Zamfara State, Ahmad Sani Yerima. Johannes Harnischfeger observed that 'campaigning on a Sharia ticket in 1999 had enabled him to oust a formidable contender: former National Security Adviser Lt.-General Aliyu Gusau'.[4]

Yerima's vocal support for sharia and his implementation of it (in some form) on 27 January 2000 was not just a public display of religiosity. It was a means of deflecting attention away from the reputation he had developed at the Central Bank during the Babangida administration (1985–93), when it was alleged that he became accustomed to a luxurious lifestyle financed through the embezzlement of public funds. Yerima remains a controversial but prominent figure; it is worth noting that he has subsequently gone on to oppose national gender equality legislation and to marry a 13-year-old girl from Egypt, in contravention of Nigerian anti-child marriage legislation, and he was accused by the Independent Corrupt Practices and Other Related Offences Commission of 18 counts of corruption in 2016.[5] Despite the transparently self-serving nature of the adoption of sharia in Zamfara under Yerima, other states quickly followed suit, prompting debate at the national level about the legality of sharia law in those states; at the sub-national level, the political debate moved towards discussions of *how* sharia law should be implemented. The return to democracy and the ensuing debates over sharia law not only brought to the fore issues of states' rights (relative to the federal government), but also stirred up ethno-political tensions and ignited a debate about federalism and the role of religion in the new country.

Yerima's success inspired imitation, and 'other politicians also depicted themselves as uncompromising fighters for the cause of Islam'.[6] The result was a class of politicians who also portrayed themselves as 'apostles of sharia' to gain support in the largely Muslim north.[7] Governor Kure of Niger State was one such apostle. He defended sharia as an integral part of Nigerian federalism, asserting that:

> The acceptance of the choice ... to be guided by the sharia is an important ingredient of our federal nature. Feder-alism enshrined in our constitution is not for our fancy. As a Federal State, our laws, institutions, and people must respect our cultural diversities, which are not just regional, ethnic, or tribal, but also extend to our religious beliefs and practices.[8]

Brandon Kendhammer, in his book *Muslims Talking Politics: Framing Islam, Democracy, and Law in Northern Nigeria*, observes that many northerners saw sharia as a way to reduce corruption in government and to improve the provision of social services. He notes that 'surveys that ask Muslims to define the characteristics of a sharia inspired "government" find that most respondents cite issues like public goods provision ... and improved security far more often than the application of harsh physical punishments or restrictions on women's appearance in public spaces – the practices associated with sharia in the global media'.[9]

In the first few years of the new constitution, a number of states in Nigeria (all in the country's predominantly Muslim north) adopted sharia law. Despite the initial enthusiasm for sharia implementation among citizens in the north, the failure of sharia to radically remedy the state's shortcomings resulted in disillusionment. Instead of supplanting the corruption and patronage networks that dominated Nigeria's political sphere, sharia merely provided another version of patrimonialism; Kendhammer notes that 'politicians and patrons cast the "dividends" of sharia as products of personal charity – rewards to devout (and loyal) citizens that could be repaid at the ballot box'.[10] He also points out that many in the north grew 'increasingly suspicious as the months and years wore on that the political enthusiasm for sharia had been little more than a ploy for temporarily buying their support'.[11]

This frustration and marginalisation helped fuel discontent that empowered Yusuf to make a name for himself as a dissident – despite his connections to mainstream Salafists who campaigned for sharia and local politicians who supported its adoption. While the adoption of sharia certainly cannot explain the rise of Boko Haram, the continued poor government performance in the north and the widespread disappointment in the failure of both democracy and sharia to 'deliver' for ordinary Nigerians certainly created conditions in which a reform movement could arise. After all the public debates, deliberations and campaigns about sharia, very little changed for many Nigerians in the north; before sharia was officially implemented across the north, an estimated three in four cases were adjudicated by local courts, many of which were governed by customary laws that often included sharia.[12] Boko Haram's precursors, many of whom held similar grievances against the inadequacies of the local political and religious elites, illustrate the ways in which Yusuf 'fits into a long local history' in which 'an Islamic scholar "on the make"' can challenge the local elites through rhetoric, organising and violence.

The marginalisation of the public in the aftermath of the politicisation of religion is a pattern that has been observed globally, in places where professed religiosity has been politicised to garner electoral support. Harnischfeger is worth quoting at length to explain the enthusiasm for sharia as a reaction to poor secular governance outcomes:

> Since citizens have never found ways to control their rulers, they can only hope that politicians will submit at least to the authority of God. Theocratic rule is regarded as an alternative to democracy; it derives its attraction from the sense that Western concepts of modernisation have led to a dead end. While party democracy seems to encourage strife and ruthless competition, sharia is conceived as a force that may check the excesses of the ruling class. The immutable law of God, which is the same all over the world, will be the yardstick by which all segments of the society, rich and poor, must be judged.[13]

Boko Haram's precursors in northern Nigeria

A brief review of these movements will illustrate the patterns of state–society governance in an atmosphere of religious contestation, as well as contextualise Boko Haram as an anti-state movement with local characteristics. This somewhat storied history of charismatic leaders inciting groups of young, underemployed men in the name of religious reform may partially explain why the government's response to Mohammed Yusuf's anti-state preaching was initially so slow. At the time, many thought that the movement was just the latest iteration of a charismatic preacher who would stir up the area's youth before losing momentum. Paul Lubeck, a noted scholar on Islam and globalisation in northern Nigeria, described the 'Yan Tatsine riots of the 1980s as part of a recurring phenomenon, observing that 'with considerable regularity during the dry season which propels the rural poor into the urban centres of northern Nigeria, religious riots have erupted in or adjacent to five cities: Kano (1980), Kaduna (1982), Bulum-Ketu near Maiduguri (1982), Jimeta near Yola (1984) and Gombe (1985)'.[14] Lubeck argues that 'in each instance the conflict was remarkably similar. When confronted by the state authorities, an Islamic sect, the 'Yan Tatsine, unleashed an armed insurrection against the Nigerian security forces and those outside the sect, resulting in widespread destruction, in thousands of deaths and in millions of naira of property losses'.[15]

The 'Yan Tatsine rejected modernisation and condemned the perversion of Islam through secularism and modernity. The movement itself is named after the virulently anti-modernisation preacher dubbed 'Maitatsine', which translates loosely as 'one who condemns', due to his frequent public protests against the effects of modernity. Their grievances against modern culture and their Luddite orientation against technology have been sustained over the decades. Since the 'Yan Tatsine riots, there has also been religious instability fomented by the Kala Kato group, led by Malam Isiyaka Salisu, who instructs his followers that 'only the Qur'an provides a reliable guide for Islamic worship', and states that he and his followers 'don't use Ḥadīths as a guide to the way we worship Allah'.[16]

Although rioters across time have justified their movements on religious grounds, protests are widely believed to be a response to perceived governmental neglect and economic decline. In Nigeria, these protests have largely been urban phenomena, reflecting migrations to the cities of the north in the face of agricultural stagnation and climate change. Lubeck notes that urban centres in northern Nigeria remain 'the epicenter of a burgeoning public sphere in which informed publics debate highly contested Islamic discourses regarding social justice, urban public space, legitimate government and gender relations'.[17]

The emphasis placed on religion as an identity marker and as a political movement in the Nigerian Fourth Republic led to scriptural interpretation and the recruitment of members into various religious groups gaining significance. This has not been confined to Islam. Christianity, particularly of the Pentecostal variety, has gained currency in the country's south (perhaps unsurprisingly, given the oil revenues that have poured into the region, prosperity gospel has also seen an upturn in support) at the same time as religious markers have become more prominent in the north. While the north/south divide falls along Muslim/Christian lines, there are also important intra-group fault lines. One of the most salient divisions within Islam is between members of the Sufi orders (typically considered to be well connected in economic and political circles) and reformist movements alleging that the misinterpretation of Islam is responsible for the ills befalling the country. The reformist groups condemn the *shirk* (idolatry/association) of the Sufi orders, arguing that these variations are deviations from the prescriptions of the Qur'an and thus un-Islamic. These innovations were often the result of Islam being melded with local practices in order to ease the process of conversion. The rise of reformist groups also reflects the tarnish that had appeared on the reputation of popular Sufi orders in northern Nigeria (in particular the Qadariyya and Tijaniyya orders, which dominate the region), which are often perceived to be 'entangled in the web of corruption that links villagers with the local government administration'.[18] The strength of the Sufi brotherhoods' economic and political networks is thus a double-edged sword, giving them influence while making them a target of reformists.

The 'Yan Izala is the most prominent of the Salafi reformist groups in the country. The 'Yan Izala gained momentum as an alternative to, and a critique of, the Sufi orders.[19] The group was established in 1978 by Sheikh Ismaila Idris and gained traction under the leadership of Abubaker Gumi. According to Ousmane Kane, it is the specific characteristics and ideological orientation of the 'Yan Izala that are responsible for the prevalence of the practice of *takfir* (or excommunication) in northern Nigeria compared with the rest of West Africa.[20] Adeline Masquelier observes that the

> 'Yan Izala's vision of an alternative Muslim civil society that promotes a philosophy of 'each man for himself,' stresses education for all, and redefined women's roles provides a privileged vantage point from which to explore the role of Islam in

its mediation of state-society relations ... Although Izala originated as a critique of Sufi doctrine, it also gave voice to a host
of concerns that arose out of the profound sociopolitical and
economic transformations of the last decades.[21]

Kane is more explicit in drawing connections between the 'Yan
Izala's theology and its at times antagonistic relationship to the
prevailing social order. He asserts that 'the two concepts – asso-
ciationism (*shirk*) and proclaiming others as unbelievers (*takfir*)
– provided the Izala religious entrepreneurs and their sympathizers
a religious justification for opposing the domination of the traditional order by which they felt oppressed'.[22]

Emmanuel Gregoire also observes that Izala arose out of social
changes that gave rise to a new wealthy class, the *Alhazi*, 'whose
conceptions of society and social relations differ from those of
their elders ... [they believe that] Hausa society is too hierarchical,
and consequently they challenge the power and authority of the
elders'.[23] However, the Izala did not merely criticise the existing
order. Recognising that the costs of weddings, birth ceremonies and
death ceremonies were burdensome, some preachers in the group
did not charge to perform these rituals.[24] The Izala also, in some
instances, abolished the need for a bride price to be paid prior to
marriage.[25] The reduction or elimination of these fees amounted to
a boon to the lower social classes.

The 'Yan Izala's prescription to cure society's ills was to increase
the role of Islam in society – along the lines of the reformist interpretation of the Qur'an that they abided by. This vision had specific
gendered implications, including an insistence on a specific style
of veiling for women in the north.[26] The Izala position that women
should vote (if only to further the cause of sharia) and should be
taught how to read (if only to better educate their children in Islam
and the Qur'an) was a significant political development in the north.
But even now, after decades of Izala influence, enfranchisement and
empowerment campaigns by international donors, a literate woman

remains rare and female political representation is essentially unheard of. The 'Yan Izala also attracted significant youth support. Many were attracted to the Izala 'because it levelled social differences. Nobody should bow before his parents and other authorities, and nobody should command respect only because of his wealth.'[27]

However, recent years have seen a significant fracturing within Izala and the rise of competition from other Salafi groups. Yusuf's departure from Ndimi mosque and the establishment of Boko Haram could be considered such a fracture. The catalyst for the split from the 'Yan Izala and the radicalisation of Yusuf was the lack of substantive change following the implementation of sharia law under the then newly elected Governor of Borno State, Ali Modu Sheriff.

Another factor facilitating violent protest has been the collapse of the economy in the country's north. This has been felt particularly in urban areas, leading to widespread unemployment and underemployment. Formerly boasting industrial centres, trading hubs, and a relatively robust agricultural sector, the north's economic base was devastated when Nigeria began exporting petroleum from the Niger Delta in the country's south. The country rapidly became dependent on oil revenue – an estimated 70 per cent of the government's revenue comes from oil money.[28] States competed fiercely for access to oil revenues, eventually resulting in a politically negotiated, complex allocation formula that satisfied few and often entrenched regional divides. Between 1973 and 2010, the number of factories in Kano registered with the Manufacturers' Association of Nigeria fell from 350 to 103.[29] Government services, never fully implemented in the region even in the colonial era, became even more egregiously inadequate. As recently as 2012, there was a 77.5 per cent difference in literacy rates between Lagos State and Borno State.[30] Neither private industry nor the government provides sufficient services or opportunities.

As industry declined across the north, city streets swelled with *almajirai*, young Qur'anic students placed in the care of a *malam* ('teacher') by their parents. Although it is intended that these children study the Qur'an, *almajirai* are typically regarded as 'street children' by northern urbanites. The tradition has religious overtones, but the reality for many *almajirai* is that their families are unable to provide care for them and have little choice but to send them away. Hannah Hoechner's work on *almajirai* in Kano emphasises that there are non-material incentives behind the system. She notes:

> The poor state of 'modern' secular education, the rhythms and requirements of peasant households, frequent family break-ups and widespread poverty all contribute to almajiri enrolments. Yet, people speaking about their reasons for enrolling children as almajirai rarely foreground the material constraints they face. Instead, they emphasise the life skills it is expected to impart, and declare that the hardships of an almajiri life are of educational value for the social, spiritual and moral training of their children.[31]

As a result of 'wider political anxieties about the distribution of power and resources within Nigeria', the *almajirai* have become easy targets for charismatic religious figures to manipulate.[32] Some people have blamed the *almajirai* for the frequency and violence of urban religious uprisings, ranging from 'Yan Tatsine to Boko Haram. One prominent NGO director insists that the first emirs in Boko Haram were in fact *almajirai* who had been co-opted into the movement.[33] This accusation is levelled despite the fact that Salafism, from which Boko Haram emerged, is critical of the *almajirai* system.

Almajirai, while sometimes regarded with suspicion, are generally viewed as a feature of the north's social landscape – particularly in the context of widespread economic stagnation. The system has been blamed for the proliferation of street children, begging for alms to pay their would-be teachers. The current *almajirai* system and consternation about the demographic threat they present, a result of the overwhelming maleness and poverty of participants, highlight the economic plight of many in the north and the importance of religious communities in the aftermath of economic contraction and political uncertainty.[34]

Thus, regardless of whether or not claims of disproportionate *almajirai* participation in religious riots are true – in fact, it is difficult even to estimate the numbers of children involved – it is clear that in the recent decades of economic decline and political change, religion and religious identification have taken on a new urgency in the north.[35] Frustrations have increasingly been expressed through religious mobilisation, a process facilitated by the fact that religious groups are often the most reliable providers of social services and best positioned to advance political agendas.

Boko Haram is undeniably a product of its historical context. A number of observers, particularly in the early years of Boko Haram, saw the group as a reincarnation of the 'Yan Tatsine riots.

Indeed, the grievances and style of preaching adopted by Mohammed Yusuf, the founder of Boko Haram, in the early years of the sect's operations were not radically different from those seen in the previous riots. But Yusuf also drew inspiration from the Salafist 'Yan Izala movement and ideology; Boko Haram's ideology is best characterised as Salafi-Jihadism. The adoption of *jihad* and of violence tactically differentiates Boko Haram from its predecessors and reflects the transnational, modern influences that have also shaped the group.

Chapter 3

BEING A GIRL IN NIGERIA AND THE GENDER POLITICS OF BOKO HARAM

Structural violence against women and girls is pervasive throughout Nigeria, but particularly acute in the country's north. While the abuses women and girls suffer at the hands of Boko Haram are more visible than the daily discrimination against women, insurgent abuse against women is ultimately an extension of the patterns of neglect and abuse that women have suffered for decades. As one former US official who worked on Nigerian issues for more than a decade joked darkly: 'Boko Haram abducts girls into a life of forced marriage and domestic servitude, taking them from their potential lives of forced marriage and domestic servitude.'[1] Mfoniso Akanamos, a lawyer from the north, observed while speaking on a panel of civil society advocates in Yola, Adamawa State, that 'society is uniquely lopsided against the female'.[2] Nigerian communities are primed for violence by the economic, political and social marginalisation of women that occurs on a daily, systemic basis.

Akanamos' observation, informed by her legal background and her experiences as a high-achieving woman in the north, is borne out in the data available about the status of women across Nigeria. In 2015, the country was ranked 152 of 188 countries in the Gender Equality Index, an 'index for measurement of gender disparity that was introduced in the 2010 Human Development Report 20th Anniversary Edition by the United Nations Development Programme

(UNDP)' and that uses metrics related to reproductive health, empowerment and employment to gauge gender parity.[3] Although the UNDP metric is imperfect, Nigeria's lacklustre performance relative to the other countries observed (many of which are poorer than Nigeria) is suggestive.

At nearly every stage of a Nigerian woman's life she is affected by systemic and pervasive gender inequality. A young woman's access to education in Nigeria is largely dependent on two factors: her family's wealth and the region in which they live. Despite variations within these two factors, the composite scores demonstrate a dismal state of affairs overall with regard to girls' education. The 2013 Demographic and Health Survey (DHS) revealed that 53 per cent of women between the ages of 15 and 49 are literate, compared with 75 per cent of men of the same age. The report notes that 'the gap in literacy levels between women and men is notable in the North Central, North East, and North West zones'.[4]

According to a 2007 report, *Educational Inequalities and Women's Disempowerment in Nigeria*, the persistent inequalities in school enrolment resulted in a female adult literacy rate of just '59.4% as against male, 74.4%'.[5] The same report noted that only 57 per cent of girls were enrolled in primary, secondary and tertiary schools, as opposed to a rate of 71 per cent among young men; the 2013 DHS found little progress in the intervening years, reporting a net attendance rate in primary education of less than 57 per cent for girls and less than 62 per cent for boys.[6] These rates are even lower in the country's north. A review conducted by the UK government found that, as a result of poor educational facilities and truncated experiences of formal education, two-thirds of 15–18-year-old girls in the north could not read a sentence (the proportion fell to less than 10 per cent in the country's south). The inequality is even more evident in the 'eight northern states, [where] over 80% of women are unable to read (compared with 54% for men)'.[7]

Even the girls who are lucky enough to have the chance to enrol in school in the first place leave earlier than their male counterparts, contributing to Nigeria's dubious honour of having the largest number of out-of-school children in the world. Only 4 per cent of girls in northern Nigeria complete secondary school. Some girls are sent to be *almajirai*; in 2007, a USAID subcontractor found that 30 per cent of the *almajirai* are female.[8]

So what do girls do, if they are not in school and not *almajirai*? All too frequently, in lieu of being students, girls become wives. More than half of women in the north are married by age 16 and they 'are expected to bear a child within the first year of marriage'.[9] Survey research found that 43 per cent of men and 36 per cent of women nationally believed that 'only when a woman has a child is she a real woman'.[10] Girls Not Brides estimated in 2016 that 17 per cent of girls were married by age 15 across the country, a rate that the UK estimates has been on the rise since 2003. The prevalence of child marriage in the country's north aggravates gender imbalances and subjects women to health risks and domestic violence. Uju Peace Okeke, a Nigerian lawyer, observed that child marriage has been correlated with 'health risks associated with early sexual initiation like obstetric fistula ... complications during childbirth, Vesico Vaginal Fistula (VVF), secondary infertility, maternal and infant mortality', concluding that 'child marriage is a form of modern day slavery', as child brides are often 'victims of sexual and other forms of domestic abuse'.[11]

In north-east Nigeria, polygamy is widespread, often characterised by wide age gaps between the husband and his wives. The system of polygamy is not only legal in the country, but is also a critical part of the social hierarchy. Marriage, as previously discussed, is a crucial means through which men perform masculinity publicly and attain social status. The intricate process of the marriage rituals in Borno State, as reported by the Imam of Madina mosque (a headquarters of the popular Tijaniyya Brotherhood in Maiduguri), has five steps of courtship and three additional ceremonies on the wedding day to complete the marriage. In none of these steps is it clear where a young woman could exercise autonomy; the negotiations regarding bride price are conducted with the girl's family and her suitor (and, at times, his family). The first step, *tambaya*, when a young man presents his case, involves the presentation of 'kola nuts, biscuits, and candies' to the family of the girl. Subsequent steps require the suitor 'to provide gift materials (textile materials, shoes, watches, cosmetics, inner wears etc) to the fiancée and her family to show how interested he is in their daughter and as well block other probable suitors'.[12] An unfortunate consequence of this process is that it incentivises early marriage between young women (and even girls) and older, socially and economically established men. It also leads to social instability, as wealthy men who take a number of wives destabilise the marriage market by reducing the availability of young, desirable brides.[13] The obstacles faced by young men seeking wives foster intergenerational resentment and can also serve to prime communities for conflict. The result of the marriage market in the country's north is higher rates of child marriage in that part of the country than in other regions.[14]

The prevalence of child marriage contributes to the high rates of maternal mortality in the country. According to the UK government's report, 'one Nigerian woman dies in childbirth every ten minutes', making it one of the most dangerous places in the world for a woman to give birth.[15] As with so many other indicators in Nigeria, there is significant regional variation in maternal health outcomes. The north-east region suffers from the highest percentage of maternal mortality, with rates five times the global average at 1,549 per 100,000 live births.[16]

A number of factors drive this astronomical rate of death in childbirth. A lack of assistance or professional medical facilities is one such factor. According to a 2012 study, one in three 15–19-year-olds in northern Nigeria gave birth without assistance from 'a health professional, traditional birth attendant, or even a friend or relative'.[17] The frequency of unassisted childbirth is illustrative of the overall lack of health services available to women in the north-east. Another factor raising the rate of maternal mortality, directly related to the prevalence of child marriage, is the young age of mothers in the north. Girls giving birth before the age of 15 are more likely to die than women who delay childbirth until their twenties. The structure of polygamous marriages, common in the north, is also thought to contribute to maternal mortality by reducing the spacing between children, as wives 'strive to have more children than their co-wives in order to ensure greater security in their marriage and old age'.[18] Just as men prove their worth and masculinity in the courtship period through their economic resources, once married, women are expected to demonstrate their femininity and value through childbirth. Nationwide, it is estimated that the average Nigerian woman gives birth to roughly six children over the course of her life.[19] Not only do these expectations cement rigid gender roles, they put women's health at risk through the cumulative strain that such frequent childbirth imposes, compounded by the lack of accessible healthcare in many areas.

Once a woman is married and has given birth to a child (or, more likely, the first of many), she still faces a number of threats in her home. According to a study conducted in 2008, one in every three women in Nigeria reported having experienced 'some form of violence, including battering and verbal abuse, emotional and psychological abuse, marital rape, sexual exploitation, or harassment within the home'.[20] These rates of domestic violence are probably under-reported in the north-east due to the sheer lack of outreach on this issue in the region. Not only is it difficult to access rural women, women are often reluctant to discuss domestic abuse or do not recognise events as being domestic abuse.

This normalisation is reflected in the widespread acceptance of domestic abuse throughout Nigeria. A 2012 national survey revealed that, nationwide, 11.9 per cent of 15–24-year-olds thought that 'wife beating is completely justified'.[21] The geographic distribution of responses is striking: in the north-east, 21.2 per cent of respondents agreed with the statement, compared with 17 per cent in the north-west, and just 3.5 per cent in the south. Another survey found that this domineering attitude towards women is reinforced by the prevalence of bride price as part of marriage. According to survey data, 'some 42% of men and 38% of women also agreed that paying bride price "gives the husband the right to do whatever he wants with his wife"', including domestic abuse and verbal harassment.[22] Despite this connection, 98 per cent of women still believed that bride price was an 'important' institution that should remain.[23] The courtship traditions in the north (which centre on the provision of gifts and bride price to the wife's family) play into notions of masculinity and femininity. Being a 'real man' in Nigeria is closely connected to a man's ability to be economically successful; an unfortunate by-product of this is the notion that a wife is another good available for purchase and use. Bride price is both a tradition of marriage and a way of commodifying women. Women's support for this tradition is, at first glance, perplexing; however, like any number of performative aspects of femininity, attracting a high bride price is a means of demonstrating social status. For those lower social classes who are unlikely to attract a high bride price, rejecting this tradition under the guise of religiosity is a way of maintaining or striving for social status through alternative routes.

Kano State, in north-west Nigeria, has recognised the threat to stability stemming from low rates of marriage (which are caused by economic stagnation and rising bride price in the region) and has instituted a 'dual marriage registry', where men seeking wives register on one list and single or widowed women register on another. The state then arranges low-cost weddings for matched pairs. Dr Bulama Gubio, of the Borno Elders' Forum, praised the programme, in which the 'government pays the bride price and gives a little newlywed support to them – just a few household goods to get them started'.[24] While the infrequent mass marriages that take place in Kano cannot be considered the single element that shielded the state from higher levels of recruitment into Boko Haram, the presence of a more responsive government and the delivery of an evidently crucial social service should not be ignored entirely as an inoculating factor.

Another post-marital feature of some women's lives in the north of the country is the practice of *purdah*, or wife seclusion. In Islam, this practice ranges from 'complete seclusion, partial seclusion, [to] voluntary "seclusion of the heart"'.[25] Relative to other regions, a greater number of women in northern Nigeria are kept confined in their husband's compound, despite the poverty in the region. It is interesting to note, as Kane does, that in no other West African Muslim country does 'seclusion exist in such a significant way'.[26] Like paying a high bride price, keeping one's wife in *purdah* is a sign of social status and is something people aspire to. Unlike bride price, which is widespread, wife seclusion is the purview of the rich. In addition to this, there is also an urban–rural divide, as 'poor women [are] involved in subsistence agriculture, or seeking jobs as farm labourers, [so] purdah has become a practice for only the wives of religious teachers, wealthy farmers and merchants'.[27]

Clearly, preventing women from engaging in the public sphere limits their economic opportunities and political mobilisation; less obviously, *purdah* limits the ability of women to acquire ID cards, indigeneity certificates and travel documents. It also limits women's ability to have discussions concerning what is happening to them and their children within their homes or talk about health issues. Women in *purdah* 'are often unable to get proper medical care, especially during pregnancy, and regular physical health check-ups', despite activism to promote better health outcomes for women in *purdah*.[28] Although it is an aspirational situation, *purdah* ultimately curtails women's public roles, and the prevalence of domestic abuse suggests that women are not necessarily compensated in the domestic sphere for their limited public roles.

This is not to suggest that women are totally absent from the economic or public sphere and confined to their homes. Women participate in economic life in Nigeria in ways that are often difficult to quantify or detect. Even women in *purdah* often sell fried snacks or non-perishable items, or engage in home-based services without violating the terms of their seclusion.[29] According to a report on education and women's disempowerment, women (both those who do and do not undergo *purdah*) are 'underrepresented in the formal sector but [play] an active and vital role in the country's informal economy'.[30]

Legally, women often have little recourse to empower themselves economically. Discriminatory credit practices and property laws limit those attempting to start their own businesses, in both the formal and the informal sector. The lack of female land ownership (in 2006, it was estimated that only 7.2 per cent of women owned land – a decline from 2003, when 13 per cent of women owned land) not only makes their ability to secure an agricultural livelihood difficult; it also limits women's ability to access credit due to a lack of collateral.[31] This situation is even starker in the north-east, where a mere 4 per cent of the land is registered to women.[32] Only 15 per cent of women across the country have a bank account, making entry into the formal sector difficult and further complicating women's access to credit.[33] The result is that 'Nigeria has one of the lowest rates of female entrepreneurship in sub-Saharan Africa'.[34]

As women age and their partners and family members pass away, they face a number of hurdles in accessing their inheritance. Despite the Land Act of 1978, which nationalised land in Nigeria, patrilineal systems of land management, in which 'women's rights of access are still regarded as secondary to those of men', still dominate in rural areas and throughout the north.[35] Widows are left in a particularly difficult position, as they lack the ability to claim their due inheritance and are left without their primary financial provider. Although there are provisions for widows in Islam, discrimination against them remains.

Part of the reason why the legal system is so stacked against women and girls in Nigeria is that there are so few women in government. In all tiers and branches of government, women are under-represented, despite the country having adopted a National Gender Policy in 2007 to advance 'gender mainstreaming' policies.

As the final chapter of this book will discuss, few women run for office in Nigeria and even fewer are elected. In the uncertain days leading up to the watershed elections of 2015, the *Daily Independent* reported that the only predictable part of the election results was that 'few women will be elected into political offices in Nigeria'.[36] The article argued that the lack of female representation was 'not because they do not want to serve their country, but the political structure and the patriarchy [*sic*] nature of the society always work against them'.[37] The piece drew on statements made in 2011 by Dr Abiola Akiyode-Afolab, a leading human rights advocate and executive director of the Women Advocates Research and Documentation Centre (WARDC). She argued that:

> Several factors exist in political parties in Nigeria which limit the aspirations of women and impede their access to leadership positions, these factors include; god fatherism, male dominated party executives, labeling, violence, money politics as well as other social and cultural factor [sic]. The failure to remove these barriers will further perpetuate under-representation of women in governance.[38]

Women in northern Nigeria only formally gained the right to vote in 1976, by way of a military decree, and attitudes and public opinion lagged behind this legal reform. The result is that women are disproportionately disengaged from the political process.

Despite all that has changed in the Nigerian political system, including the historic democratic transition of power from the People's Democratic Party (PDP) to the All Progressives Congress (APC) in the 2015 presidential elections, women's political marginalisation has remained a constant. A common refrain in feminist circles globally is 'You have to see it to be it.' Women's empowerment in Nigeria suffers from the lack of role models in business, politics and other positions of power.

National consequences of women's marginalisation: priming the country for conflict

All of these disappointing metrics that track women and girls in Nigeria over the course of their lives point not only to a society that is unfavourable to women, but also to one that is deeply unstable and prone to violence. In the ground-breaking book *Sex and World Peace*, Valerie Hudson, Bonnie Ballif-Spanvill, Mary Caprioli and Chad F. Emmett demonstrate quantitatively and qualitatively how gender inequality facilitates instability and violence worldwide. Their text uses a global database to demonstrate the 'priming effects of gender inequality', while setting out a system of metrics that takes into account the economic, political and social status of women within countries.[39] Beyond listing statistics relating to maternal health and female representation in legislative bodies, Hudson and her co-authors discuss how cultural conceptualisations of women impact on behaviour, which in turn can prompt social cohesion or discord.

One of the most salient points made by the text is in regard to the social importance of controls on women's reproductive health. As mentioned previously, marriage in the Lake Chad Basin is an important marker of social status and a rite of passage for young men; it is also a means of transferring, limiting and controlling women's sexuality and reproductive power – particularly given the prevalence of early marriage and the perceived value of virginity in the region. Hudson and her co-authors argue that if a woman's 'sexual relations and attendant behavior, such as manner of dress', are outside the social norm, 'her activities are viewed as bringing chaos and instability to the group'.[40] The threat that deviation poses alters gender relations, as 'the need to protect a woman becomes more and more associated with the need to protect her chastity – not her life, not her freedom', culminating in a system in which 'her life and her freedom are both subordinate to the goal of ensuring her chastity'.[41] The statistics illustrating the prevalence of child marriage and the widespread acceptance of spousal abuse reveal attempts to control women by circumscribing their autonomy early and often. Control over women has become an important symbolic battlefront between Boko Haram and the Nigerian government, as will be discussed in Chapter 4.

The rise in social violence in the aftermath of Nigeria's transition to democracy in 1999 is puzzling, at first observation. One clue may lie in the fact that 'the income gap between men and women grew after democratization', following changes regarding 'reproductive roles, lack of access to productive assets, and issues related to education' that marginalised women.[42] The democratic transition did not necessarily advance gender parity; in many instances it aggravated long-standing grievances and marginalised certain groups, thereby sowing the seeds of social violence and propagating the growth of violent non-state actors such as Boko Haram. As Cynthia Cockburn observes:

> what disposes society to war is the dichotomous and complementary nature of the gender relation, in which the sexes are specialized in such a way that each lacks half of the human range of qualities. Males are designated protector, females (and young) as protected. At the same time, perversely, males are cast as wielders of the means of coercion, women as 'natural' victims. In such a gender order, war can seem the fulfilment of gendered destinies.[43]

Any post-conflict redevelopment process must address these fundamental gendered fragilities; however, there are only a handful of models for Nigeria to emulate. As Aili Mari Tripp, Myra Marx Ferree and Christina Ewig noted: '[G]ender-based exclusions from security discourses and practices are not unusual or unique. The absence of a gender dimension in the establishment, revision, and operation of new legal and political institutions in post-conflict societies has been generally acknowledged.'[44] Tripp has stated that 'conflict had a significant and independent impact on women's political representation in sub-Saharan Africa and correlates strongly with the sharp increase in female legislative representation in sub-Saharan Africa, which tripled between 1990 and 2010'.[45] The question of whether Nigeria can use this crisis as a launching pad for gender parity reforms or whether it will be a missed opportunity is addressed in the final chapter. What is evident is that the current gender politics regime in the country is oppressive to women and deeply unstable.

Birthing the movement: gender politics of Boko Haram

The systemic discrimination against women in Nigeria, particularly in the north-east, created conditions in which women 'bargained with the patriarchy' to advance their status within the social and legal limitations of their community. Boko Haram, particularly under Mohammed Yusuf, worked to capitalise on the marginalisation of women in order to garner their support. According to Hamsatu Allamin, who works with the British Council's Nigeria Stability and Reconciliation Programme (NSRP), Yusuf's 'early preaching empowered women through Islamic education'.[46] His insistence on female education prompted many of his early, wealthy followers and patrons to turn their homes into schools for women. One of Yusuf's most important patrons, Baba Alhaji Fugu, hired him to teach his daughters. Fugu became Yusuf's father-in-law after Yusuf married one of the daughters whom Baba Fugu had hired him to instruct. It was this relationship between Yusuf and his father-in-law that allowed him to establish his own mosque, on land given to him by his indulgent patron.

In these years, he preached that 'the democratic government is not *for* us', and a group of men who still live in the Railway neighbourhood of Maiduguri, where Boko Haram's *Markas* (base) was located until its destruction during the security clampdown of July–August 2009, recall that his 'top priority' was the establishment of sharia law in Borno State. The 500 or so people who came to his sermons, many of whom were women, were enthusiastic about the implementation of a legal system that was more responsive to their needs. This finding corroborates Kendhammer's assertion that the push for sharia was, in essence, a demand for more responsive governance.[47]

Beyond his preaching, Yusuf established a social infrastructure among his followers that was relatively female-friendly, given the status of women in the north-east. Ahmed-Ghosh argues that, when questioning how women become involved with extreme religious groups the world over, it is important to understand that women 'may see religious movements as serving their own interests, interests which focus on maintaining the household and the community'.[48] Particularly in sects with a group-help component, membership 'is not just a matter of religion, but also of an institution that is perceived as privileging them and providing the stability they need to survive'.[49]

This infrastructure included Islamic education targeted towards women. The opportunity to receive Islamic education, particularly of a high quality, was cited by a number of people as a reason why women and girls joined Yusuf's sect in the early 2000s. This stance reflects the group's roots in the 'Yan Izala, which advocated for women's education and political participation in order to pass sharia law and to better prepare women for their eventual (and paramount) roles as wives and mothers. Yusuf's early preaching repeated the Izala sentiment that, without quality Islamic education, women would not be able to rear the next generation properly. For women, access to Islamic education provided improved social status and livelihood opportunities, as well as making them more desirable marital partners.[50]

At his mosque in Maiduguri and while travelling to villages across the north in the early 2000s, Yusuf organised gender-segregated preaching and paid attention to women and girls. One woman from Banki, who followed her son into Boko Haram, recalled that, on his visits to her village, prior to her joining the sect, 'if it concerned men, then men attended; if it concerned women, then the women were called to attend'.[51] Her understanding of Muhammed Yusuf's early message is clear: 'The priority was women. It was some of the first things they would say that they would change.'[52] According to discussions I had with men who heard Yusuf's early preaching, they were told to encourage the women in their lives to attend the female preaching sessions. When men formally joined the sect, they often brought along their wives (willingly, or after a bit of persuasion).

Yusuf's ideological orientation and the gendered division of labour required for the group's operation meant that members needed to be married, with Yusuf facilitating marriages between his group's members in this early period. According to residents of the Railway neighbourhood, over the years, Yusuf facilitated over 500 weddings. 'They were mostly very simple, not very expensive marriages,' a former attendee at the ceremonies recalled. 'He saw that the youth are stranded and he capitalised on it.'[53] Another man who lives in the Railway neighbourhood remarked that, even though the neighbourhood was relatively impoverished, 'traditional marriage is so expensive that even if you want to, sometimes you can't. The whole thing can cost 1 million naira.'[54] Even today, the area surrounding Yusuf's (now demolished) mosque is strikingly poor. Walking along the dirt roads, the pleasantly worn characteristics of Maiduguri, with its stencilled signs, bustling commerce and peeling paint, are absent, replaced by unpainted, somewhat dilapidated buildings. To add insult to injury, the neighbourhood is within a short drive of the resplendent emir's palace. The appeal of Mohammed Yusuf's system, in which, as one man recalled, 'if you don't have the dowry but you can recite the Qur'an and promise to teach your wife, you were permitted to marry', is immediately clear.[55]

Surveys of men in Nigeria reveal that masculinity is undeniably bound to a man's ability to generate income and provide for his wife. In the north-east, the compulsion to take a wife is particularly acute, as polygamy is common and the number of wives and children that a man has is a mark of status. Barriers to employment become barriers to marriage, doubly denying those without employment a sense of manhood and autonomy. Pride in the family is such that other challenges to a sense of fulfilled masculinity can be overlooked. During my time in Maiduguri, I met a displaced man who was struggling to feed his children and whose only source of income as a volunteer vigilante was the small, unreliable sums of money passed to him sporadically by the communities he defends; despite his precarious economic situation, he boasted proudly to me that, through it all, he has still managed to continue impregnating his three wives. He, his wives and their 19 children live in two bedrooms in a concrete settlement in a commercial part of town, with mats for sleeping stacked against the walls and flies darting across every surface. With a wide grin, he asked, 'Am I not a rich man?,' as his children assembled in the room in tattered clothes, with round bellies.

The lack of employment opportunities for young men in many northern cities, compounded by the prevalence of polygamy among the city's older elites and the stark (and very visible) contrast between the living standards of those with jobs and those without, made conditions rife for intergenerational conflict. Although the burden of paying for marriage falls on men in Nigeria, a limited marriage market also has serious ramifications for women. Just as marriage is a rite of passage that signifies entrance into adulthood for men, 'a girl becomes a woman on her wedding day', as Zainab told me. She argued that life improved after marriage: 'It's different when you're married. You're your own person. You don't have to listen to your parents; you're now independent.'[56] Even the selection of a member of Boko Haram as a husband often provided a means for women to exercise some authority. Aisha, a 17-year-old girl who voluntarily joined Boko Haram, recalled that she was able to marry a childhood friend who had joined Boko Haram and had become fairly high-ranking – despite her family's disapproval. 'I liked him very much, he was brilliant and handsome, but my parents did not want me to marry him. I did not even tell them I was getting married. They knew he was fighting *jihad*.'[57] Despite the lack of familial support, she proudly boasted that, when she became his second wife, 'we had a very big wedding'.[58]

Not only did marriage into the sect provide a way for women to escape their parents' homes and develop their identities, it also provided them with rare financial autonomy. Yusuf and his followers preached (and, evidentially, followed) a return to the Islamic interpretation of giving bride price directly to the woman. Hamsatu explained that, according to this Qur'anic interpretation, 'Islamically, the dowry for the bride should go directly to the woman. Even your parents are not supposed to touch the dowry – you are supposed to use the money as you see fit.'[59] Common practice, however, has deviated from this interpretation and bride price is widely given directly to the parents of the bride or to a male guardian. Women rarely get to exercise any control over their dowry or the negotiation surrounding it. The drive towards marriage was strong for both men and women in Yusuf's cohort, and his Qur'anic interpretation was a valuable conduit for them to subvert the oppressive aspects of the Nigerian marriage market. Hamsatu glibly concluded that, while the preaching and financial support of the group were appealing to many, 'others joined because before they could not get near these women in their dreams and now they get to take them as their own wives'.[60] Although the intensity and style of fighting of Boko Haram changed when Abubakar Shekau took control, the character of the (voluntary) marriages between sect members was not radically altered. Aisha, who was married in 2013 to an emir in Boko Haram, was thrilled that her bride price – a hefty 100,000 naira (due to both the status of her husband and her desirability as a partner) – was paid directly to her. Other women who married during this period recalled that, although 'Boko Haram weddings are smaller, you get the dowry and it's not too small'.[61]

Yusuf's preaching also emphasised taking proper care of one's wife even after marriage, a practice that continues under Shekau's tenure. Falta, who joined to follow her son, is obviously a biased source but is also a rarity in her willingness to associate freely with the insurgency. She recalled that 'some men treated women well before *aqidah*, but after *aqidah* they added special treatment and all of the men started treating women better'.[62] Zainab was married somewhat hastily to a member of the group by her father; she recalled that her future husband 'saw me walking home from lessons one day and sent someone to my father. At the time I was seeing someone else that I liked better … We had been dating for four months, but once the tailor saw me it took only ten days to get married.' She was better pleased by her marriage the longer she stayed with her husband, stating simply: 'I was happier about the marriage when he showed me all the things he had gotten me for our house. A big family size bed, a chair, cupboard and utensils, clothes.'[63] Even better, 'after the wedding, he gave me anything I wanted … it was nice. We had nice conversations and I would tend to my children and do my chores.'[64] The sect's gender politics, while regressive and patriarchal by secular Western standards, often represented a significant improvement in women's status within the local context of Borno State.

The Boko Haram commander's wife stated unequivocally that 'there was 100 per cent better treatment as a wife under Boko Haram. There were more gifts, better food, and a lot of sex that I always enjoyed.'[65] This advancement, relative to the typical experience of a woman raised in northern Nigeria, can be witnessed at nearly every developmental stage: Boko Haram advocated for Qur'anic education for all children (including girls), advocated for bride price to be paid directly to the bride, advised men to act as protectors and providers for their wives, and imparted to their male followers the importance of caring for their older, female relatives. The insurgency's appeal to women becomes clearer when considered as an alternative to the narrow opportunities women in northern Nigeria would otherwise face.

Despite the clear benefits of membership for women, many (even regional experts) were initially surprised by Yusuf's success in galvanising support among young women in the early 2000s. Gerhard Müller-Kosack, an anthropologist who specialises in the communities in the Mandara Mountains along the Nigerian border with Cameroon, which have been particularly affected by the insurgency, was stunned by the change in the women in the community following exposure to Boko Haram's ideology. He noted: 'It was the women at the forefront of the change.'[66] Not only had the women adopted the full covering in their dress, they were also engaging in overtly political actions. Müller-Kosack returned to find that his endeavours to build and furnish a school had unravelled: 'All the books had been burned – the young women, it was they who made a pile of them and burned them in front of the school.'[67]

The female adoption of Boko Haram's ideology and standards of public dress reflects the broader history of Islamism in Nigeria, where women have used new social movements to advance their own interests. In *The Hijab in Nigeria*, Hauwa Mahdi notes:

A silent revolution in Muslim women's veils has been taking place in Nigeria for the last 30 years. Up to 1975 hardly any Muslim woman in northern Nigeria wore the *hijab*, while today one could not miss the growing number of women who wear it … From the mid 1970s, the *hijab* began to be worn by women in institutions of higher education in Nigeria. Because of where and who the wearers were, one could infer that the *hijab* has its origins in the values of the urban middle class. By the late 1980s, its use had spread to other classes of urban women and gradually to some of their rural sisters. By the 1990s, the idea of the *hijab* had begun to pose a challenge to governments' uniforms policy in the public service sector such as the nursing profession. With the introduction of Islamic law in 1999, some of the Muslim states introduced the *hijab* as a compulsory part of girls' uniforms in state schools. The *hijab* is becoming visually louder and a compulsory part of female dressing in the certain public space [sic].[68]

Although some critics have suggested that the *hijab* reflects an oppressive moral standard, it is evident that some women in Nigeria have adopted it as a means of asserting their autonomy. Further, given that many women in northern Nigeria live under – or are expected to aspire to – *purdah* or wife seclusion (a practice that limits their interaction outside the home), it is possible that the *hijab* allows them to engage in the public sphere without sacrificing their moral reputation. The adoption of the veil was, for some women, an empowering act. Those who are waiting for 'feminism' (meaning Western feminism) to arrive in northern Nigeria should be aware of the ways in which women throughout the region have organised and advanced their own interests. A report by the Wilson Center on women's rights in northern Nigeria observed that: 'Women's rights movements in Hausa-speaking Nigeria have been present before the establishment of the Caliphate. This rich history gives Muslim women from the North a voice that is distinct from Western feminist movements and sometimes contrary to them.'[69]

It appears that women's support for sharia law and their adoption of political religiousness were a reaction to the perceived failure of the secular government and traditional leaders – largely the same factors that motivated their male counterparts. Their support, perhaps, should be less surprising given women's relatively more tenuous position. State services for women, including education and health support, are limited in the north-east, and a number of customary traditions put women at a disadvantage if their male patrons (fathers, husbands, brothers) die.

Although the plight of women in the north-east will be detailed in the following chapter, it is worth noting here that sharia was a means of advancing women's rights relative to the status quo. According to the US Department of State's 2015 report on human rights in Nigeria, many customary practices in the region did not recognise a woman's right to inherit her husband's property, with many widows rendered destitute when their in-laws took virtually all of the deceased husband's property.[70] In addition to a lack of reliable property rights, 'domestic violence was widespread and often considered socially acceptable', to the extent that 'police normally did not intervene in domestic disputes, which seldom were discussed publicly'.[71] In contrast, sharia law offered women some hope of justice. The report noted that, under sharia, widows maintained property rights and that a number of NGOs had recorded women successfully defending their rights in sharia courts when they were finally implemented.[72] One of the first initiatives of the Federation of Muslim Women's Associations in Nigeria (FOMWAN), one of the most prominent civil society groups in the north-east and perhaps the best known women's rights group in the region, was a campaign for 'the creation of sharia courts for personal law outside the old Northern Region so that Muslim women in these areas could gain access to the protections of Islamic inheritance and divorce law'.[73]

In sum, Boko Haram's appeal to women in these early years extended beyond the social services that were provided by and built upon women's support for sharia law and, more generally, reform. Involvement in Boko Haram helped women advance their own interests and political agenda in a manner that also provided moral support for such activism. Membership was not only a means of advancing individual interests, but also a spontaneous collective political response to inadequate government care. While subsequent chapters detail the nuances of the ways in which Boko Haram was able to capitalise on women's marginalisation by providing an alternative identity and moral code, it is sufficient to state here that the dominant narrative of women being coerced, conscripted and abducted into the sect is an incomplete one and reflects a significant operational transformation from the group's initial recruitment tactics. While kidnapping and coercion are undoubtedly a feature of this insurgency, they do not capture the totality of the female experience with Boko Haram.

Yusuf's wives as allegory

It is worth noting that Yusuf's four wives provide an interesting microcosm of the myriad ways in which women joined Boko Haram of their own volition. He married his first wife, Hajia Bintu, when he was 25 and she was 19. The two were cousins. Yusuf's childhood friend reminisced about the traditional wedding, describing it as 'a very colourful big wedding' where 'even Yusuf was very happy and dancing'.[74] Hajia married Yusuf 'before he was a radical' and she was essentially brought into the group through her pre-existing relationship with Yusuf.[75] Like Hajia, many women across the northeast discussed how their husbands and other family members were their conduit into the insurgency following the men's conversion. His second wife, Fatima, was married to Yusuf after he was hired by her father, Baba Alhaji Fugu (later identified as one of the patrons most important to Yusuf's rise), to serve as a tutor for his daughters. Fatima's father resisted their partnership at first, but was convinced by his friends that Yusuf would be a good provider. This sort of familial resistance was a common refrain among the women who had chosen members of Boko Haram as their future spouses.[76] Yusuf's third wife, Hajia Gana, was introduced to Yusuf by members of her family after he came to preach in her village. Her family's enthusiasm was the driving force behind her marriage. Like Hajia Gana, some women described to me how their family members married them to insurgents – brothers and fathers sympathetic to the sect were often eager to increase their prestige within the insurgency by arranging marriages.[77] His fourth and final wife was perhaps the most colourful character of the group: older than her husband by a handful of years, she was the widow of a popular civil servant and sought out Yusuf as a partner.[78] This final wife represents the considerable number of women who, after being exposed to the insurgency and the benefits of membership, took the initiative to seek membership.

Yusuf's wives' eventual fates may also provide a metaphor for some of the outcomes for women who have been involved with

Boko Haram. According to Yusuf's childhood friends and residents of the Railway neighbourhood where he founded his mosque,
Yusuf's first wife has left the group and is living quietly among the
community in Maiduguri. Her experience suggests the capacity for
reintegration of women previously in the sect.[79] His second and
third wives have remained in Boko Haram, reportedly remarried to
Shekau after Mohammed Yusuf was killed, echoing the stories of
women who described intra-sect divorce and marriage as relatively
common. Their experiences represent the women who maintain
their loyalty to the sect or who are forced to remain in the group
through the internal Boko Haram marital dynamic. The fourth wife,
twice widowed by 41, was remarried to a Boko Haram commander
and killed during fighting in Bama, a town not far from Maiduguri;
she represents, perhaps, those women who have been caught in the
crossfire between the state and the insurgents.[80]

As Chapter 4 illustrates, marriage, access to education,
improved status, and family revenge were all powerful drivers
of women's recruitment into Boko Haram. Subsequent chapters
address the fates of these women, as casualties, displaced women,
prisoners and fighters.

Chapter 4

GIRLS AS SYMBOLS: THE CHIBOK ABDUCTIONS AND THE SILENT MAJORITY

> Men fighting wars that problematise identity may burden women with the cultural symbols of the religion/nation/ethnic group their leaders say is under attack
>
> *Sheila Meintjes, Anu Pillay*
> *and Meredeth Turshen*[1]

While it is true that Boko Haram wreaked havoc on communities across the Lake Chad Basin for years before its atrocities captured international attention – and women in Nigeria have suffered a myriad of discriminatory and outright abusive systems largely in silence for generations – it is undeniable that the Chibok abductions marked a turning point in the course of the insurgency and the government's response. Despite the event's notoriety, a number of questions remain. What exactly transpired that night? Why did this abuse capture such unprecedented media attention? How were these girls transformed from victims into symbols that spawned a Chibok political-philanthropic complex capable of raising untold amounts of money and galvanising worldwide support? What has happened to the Chibok girls, and the thousands of other women abducted by the insurgents over the course of the conflict? What incentivised this tactic and where else has it been used? How have the Chibok abductions shifted the conversation about Boko Haram in Nigeria and around the world? This chapter attempts to shed light on these questions.

Chibok: abduction, manipulation and global condemnation

In the late hours of 14 April 2014, insurgents stormed the dormitories at the Government Girls Secondary School in Chibok, a remote town in Borno State. Members of Boko Haram pretended to be guards and instructed the girls to climb into their trucks. As the insurgents carried off the 276 girls, who had been at the school to take their Senior Secondary Certificate examination, they burned down houses in Chibok.

An 18-year-old who was abducted that night but managed to escape as the insurgents left Chibok recalled that:

> Two men told us we should not worry, we should not run. They said they had come to save us from what is happening inside the town, that they are policemen. We did not know that they were from Boko Haram. The rest of the men came and started shouting 'Allahu Akbar' and at that moment we realized, they were Boko Haram. We were told to be quiet. One of them told us that the horrible things we heard happening elsewhere, like burning houses, killing people, killing students, kidnapping people, would happen to us now. We all started crying and he told us to shut up.[2]

The residents who did not flee Chibok that night reported being filled with fear and dread as they heard the insurgents come into town on their motorbikes. At the school the next day, local residents who had remained in the town and had avoided being targeted by the insurgents reported: 'We saw the classrooms burnt, ashes everywhere and everything dumped – schoolbooks and Bibles.'[3]

Over the next few days, tallies were taken of the number of girls who had been abducted, and the dozens of girls who managed to escape the insurgents trickled back into town. These girls relayed that 'the men had come in army uniforms so, at first, they had not realized it was a Boko Haram attack'.[4] The men had entered the school, 'shot in the air and then threatened two Muslim students and instructed them to show them where the brick-making machine was'. If the students refused, the men said that they would 'kill all the students, starting with the Muslims', according to a witness interviewed by Human Rights Watch. Escapees reported that they believed Boko Haram had originally targeted the school just to steal a brick-making machine, food and other supplies; the insurgents changed their plan once they 'realized they had access to the young women and girls and faced little resistance'.[5] The insurgents, seeing the opportunity to abduct the girls, called to arrange more vehicles to carry them away.[6] In *Those Terrible Weeks in Their Camp*, Human Rights Watch reported that:

[after looting and burning the school grounds, the men put as many students as they could fit into one truck. The remaining young women and girls were forced to walk for about 10 miles at gunpoint on the route to a Boko Haram camp in the Sambisa forest, until they were eventually accommodated in other vehicles that later arrived. Three girls, for whom there was still no room, were released.[7]

As the insurgents fled the scene, some girls leapt from the trucks en route to the camps in the forest, hiding from insurgents and fleeing back to their homes.[8]

The tragedy was made all the more frustrating by reports that the Nigerian army had more than four hours' notice that such an attack was going to take place, but failed to secure the area.[9] Conspiracy theories gained traction as more details about the night were revealed: only 15 soldiers were at the school that night, 'instead of the usual 100' (an exaggeration of the security presence in the town – let alone in the school), and the 27 police officers stationed at the school were intoxicated; the school's headmistress was in Maiduguri seeking treatment for her diabetes; and the school's generator had run out of diesel.[10] The confluence of unfortunate events was taken as a sign of government complicity in the abductions and interpreted as just another example of the marginalisation of communities in the north.

In the days following the abduction, even establishing how many girls had been taken proved a difficult task. The Borno State government first claimed that 129 had been at the school that night, with 14 having escaped the insurgents, leaving 115 to be rescued from Boko Haram. A few days later, a local Christian priest, Enoch Mark, who had three members of his family abducted, told reporters that the insurgents had claimed more than 300 girls. The official count that 276 girls had been abducted was only arrived at on 2 May 2014, at which point only 219 remained in their control.[11] Further adding to the confusion was the 16 April announcement by the Nigerian defence spokesman at the time, Chris Olukolade, that the military had rescued 107 of the 115 girls.[12] A political tussle ensued when the school's principal refuted this claim. On 18 April, the military retracted its statement, with Olukolade stating that his announcement had been made 'in good faith and not intended to deceive the public'.[13] While conspiracy theories are tempting, it is perhaps more accurate – and even more dispiriting – to conclude that this state of affairs was the norm in the north-east at the time. Security forces were stretched thin, poorly compensated and largely ineffective, making such an attack possible.

The reaction to the abduction was swift and shockingly widespread, given the lack of attention outside of Nigeria paid to the crisis in the north prior to this event. The Chibok abductions seemed to represent a microcosm of the frustrations with Goodluck Jonathan's administration and its response to the crisis in the country's north-east. Technological innovations, especially social media, gave

parents and activists an unprecedented platform to air their grievances in relation to the government's lumbering response. Protests
in cities across Nigeria on 30 April and 1 May 2014 highlighted the
government's callousness. Patience Jonathan, then the First Lady,
reportedly ordered the arrest of one of the women protesting. One
of the protest leaders arrested, Saratu Ndirpaya, told the Associated
Press that Patience Jonathan had accused them of being members of
Boko Haram or merely political dissidents, and had asserted that
the Bring Back Our Girls protestors 'just wanted the government of
Nigeria to have a bad name'.[14]

Despite the government's reluctance to engage with the activists, the movement gained unexpected momentum following the
creation of the hashtag #BringBackOurGirls by a lawyer in Abuja.
The phrase trended globally, at the time setting a record for the
most tweeted hashtag in Twitter's history, with 2.3 million tweets by
11 May 2014.[15] Politicians and activists around the world, including
First Lady Michelle Obama and girls' rights advocate Malala
Yousafzai, used the hashtag, thereby raising the profile of the crisis
and placing even more pressure on the Jonathan administration.
The international community's perception of Nigeria's administration seemed to shift towards the idea that it was incompetent or
wilfully uninvolved in the north-east. Certainly, the Chibok abductions called into question the ability of the Nigerian government to
put down the insurrection. Former US ambassador to Nigeria John
Campbell concluded that the abductions suggested that the insurgency's strength 'appears to be increasing. The government's ability
to provide security to its citizens appears to be decreasing.'[16]

The global attention translated into greater access to Nigerian
politicians for the parents of the abducted girls. However, it became
clear that this access was granted only grudgingly – and that it
would not necessarily be matched by the sort of intervention, assistance or compassion that the activists were demanding. Some in
Jonathan's administration accused the activists of 'fabricating the
abductions' and of being supporters of the insurgency.[17] *The Econ-*

omist suggested that 'the worst aspect of the Nigerian government's handling of the abduction is its seeming indifference to the plight of the girls' families', observing that 'it took more than two weeks before Jonathan addressed the matter in public'.[18]

The outright disdain that many in the Jonathan administration had for the #BringBackOurGirls movement was well illustrated by the 4 May arrest of Naomi Mutah Nyadar, an organiser and vocal advocate for the group. Nyadar was arrested following a meeting between Nigeria's First Lady and the family members of and advocates for the abducted girls.[19] The President's spokespeople claimed that the arrest was made on the basis of impersonation; allegedly, Nyadar had 'claimed that she was one of the girls' mothers, so she's just being questioned by the police'. Another member of the #BringBackOurGirls movement, whose two nieces were taken, defended Nyadar, stating that the government was 'claiming it is a hoax and that her daughter was not abducted. But when we say "bring back our daughters" the campaign means it in the broader sense of "daughters of Nigeria."' The activist concluded: 'They are so clueless.'[20]

In contrast, Boko Haram's leadership was not as slow to identify the value of the international attention to the plight of the abducted girls. On 5 May, the insurgents released a video featuring Abubakar Shekau elaborating on how the group intended to use the girls. A second video message, released on 12 May, showed over 100 of the girls and demanded that, in exchange for their release, the government free detained Boko Haram members. Listing the places where members were detained, Shekau stated: 'We will not release them while you detain our brothers.'[21]

The videos' messages seemed tailored to incense Nigerians and the global community of activists who had rallied around the hashtag. Infamously, the second video featured the girls (many of whom were Christians, reflecting the history of Christian missionaries in Chibok) in *hijabs*, while Shekau stated emphatically: 'Allah has instructed me to sell them.' He went on to say that the girls should have been married, not in school, given their eligible ages.[22] The release of this video can be considered a critical moment in which the Chibok abductions edged towards being a symbolically significant event and away from being merely a tragedy or a routine violation of women's rights.

News of a potential deal to free the girls in 2014, brokered between Boko Haram and the government, became public only following the government's abandonment of the plan. According to *The Telegraph*, 'officials from the Geneva-based organization have sat in on talks between the Nigerian government and a senior Boko Haram leader currently held in one of the country's maximum security prisons', in addition to visiting 'a number of other jails, identifying a list of 16 senior commanders that Boko Haram wants freed in exchange for its hostages'.[23] The Nigerian press reported that, 'at the 11th hour, officials scrapped the exchange in a telephone call from a crisis summit in Paris where Nigerian President Goodluck Jonathan met foreign ministers including those from Britain, the United States, France and Israel'.[24] At the summit, 'it was agreed there that no deals should be struck with terrorists and that force should instead be used against them'.[25] The vagueness of the details surrounding the potential deal and the generally strained relationship between President Goodluck Jonathan and the international community called into question the plausibility that such a deal was ever brokered and then called off. Regardless of the veracity of the claims, the situation enraged the population.[26]

Nigerian #BringBackOurGirls activists maintained their momentum, continuing protests in Abuja, in spite of government efforts to prevent such action. These protests kept attention focused on the plight of the girls, most dramatically through a tally of the number of days since the girls had been abducted. Their activism ensured that the Chibok abductions were addressed in the watershed 2015 presidential elections. The events surrounding the night of 14 April helped establish a narrative of Goodluck Jonathan as ineffective, uncaring and incompetent. This perception helped usher

General Muhammadu Buhari into the Nigerian presidency, following electoral delays related to instability in the north-east. The Buhari administration has been at pains to avoid the mismanagement of the Chibok abductions that occurred under the Jonathan regime. In his inaugural address in May 2015, Buhari asserted that his 'government will do all it can to rescue [the Chibok girls] alive' and stated that he could not declare that he had 'defeated Boko Haram without rescuing the Chibok girls and all other innocent persons held hostage by insurgents'. Further illustrating the national importance the issue had assumed, within two weeks of being sworn in, President Buhari, his wife Aisha Buhari, and the Vice President's wife, Dolapo Osinbajo, held a meeting with some of the mothers of abducted Chibok girls.

The Buhari administration's improved interaction with the #BringBackOurGirls activists was coupled with a renewed military campaign in the north-east against Boko Haram. Despite Buhari's initial characterisation of the rescue of the Chibok girls as a defining event in winning the war on Boko Haram and his announcement in December 2015 that he was willing to 'negotiate with Boko Haram for the release of the Chibok girls without any preconditions', by Christmas 2015 he was claiming that the insurgency was 'technically defeated' although the Chibok girls had still not been found.[27] Unsurprisingly, this shift in posture led to anger among activists, who concluded that Buhari was as out of touch as his predecessor. Frustration continued to mount as the two-year anniversary of the abduction approached. The 'proof of life' video released near the anniversary of the abductions helped keep the girls in the news cycle, putting additional pressure on the Buhari administration to live up to its campaign promises. A confrontation between the police and #BringBackOurGirls protestors in early September 2016 led many to accuse Buhari of being as callous as Jonathan.[28]

Despite these setbacks, the Buhari administration has had more success in bringing back the Chibok girls than the Jonathan administration. In May 2016, Amina Ali Nkeki emerged from the Sambisa Forest with her child and her Boko Haram husband. Nkeki was the first of the Chibok girls to escape after being brought to the insurgents' camp and her 'rescue' (perhaps better described as an escape, given that she and her husband left the insurgency without support from the military) was greeted with international celebration and global press coverage.[29] Critics noted that her rescue became part of the Buhari administration's public relations offensive, citing the media attention paid to her reunion with her mother and the high-profile meeting between the girl and President Buhari in Abuja.[30] Following the meeting, it was unclear what the girl's future would be, and the government's statements about the care and protection she would be given were conspicuously absent when discussing what would happen to her husband – or even what sort of care would be given to the daughter she had given birth to while in captivity with Boko Haram.

In October 2016, news broke that the Nigerian government had successfully negotiated the release of 21 of the Chibok girls, suggesting that the Buhari administration had reinitiated the negotiations between the Nigerian government and insurgents reportedly scrapped under Jonathan. Few details have emerged about the process, other than the fact that the International Red Cross and the Swiss government brokered the talks.[31] Of the 21 girls who were released, at least eight have had children. The government did not disclose how long the negotiations had taken, what subjects were covered, or how it had identified legitimate spokespeople from Boko Haram. Importantly, no information has been released regarding what Boko Haram received in exchange for the release of the girls. The reports of a prisoner swap were denied and condemned by the Nigerian government, but the denunciations were not accompanied by any additional information about the terms of the negotiation.[32] Others have speculated that the government paid a ransom to the insurgents, a claim also denied by government spokespeople.[33] Although it is irresponsible to disseminate false news, it is frankly unthinkable that the insurgents would cede such a valuable negotiating chip without receiving something in return. This is particularly unlikely as a few months later, in May 2017, 82 Chibok girls were exchanged for five Boko Haram commanders.[34] The Buhari administration's continued negotiations with Boko Haram, endeavouring to bring home the Chibok girls, is a testament to the dedication and effectiveness of the #BringBackOurGirls movement.

'In these girls we see our daughters': branding Chibok[35]

The international community's condemnation of the attack was accompanied by the development of partnerships between Nigerian activists and international advocacy groups. A number of the Chibok girls who managed to escape from Boko Haram have been given scholarships to universities and schools; these high-profile admissions were often paired with fundraising drives and renewed activism on the issue of girls' education. Michelle Obama's statement that 'in these girls, Barack and I see our own daughters. We see their hopes, their dreams' was met with global approval. The sympathetic profile of the girls, their universal appeal as daughters and innocents, galvanised action to save the abducted girls and to support the girls who had managed to escape from the insurgents.[36]

As a result of partnerships between Nigerian and American activists, ten of the girls were granted visas and scholarships to attend private schools in the United States. Although the ten girls were initially divided between two schools on the West Coast, eventually they were all enrolled in a single school in Virginia. According to a journalist who has worked closely with the Chibok girls, their relocation to Virginia was in response to inadequate care, the concern being that the girls were seen more as a fundraising opportunity for the schools than as young women in need of serious educational intervention.[37] The situation escalated to the point where the federal government of Nigeria felt compelled to take guardianship of the Chibok girls attending school in the United States, although the full details of the logistics of this guardianship have yet to be released.[38]

Even after the government intervened on the girls' behalf, problems continued. In September 2016, the Minister of Women's Affairs, Aishatu Hassan, released a statement that the government had been made aware that the girls were being treated as spectacles rather than as students. She stated plainly that 'the girls were being used as tools for making money – not prostitution – but in the sense that they will be taken here and there where they go and relay their experiences during the insurgency, especially the invasion of Chibok town by Boko Haram and how they were abducted'.[39] When the girls complained that they 'were taken to U.S. on an arrangement that [their interim guardians] were going to send them to school and that they were going to pay for their school', not to be used as fundraising tools, they were allegedly told that 'they were not allowed to remain in school'.[40] The families of the girls were distressed by their treatment. Yakubu Nkeki Maiva, the chairman of the group of parents of the abducted girls, lamented: 'When they were taken abroad we were told that they were going there to study and not going on tourism. We want them to return home with certificates and not tourists' experiences.'[41]

The American University of Nigeria (AUN) in Yola, the capital of the north-eastern Adamawa State, also admitted 21 of the Chibok girls who escaped the insurgents on a programme that will allow them to finish their interrupted studies and then, if they choose to do so, to enrol in the university.[42] AUN coupled this act of charity with a significant fundraising and public relations campaign, including fairly regular blog updates about the status of the Chibok girls. One remarkably transparent post, entitled 'Chibok Girls at AUN Learn, Explore, and Thrive', recounted the girls' enjoyment of a nature trail on the school's campus before closing with an appeal for donations:

Inspired by their outing, the girls and faculty members now have plans to make another nature trail in another part of [the] campus. The girls are so excited to explore and learn. We are grateful that with your help, we have been able to take them in and give them that opportunity.

In the first year of hosting the Chibok girls, AUN reported that more than $100,000 had been raised in the girls' name, a sum that is surely only a small proportion of what has been raised globally. These acts of charity on both sides of the Atlantic were opportunistic; the appeals frequently positioned the Chibok girls as symbols, rather than victims.

The Chibok girls have also become a political symbol, in addition to a boon for fundraising. The Buhari administration galvanised support for the war effort by manipulating the image of the Chibok girls to serve the administration's needs. As Deepa Kumar argues, reflecting on the gendering of war narratives throughout history, 'the most prominent role that women play in war narratives is that of victim. Women can suffer rape, torture, or death during war, giving the male soldier the special duty to protect her from such consequences.'[43] The quest to 'bring back our girls' has been drawn into a larger narrative about the war against the insurgents. It is significant that, according to public reports, the Nigerian government has only engaged in negotiations with the insurgents about the release of the girls.

The soldiers, some of whom have been accused of gross human rights abuses and rampant corruption, are cast as heroes (and absolved of these violations) in their mission to return the Chibok girls and put an end to the insurgency. This narrative is not dissimilar to the one that accompanied the rescue of Jessica Lynch during the war in Iraq; Kupar observes that Jessica Lynch, part of a minority in the US military as a woman:

became a symbol of the West's 'enlightened' attitude towards women, justifying the argument that the US was 'liberating' the people of Iraq. In short, the Lynch story, far from putting forward an image of women's strength and autonomy, reveals yet another mechanism by which they are strategically used to win support for war.[44]

The girls kidnapped from Chibok fit neatly into this narrative, given their abduction from a government school and the innocence conveyed by their youth.

Just as the Buhari administration and international NGOs have attempted to shape media coverage of the Chibok abductions to their benefit, so too has the leadership within the Boko Haram insurgency recognised the narrative and symbolic value of the girls. It is worth noting that the 5 and 12 May videos marked the shortest amount of time between Shekau's appearances in propaganda videos. The full transcripts of these videos are revealing about the sort of image that the sect wishes to project, as both a deeply pious sect and the vanguards of 'true Islam'. In the videos, Shekau asserts that he would be well within his rights as a Muslim in *jihad* to sell off the girls, and he suggests that he may do so. While these threats are levelled, there is nothing to show them being carried out. What is shown are more than 100 of the girls in conservative Islamic dress, interspersed with armed militants. Shekau asks his audience: 'Don't you know the over 200 Chibok schoolgirls have converted to Islam? They have now memorized two chapters of the Koran. They have seen themselves in the Books of Luke and John that Christians have corrupted the Bible. Girls from Chibok confessing Islam is the true religion!' He then reports that, following this conversion: 'We married them off. They are in their marital homes.'[45] The transformation of Christian schoolgirls into Muslim wives of Boko Haram insurgents is a powerful image and the insurgency was media savvy enough to leverage the fear this image generated to gain international influence.

The release of a 'proof of life' video as the second anniversary of the abductions approached illustrates the longevity of this media campaign. According to CNN, which released the video, it featured '15 girls in robes identifying themselves, [and] is believed to have been made in December in the course of negotiations between the government and parties claiming to represent Boko Haram'. This video was reportedly combined with a new request – $50 million in exchange for the girls – although this demand has been greeted with scepticism by many, who believe that Boko Haram would not trade the girls for that sum.[46]

As a terrorist organisation fighting an insurgency, it is in Boko Haram's interest to instil fear. As Adotei Akwei, Amnesty International's managing director for government relations, observed in 2014: 'Armed groups tend to compete with each other about how badly they can intimidate a population.'[47] The potent symbolism of the Chibok girls, combined with the global attention that news concerning them receives, makes the girls a valuable resource for the insurgency. Lauren Wolfe, with the Women Under Siege reporting project, noted that 'Boko Haram has chosen a group – girls – that is historically vulnerable, yet whose members carry precious undertones about the purity of most societies. And with that designation as the bearers of purity, girls become a group that is little more than a symbol.'[48] Unfortunately, much of the activism concerned with their return not only fetishizes the girls, dehumanising them as they are elevated to near-mythic status, it may well prevent the Chibok girls from being freed. A Nigerian military commander is quoted as observing that:

> Boko Haram sees the Chibok girls as their trump card. We think they are keeping them with their main leadership. The day we get the Chibok girls will spell the end of Boko Haram, but I fear they will kill all the girls in mass suicide bombings in the process.[49]

Not only have the Chibok girls been used by the insurgents to project a fearsome image; within Boko Haram's ranks too, the 'Chibok brand' has been adopted in order to maintain order and instil fear. Women who were held as slaves reported that the female enforcers of the insurgency's sharia laws in the camp were referred to as 'Chibok girls'. According to a report by the BBC, 'people were tied and laid down and the girls took it from there ... the Chibok girls slit their throats'.[50] Amira, a woman from Adamawa held by the insurgents, claimed that these so-called Chibok girls 'were trained as soldiers and given guns'.[51] She recalled that 'if you were stubborn and refused them, they can kill you', which, she reported, they often did. Other women, living as IDPs in Maiduguri, reported that the insurgents would admonish them for not being 'good like a Chibok girl' if they disobeyed Boko Haram's dictates.[52]

The wives of former Boko Haram members were strikingly knowledgeable – or claimed to be – about the location and status of the Chibok girls, further suggesting that the girls have obtained an almost mythic status among the sect's members. Another woman named Amira, who was married to an insurgent commander, asserted emphatically in June 2016 that the 'Chibok girls are all alive' and that they are being 'held until Boko Haram's leaders are freed', parroting the insurgency's propaganda.[53] Others concurred that the girls were alive, and asserted that they were being held with Shekau at one of the camps in the Sambisa Forest. Whether or not these claims are true, they reveal the importance of the Chibok girls as part of the insurgency's identity, narrative and internal organisation.

More than the Chibok girls

Despite their global profile and potent symbolism, the Chibok girls represent merely the tip of the iceberg of Boko Haram's wide-spread abductions of women and girls in the region. A vigilante in Maiduguri observed, in an exasperated tone, 'the whole world focuses on Chibok but that is a mistake' that skews understanding of the conflict.[54] As already quoted in chapter 1, a report conducted by Amnesty International estimated that, between 2014 and spring 2015, Boko Haram abducted more than 2,000 women.[55] This number is certainly higher now, as the insurgency has continued to abduct women and girls as part of its raids and has expanded its territorial presence into Chad, Niger and Cameroon. Further, it is not clear if the Amnesty estimate includes the multitudes of women who were abducted only for a handful of days, or less, before escaping.

In fact, the Chibok abductions were not even the sect's first foray into mass kidnapping, although they were certainly the most publicised and largest of such attacks at the time. Human Rights Watch identifies the abduction of 12 women from a police station in Bama in May 2013 as the first 'case of abduction of more than one woman in a single attack, and signaled the beginning of a campaign of violence against women and girls'.[56]

Another significant pre-Chibok abduction was a February 2014 attack in Konduga, in which 25 women were abducted and 53 people were killed.[57]

In a video released in February 2014, Shekau admitted that 'we kidnapped some women and children, including teenage girls', but defends the abductions on the grounds that the government has targeted the female relatives of insurgents, noting that 'in a single house in Damaturu, eight of our women and 14 children were arrested'. He stated that 'no one in the country will enjoy his women and children' unless the demand that detained members be freed were met. This tactic was seemingly effective: in May 2013, 23 women, some identified as wives of high-ranking Boko Haram fighters, were released. A source quoted by Human Rights Watch suggested that an additional 180 women were still detained, and Boko Haram's rhetoric continued to agitate for their release.[58]

The question of why the sect began tactical abductions when it did remains largely unanswered; however, there is considerable evidence (alluded to above) that these attacks were made in retribution for the detention of Boko Haram militants. A study conducted by Jacob Zenn and Elizabeth Pearson argues that 2013 'marked a significant evolution in Boko Haram's tactics, with a series of

kidnappings, in which one of the main features was the instrumental use of women ... in response to corresponding tactics by the
Nigerian security forces'.[59]

A year before the Chibok abductions, in May 2013, the insurgents
led a 'massive assault' on police barracks in Bama, in central Borno
State. During this assault, in which the insurgents killed more than
100 people, 12 women and children were captured. These women
were visiting relatives at the police station and, once released, told
Al Jazeera that the insurgents 'told them explicitly that their abduction was a response to the government's detention of their own
wives and children'. This line of justification was also presented by
Abubakar Shekau in a video in which he claimed responsibility for
their kidnapping. Zenn and Pearson observe that the claims of retribution were not entirely unfounded, as more than 100 women and
children had been detained by the Nigerian authorities:

> among them Shekau's own wives ... the wife and children of
> the commander for Kano, Suleiman Muhammed; the pregnant
> wife of the commander for Sokoto, Kabiru Sokoto, who gave
> birth while in prison; and the wife of the suicide-bomber who
> attacked the 'This Day' media house in Abuja in April 2012.[60]

This sort of justification was carried throughout the insurgency's propaganda for a number of years; Zenn and Pearson report that
the 'capture of Boko Haram militants' family members was cited
as a grievance in almost all Shekau's video statements in 2012 and
2013'.[61] They note that Shekau levelled serious accusations against
the government concerning its conduct surrounding these 'kidnappings'.[62] Shekau also 'speculated on the possible sexual abuse of the
Boko Haram family members by security forces', and 'made clear
the intention to target "enemy" women in return'.[63] They conclude
that 'these events demonstrate an established cycle of government
detentions of women related to Boko Haram, and the group's retaliatory abduction of ... women'.[64]

Although Zenn and Pearson's analysis certainly provides valuable insights, it does not capture the full scope of Boko Haram's grievances concerning the detention and harassment of its members, which are long-standing. One should recall that a catalysing event in the group's history was a confrontation with the police over the use of helmets on motorbikes, combined with a perception of unjust persecution. Since 2010, Boko Haram has engaged in raids on prisons to free its members. The first such prison break was in Bauchi State, where the sect released an estimated 700 prisoners and released an accompanying video.[65] In this and other propaganda videos that address the status of detained adherents, the insurgency highlights the inhumane conditions of the Nigerian prison system and the abusive practices of the Nigerian police. This line of attack is fertile ground for the insurgency as it tries to rally local support; Afrobarometer survey data suggests that fewer than one in three Nigerians trust the police.[66]

This lack of trust is a result of a dismal lack of professionalisation in the police force. Discussions with Nigerian NGOs reveal that the Nigerian police are unable to conduct police work effectively because of their lack of training and resources. As a result of the inadequate budget for the Nigerian police service, most police facilities 'cannot meet the minimum prescribed standards'.[67] This failure is particularly disheartening when one considers the modesty of the standards: for example, every police station is expected to have at least 'one truck, jeep, or similar vehicle, one station wagon, and one motorcycle'.[68] The weaponry given to officers is frequently outdated; observers frequently note that 'robbers are usually better armed than police officers'.[69] Communications technologies are also observed to be lacking, preventing police officers from mobilising and coordinating effectively. In addition to inadequate physical capital, the police force's human capital is underdeveloped. Nationwide, there is a shortage of DNA experts, forensic labs and workers, and ballistics experts. As a result, most 'evidence' in Nigeria is based on confessions, which are generally unreliable and often obtained through coercive means.

Despite the lack of resources allotted to the Nigerian Police, its officers are 'granted wide powers of arrest: all that is required is "reasonable suspicion" that an individual has committed, or is about to commit a crime'.[70] There are no institutionalised means by which victims of police maltreatment can seek redress. Although the leeway given to the Nigerian Prison Service (NPS) and the Nigerian Police Force (NPF) was intended to deter crime, 'it is a well-known fact that there is widespread abuse', including the detention of 'relatives, friends, associates, and even neighbors when the person in question cannot be located'.[71] Even when complaints are formally lodged against officers, judicial oversight is hampered, as 'judges must rely on investigations conducted by the same NPF whose personnel are accused of committing abuse in the first place'.[72] This results in a system in which 'the government routinely fails to exercise due diligence' and 'NPF personnel enjoy a stunning degree of impunity'.[73]

In March 2014, the insurgents launched an attack on Giwa Barracks, a military outpost, makeshift prison and well-known symbol of police–military cooperation and excess. Amnesty International has repeatedly highlighted the persistence of extrajudicial violence, torture and inhumane conditions in Giwa Barracks. During this prison break, it was reported that all of those who were held in Giwa were given the option of joining Boko Haram's ranks or returning home. Reports suggest that, following the release of the prisoners, Boko Haram withdrew and 'shortly thereafter the security forces reoccupied the facility'.[74] Particularly chilling are the allegations that, following the prison break, the official security forces and the CJTF 'hunted down all of those who had escaped and murdered most of them'. Reports by Amnesty International estimate over 600 fatalities in the aftermath.[75]

Boko Haram has capitalised on the abuses of the police and the military in its propaganda, particularly in videos and pamphlets released after prison raids that emphasised the military's targeting of vulnerable populations. In 2011, Shekau released a statement using the events of 2009 as a rallying cry, to avenge both Yusuf's killing and the murder of Nigerian civilians:

> You all saw on Al Jazeera TV how unarmed men, youths, women, cripples, and even youth were asked to lie on the ground and were shot in the head and chest by security agents. You all saw our leader Mohammed Yusuf with handcuffs and shot ... you all saw how Masjid and the Holy Qur'an were being destroyed.

In 2012, Shekau released a flyer following attacks on Kano, stating: 'You should know that the security in Kano are using tricks in arresting our people ... our war is with the government ... anyone who is instrumental to the arrest of our members is assured that their own is coming.'[76]

The Chibok abductions, and others of this style, marked a turning point in the insurgency's campaign against the abusive and predatory nature of the state. No longer squarely aimed at illustrating the government's abuse, such abductions were a way of 'fighting fire with fire'. Although Shekau was still portraying the insurgency as a defender of Muslims, his audience shifted. The Chibok girls' transformation and 'conversion' to Islam was a message directed at the government, the international community and non-Muslims to instil fear, rather than to a Muslim audience to cultivate sympathy. The abduction of the girls was a means of striking back at a governmental system that was considered to target Muslims and engage in heavy-handed crackdowns with impunity. The shift towards retributive abductions, and away from emancipatory raids, seems to be a function of a handful of factors. One of these was the insurgents de-emphasising the importance of grassroots civilian support; this was evidenced by the sharp increase in civilian targeting at the time, described by Human Rights Watch as a period in which 'the group has perpetrated almost-daily attacks on villages and towns, and laid siege to highways', and in which 'Boko Haram has killed civilians, pillaged property, and destroyed schools, homes, and businesses, which were often razed to the ground'.[77] Human Rights Watch also notes that the creation of the vigilante CJTF further incentivised civilian targeting because of the blurred line between security agents and civilians, the utility of abducted girls and boys in Boko Haram's operations, and the effectiveness of female abductees (particularly the Chibok girls) as a symbol for cultivating fear.[78]

Further incentivising mass abduction as a tactic was the 'relative ease with which [Boko Haram] carried out the Chibok abductions'.[79] The low-investment strategy's high reward 'appears to have emboldened Boko Haram to step up abductions elsewhere'.[80] Human Rights Watch's cataloguing of the continued abductions in the immediate aftermath of the Chibok abductions is revealing:

> On April 16, six women and two children were abducted from Wala village and taken to a camp in Sambisa forest. Another five women from Gujba village in Yobe State were reportedly abducted on April 25. Eleven teenage girls were also abducted during attacks on Wala and Warabe villages in southern Borno State on May 6. In early June, suspected Boko Haram gunmen reportedly kidnapped another 60 women from Kummabza, in Damboa, Borno State.[81]

In June 2014, the group also raided Fulani communities, kidnapping 20 women and demanding 800 cattle as ransom.[82] This count does not include any of the many abductions the insurgents have undertaken since June 2014.

As previously addressed, this strategy was effective in cultivating an aura of fear, giving the insurgents an international profile and a more effective bargaining position vis-à-vis the state.

The plight of abducted women and girls

We are all one: my mother, my father, my aunty, were all taken by Boko Haram, so it is like I am still there.

Halima, 18, an IDP living in Dalori
alone after escaping the insurgents[83]

According to Human Rights Watch, a commander told an abducted 19-year-old girl who was taken to an insurgent camp in the Sambisa Forest:

You are no longer in Nigeria. You are now in an Islamic kingdom. Here, women's rights are respected, not like in Nigeria where women are made to work, farm, fetch water and firewood, and where you have all types of discrimination. This is the reason why we are rescuing Christian women like you. In our Islamic kingdom, there will be no discrimination because everyone will be Muslims.[84]

Although Abubakar Shekau and other leaders of Boko Haram would like to portray themselves and the insurgency as a vanguard of Muslim interests in Nigeria, the abduction and subsequent treatment of women and girls constitute a gross abuse of human rights. Human Rights Watch summarised that abducted women and girls who refused to convert were killed or 'subjected to physical and psychological abuse; forced labor; forced participation in military operations, including carrying ammunition or luring men into ambush; forced marriage to their captors; and sexual abuse, including rape', in addition to the general demands placed on women 'to cook, clean, and perform other household chores'.[85]

It is worth observing that, although the phrase 'rape, loot and pillage' has been used to describe conflicts since time immemorial, sexual violence is not ubiquitous in modern conflict. As Cynthia Cockburn notes: 'Like all other aspects of war, wartime rape is by no means "senseless violence". Rather, it is a social, relational phenomenon, with complex meanings capable of being explored, analyzed, and understood.'[86] Elizabeth Wood's review of sexual violence in (and its absence from) modern conflict reveals that, in instances where sexual violence is used, there are typically four patterns – sexual torture, sexual slavery, sexual violence as a form of terror, and rewarding soldiers with rape – each of which is revealing about the characteristics and organisational structure of the conflict.[87] Building on this work, Dara Kay Cohen has concluded that the disproportionate use of gang rape by insurgents in general suggests that rape is a means of 'combatant socialization', intended to improve the insurgents' ability to work together and a means of cultivating bonds among disparate actors.[88] Testimony of those who have been abducted by Boko Haram and released or rescued, or who have escaped, is undoubtedly harrowing; however, the lack of reports of gang rape may reveal important aspects of the insurgency's internal organisation and recruitment tactics, which will be discussed later.

The general pattern of Boko Haram's attacks outside cities is to invade a village, slaughter the able-bodied men who refuse to join them, and abduct the women who have converted or seem amenable to conversion. This pattern was constructed through the stories of women from a number of communities across the north. One girl, who was taken near Bama in Borno State, described her abduction as being prefaced by religious sorting:

All [the] young men including Muslims were told to either join the insurgents or be killed. They slit the throat of some of the men, saying they'd not waste bullets on them. Christian women wearing pants [trousers] were shot in the leg and left to die. Older Muslim men and women wearing Muslim veils were released to go, while the rest of us were driven to their camp in Sambisa forest.[89]

Other women reported that they were given the opportunity to convert. Abductions that occurred in southern Borno State, where there is a significant Christian population, were often characterised by coerced conversions. Human Rights Watch relayed the story of a young woman abducted by the insurgents and taken to a camp in Gwoza, where 'combatants placed a noose around her neck and threatened her with death until she renounced her religion'.[90] A 23-year-old who was abducted alongside her 47-year-old mother recalled that, following their abduction:

> The insurgent leader addressed us saying 'today we're going to convert you to Islam, then you can choose any one of us to marry, and we'll give you a place to stay.' My mother and I were already married so we refused but when they threatened to kill us, my mother advised we should agree because I was in the early stages of pregnancy and was too sick to eat. We were made to recite some words in Arabic and showed how to pray. Then they let us go after three days because my mother promised we will convince our husbands to become Muslims.[91]

Umma, a 60-year-old woman who was captured by Boko Haram during one of their raids on Baga, spent more than 50 days under the insurgents. She reported that she and the other women taken from her town 'were incarcerated by them; they dragged us along as they destroyed the city'.[92]

According to the women who were forced into the insurgency, life as an abducted woman 'was very stressful – we lived in hunger, we were physically abused'.[93] Umma reported that 'if you agree to believe in Boko Haram's ideology then you are taken as a wife and treated well', and said that she did not blame the girls who converted and married, but that she did not convert. It is worth observing here that both Christians and Muslims were forced to convert by the insurgents, who define 'real Muslims' only as members of their group who abide by their specific ideology. Umma was able to flee the insurgents, making her way to a displacement camp in Yola, where she hoped to find and reconnect with her daughter. Her experience of abduction, escape, and then life in a displacement camp is common for women in the north-east.

Similarly, Amina, a 22-year-old with six children, also from Baga, who now lives in an official IDP camp in Maiduguri, recalled that: 'Boko Haram ransacked everything. We were gathered in a mosque in Baga, which Boko Haram surrounded and waited for instructions from their leaders.'[94] To prevent the women and girls from attempting to overpower the insurgents – who, in many instances, they outnumbered – members of Boko Haram frequently engaged in public displays of brutality. In the mosque where Amina was sequestered with the other women in Baga, 'they shot a few people to show that they were serious'.[95] Women are often subjected to brutal displays of the insurgents' strength and capacity for violence; their introduction to the sect is often being forced to watch as the insurgents ransack their town and in some cases murder their family, friends and neighbours. An older woman, who had fought back against the captors who had picked her up while she fled Michika (northern Adamawa State), was forced to watch as an insurgent who had expressed pity for her was murdered. She recalled:

> They tried to rob me and I refused. I fought them back. One man hit me, so I struck him across the face. He hit me on my head – look, you can still see the scar a bit. One of the lookouts saw them hit me and came down from his post to tell them to stop. He even applied ointment to my hair to help the bleeding. The men who tried to rob me then took him away and killed him. They made me watch them kill him.[96]

In many of the raids on villages, following the corralling of the women and girls, orders came down from insurgent leaders that 'the women should be kept so that the men can select their favourites and the children should be taken for schooling'.[97] The women taken as wives are typically in their teens. Amina's view is that they prefer young girls 'because they are naïve and easier to control'.[98] The random acts of rape that characterise many instances of gender-based violence in conflicts are less prevalent in Boko Haram than instances of coordinated abductions.

Some women did not become wives, but rather were made into 'slaves' or 'submissives' by the insurgents. 'I was used as a slave; I cooked food when they had it and cleaned,' a young female called Kaka recalled from her new home in an IDP camp in Yola.[99] In some of the insurgency's cells, enslaved women are not married off but are systemically sexually assaulted. 'I was not a wife but the men forced themselves on me frequently,' Kaka reported.[100] Although there are certainly a number of women who have been subjected to sexual abuse and rape, the women interviewed by Human Rights Watch reported that 'Boko Haram commanders appeared to make some effort to protect them from sexual violence' and that most of these violations occurred following forced marriages.[101] Reports of non-marital rape by the insurgents are rare; some women, even those abducted by the insurgents, reported that they were not physically or sexually assaulted by the insurgents – likely due to the sect's leadership banning such assaults. Hassana, a 25-year-old girl from Baga who was captured by Boko Haram for two weeks, stated that: 'Boko Haram was scared of women. They were afraid to touch us because they had a charm and they said if they touch a woman the charm would be broken.'[102]

Despite the gravity of such abuse by 'insurgent husbands', it should be noted that, as in a number of countries, marital rape is not illegal in Nigeria.[103] Although marriages conducted in the absence of consent are not recognised in Nigerian law, there is no cultural norm against marital rape – particularly given the intra-insurgency perception of these marriages as legitimate.

Some of the wives who were forced into marriages to strangers unsurprisingly sought to flee their captivity. One particularly clever young woman, Fatiah, who managed to escape to Madina mosque in Maiduguri, recalled that she was able to play the insurgents off against each other to her advantage. She was abducted and 'claimed' by one of the insurgents to be his wife. She recalled:

> He intended to make me his wife. He would come in and say that: 'We are going to kill your husband and then I will marry you.' They all said that the men not in Boko Haram were disbelievers and deserved to die.[104]

Fatiah's would-be husband was not the only man who wanted to take her as a wife, however, and a rift between the cell's leaders developed over her. She recalled:

> Both men wanted to marry me. My second suitor helped me escape, saying that if he could not have me the other man should not be able to have me either. When my captor left, he told the guard that I was leaving the camp to do work for him and led me to the path to the forest. He said if I was stopped I should tell them that I am running an errand for him. I met my father-in-law in the woods. He and some pastoralists helped me survive in the Baga Forest.[105]

It is critical to note that however horrifying the abduction of women and girls on such a scale is, such practices are far from uncommon in insurgencies throughout the world. They have been a feature of a number of sub-Saharan African armed groups. However, prior to placing this insurgency's use of abduction in regional perspective, it is important to recognise the incentives to identifying oneself as being kidnapped and to reporting relatives as being abducted, rather than admitting to voluntary participation.

The stigma associated with the sect skews understanding of Boko Haram's practices. Hamsatu Allamin observes that many in the IDP camps joined voluntarily as wives, 'but they won't admit it out of fear'.[106] She asserts that 'some would even prefer to return to their husbands' in the insurgency, recalling two girls in December who fled an IDP camp in Konduga to try to return to the sect.[107] When the camp's guards detained them a few hours later, far from the camp, they said: 'We are going back to our husbands in Sambisa.'[108] The temptation to refer to one's family members as 'kidnapped' rather than indoctrinated, coerced, or voluntarily recruited into the sect is well illustrated by the story of Shettima. He is a quiet man in his mid-fifties living as a displaced person in Maiduguri with his two wives and two remaining children.[109] Three of his children are with Boko Haram, and, according to community members, at least one of them joined voluntarily, although Shettima denies this claim vehemently.[110] From the small room that he rents in Maiduguri, he recalled that 'we were in Marte when they took our children' in late 2013, imposing their rule of law over the residents. Shettima was allowed to continue his job as a truck driver, carrying food and other goods throughout Nigeria. The demands of Shettima's job kept him away from home frequently, but he said: 'I tried as much as possible to prevent my children from going to the preaching. I even told my neighbours not to go. But I was on the road a lot and could not always prevent them from going if they wanted to.' After an extended conversation, Shettima went so far as to say that his children had even attended Boko Haram's preaching, admitting that 'maybe when I left sometimes they went to the group'.[111] The result of their attendance at Boko Haram's preaching, grudgingly confessed by their still-grieving father, was that all five of his children 'became more religious'. He clarified that: 'It was not that they prayed more than five times a day but their behaviour changed and they became more ardent.'

According to the community members from Marte who fled with Shettima, his eldest son voluntarily joined the sect as a result of this attendance, and then helped to convert his younger siblings. Some of the community members claimed that Shettima and his wives fled with their two remaining children because 'his eldest son was planning to kill him'.[112] Regardless of what transpired in Marte, if questioned by the authorities Shettima would describe his children as abducted, rather than as voluntary recruits. He is not alone. The stigma surrounding association with Boko Haram incentivises narratives of coercion and abduction, rather than grappling with the murkier depths of structural violence in Nigerian society, intergenerational conflict, and the ideological appeal of an anti-state movement. When one displaced man living in a camp in Yola was asked about the possibility of accepting kidnapped boys back into the community, he was ambivalent. When asked about returning boys who had volunteered, however, he was adamant that 'you don't play with snakes ... no matter how small; if a snake bites you, you die'.[113] Hamsatu Allamin observed that 'we all know someone in Boko Haram and we all want to protect them', creating an atmosphere in which it pays to be economical with the truth.[114]

The stigma of association with Boko Haram affects men and women and is even beginning to tarnish the reputation of those who have been abducted, perhaps reflecting the declining legitimacy of claims of abduction. The joint UNICEF–International Alert report *'Bad Blood': Perceptions of Children Born of Conflict-related Sexual Violence and Women and Girls Associated with Boko Haram in Northeast Nigeria* found that women and children who are thought to be associated with the sect face intense discrimination. This is a result of both the cultural norms regarding sexual violence and the loathsome reputation of the insurgency. The report asserted that:

> popular cultural beliefs about 'bad blood' and witchcraft, as well as the extent of the violence experienced by people at the hands of JAS [an alternative name for Boko Haram favoured by some organisations], form the basis of this fear. This general perception has been exacerbated by stories of women and girls returning from captivity and murdering their parents.[115]

A vernacular has sprung up to convey the mistrust of women

and girls who have spent time with the insurgents; according to 'Bad Blood', they are 'often referred to by communities as "Boko Haram wives," "Sambisa women," "Boko Haram blood," and "Annoba" (which means epidemics)'. The report asserts that the conceptualisation of the women as an epidemic 'reveals fears that their exposure to JAS could spread to others. This infers that these girls and women were radicalized while in captivity, and if allowed to reintegrate into their communities, they might recruit others.'[116]

The challenges of social integration will be addressed in subsequent chapters relating to post-conflict redevelopment; however, it is worth noting here that social attitudes incentivise women to manipulate their experiences to downplay their autonomy and give a skewed perception of the scope of the insurgency's abductions.

Contextualising atrocity: strategic abduction in sub-Saharan African conflicts

Although it is possible that the numbers of 'kidnapped' and 'abducted' people throughout the Lake Chad Basin are inflated, the practice of widespread and systemic abductions is certainly not unique to Boko Haram as an insurgency. In sub-Saharan Africa abductions into insurgent groups have occurred in conflicts ranging from the Democratic Republic of the Congo and Sierra Leone to Uganda and Sudan and South Sudan.[117] A report by the US-based National Public Radio (NPR) noted that, although '[n]one of these militias can claim to have invented a tactic as old as war itself … these raids on girls and young women have become increasingly common in modern African guerrilla warfare'.[118] Chris Coulter, who has studied strategic abductions with a particular emphasis on their use in Sierra Leone, points out a number of structural factors that encourage the use of this tactic. Abductees are not merely a means of replenishing depleted fighting forces; they are also integral to the functioning of the camp. 'These people live in the bush, literally,' Coulter explained to NPR. 'They need women as support staff. Someone has to cook, clean, and do all of the other chores that you need done.'[119] If an insurgency is struggling to gain voluntary recruits – whether through ideological or material appeals – abduction is another means of filling their ranks. Another reason for the popularity of this tactic is the impunity enjoyed by the kidnappers, as a result of the 'remote regions forsaken by governments and state armies' in which groups operate, as well as a general lack of political will to confront the insurgencies.[120] The third reason, discussed earlier in this chapter, is the symbolic value of women and girls, which helps to instil fear in the population.

Although this tactic is widespread, the similarities between Boko Haram's abductions and the kidnappings committed by the Lord's Resistance Army (LRA) in northern Uganda are striking. The LRA is 'notorious for wantonly and systematically abducting people, particularly children' to be used as fighters, wives, load-bearers and 'human shields'.[121] These similarities were so apparent that, in the aftermath of the Chibok abductions, America's ambassador to the United Nations, Samantha Power, tweeted: 'In abducting more than 200 girls, Boko Haram is mimicking one of the LRA's most monstrous tactics.'[122]

A clear parallel between the LRA and Boko Haram can be found in the abduction of schoolgirls, resulting in the galvanisation of international condemnation and activism. One particular example stands out. On 10 October 1996, the LRA abducted 139 female students from a boarding school in Aboke, in the northern Apac district. The three Sisters in charge of the school feared such an attack (the school had been targeted in the past) and had requested support from a local defence unit militia, which never arrived. At 2.30 am, the school's night watchman informed Sister Fassera: 'Sister, the rebels are here.'[123] The three Sisters hid from the rebels, assuming that if they were found, the rebels would force them to open the dormitories holding the young women, which had reinforced windows and doors that the Sisters hoped could prevent the rebels from entering. Just as in the Chibok abductions, the rebels burned the school, looted its supplies, and abducted a number of girls with little resistance. When the rebels dispersed, the Sisters went to the dormitories to assess the damage, realising that over a hundred girls had been taken. The school's headmistress, Sister Rachele Fassera, tracked the rebels by following the trail of looted candy and drink wrappers into the bush, eventually managing to negotiate the release of 109 of the girls.[124] The 30 that the rebels refused to release were chosen as 'gifts' for the rebel leader Joseph Kony. Sister Fassera's bravery drew international attention. Her alliance with the parents of the abducted children (which resulted in an advocacy group called the Concerned Parents Association) caught the attention of notable figures such as Pope John Paul II, Hillary Clinton, Kofi Annan, and even Sudanese President Omar al-Bashir, whose condemnation raised the profile of the conflict in northern Uganda in general.[125] Similar to the Chibok abductions, negotiations in which the symbolic value of the abducted girls gave the rebels leverage were held between the Ugandan government and the LRA. The rebels' demand that the Ugandan military declare a ceasefire was one demand too many, however, and the Ugandan government eventually declared that they were not responsible for the girls' fate. By 2006, five of the girls had died in captivity, but 23 of the 25 surviving girls had managed to escape. The LRA has continued its campaign of abductions, with analysts estimating that 25,000 to 38,000 children have been forcibly conscripted into the LRA – although it is widely recognised that this estimate is too low.[126]

The similarities between the LRA and Boko Haram are particularly demoralising when one considers that the LRA's activities have dragged on since its founding in 1987, spilling across Uganda's borders and becoming a persistent regional crisis. Boko Haram's adoption of one of the LRA's signature tactics suggests the possibility of the crisis in northern Nigeria becoming a long-term feature of the region. The similarities between the LRA's and Boko Haram's pattern of abductions also serve to contextualise the Nigerian conflict as an African insurgency, rather than as a Middle East-style terrorist action. This comparison also suggests that not only will a significant number of women be subjected to the trials of detention by Boko Haram, but that the process of reconciliation between abductees and their communities will require significant support if people are to overcome the stigma associated with being abducted.

Chapter 5

WOMEN AT WAR: WIVES AND WEAPONS IN THE INSURGENCY

Despite the dominant media narrative surrounding Boko Haram, which emphasises the group's egregious violations of women and girls, it is important to clarify that not all women within Boko Haram's ranks or living under its control were abducted or even coerced into the insurgency. While it is appealing to portray women as passive victims, to do so would rob women of their agency. Such a characterisation obscures the nuanced gendered and religious politics that characterise the sect's roots and rise and furthermore makes the group's longevity puzzling by removing any reference to the contributions volunteered by women. As uncomfortable as it may make observers, it is evident from interviews with women who joined the sect of their own volition that participation in the insurgency could often be used to improve a woman's quality of life. Even those who were abducted and coerced into Boko Haram reported that they could use the group's social infrastructure to advance their interests.

Certainly, women throughout the Lake Chad Basin joining Boko Haram is not the first instance of women working within the narrow constraints of their social systems to find means to advance their own interests. Ahmed-Ghosh, observing the actions of women living in an enclosed, conservative Muslim community in the United States, notes that:

the reality for all women, religious or non-religious, is that they live in patriarchal cultures. Under patriarchy, there are situations where women willingly conform to Islamic norms (even if these norms are seen as oppressive by others) engaging in what I term 'patriarchy trading,' which allows them to claim some agency.[1]

Ahmed-Ghosh elaborates on this concept of 'patriarchy trading', explaining that women 'are aware of the patriarchal constraints in their religion but opt for it over what they refer to as western patriarchy which is overlaid with resentment towards Islam and is racist'.[2] In short, women assess the social options before them and make a decision about how to best advance their own interests. Which system will best provide for their needs? Which system are they best equipped to navigate? The systemic structural violence that women face in northern Nigerian society makes it easier for some to lend their support to anti-state movements (including the Boko Haram insurgency) – particularly when the insurgents make clear the 'benefits' that women can enjoy as part of Boko Haram.

Many in the West have difficulty recognising the possibility that women may adopt extreme religious ideologies – especially when these groups are even loosely associated with Islam – as a means of empowering themselves. Saba Mahmood argues forcefully and eloquently about the need to recognise the agency and autonomy of women in Islamist movements (both peaceful and violent). She observes that:

It is important to take into consideration the desires, motivations, commitments, and aspirations of the people to whom these practices are important. Thus, in order to explore the kinds of injury specific to women located in particular historical and cultural situations, it is not enough simply to point out, for example, that a tradition of female piety or modesty serves to give legitimacy to women's subordination. Rather it is only by exploring these traditions in relation to the practical engagements and forms of life in which they are embedded that we can come to understand the significance of that subordination to the women who embody it. This is not simply an analytical point, but reflects, I would contend, a political imperative born out of the realization that we can no longer presume that secular reason and morality exhaust the forms of valuable human flourishings.[3]

For many, the temptation is great to project Western norms onto radically different contexts and condemn any deviation from the secular nation-state as inherently inferior. Doing so, however, endorses grave misconceptions and asserts that participation in these systems is illogical. Once deemed as such, the responsibility to engage critically with the motivating factors of membership is abandoned. They are 'fanatics' incapable of appreciating appeals to reason or of engaging in negotiations.

It bears repeating that the lines of consent, coercion, autonomy and oppression are blurred by the structural violence that women face in Nigeria. Women's limited opportunities, a result of the repressive character of social and political norms, particularly in the north, may be seen as a coercive 'push factor', encouraging female participation in the radical group. On the other hand, attributing women's actions entirely to their environment also risks robbing them of autonomy. As Saba Mahmood summarises:

> in order for an individual to be free, it is required that her actions be the consequence of her 'own will' rather than of custom, tradition, or direct coercion. Thus, even illiberal actions can arguably be tolerated if it is determined that they are undertaken by a freely consenting individual who acted on her own accord.[4]

Another factor limiting our understanding of women's participation in radical religious groups is the discourse on 'agency', which 'is largely thought of in terms of the capacity to subvert norms', rather than consent to – or manipulate – prevailing norms.[5] The rest of the chapter will attempt to explore what consenting to Boko Haram entails and to explain what could motivate such an affiliation. Although many restrictions and roles are generally oppressive, the women kept under these conditions have identified and created coping mechanisms to improve their situation, both prior to joining the sect and once they have been inducted. Carroll McC. Pastner has this to say concerning autonomy in oppressive systems:

> Regardless of whether they are willing or unwilling participants in a social system, people 'fiddle with the rules' and situationally disregard them in order to better their own position (although social systems differ as to the amount of 'fiddling' permitted). Women in purdah are no exception and thus will manipulate and even defy normative ideals and men to a calculated extent. Their use of power is, on the whole, both indirect and negative, because legitimate access to rights and privileges is often unobtainable or difficult to achieve with de jure control in the hands of men.[6]

Despite the temptation to ignore female participation in the insurgency, it would be anomalous if Boko Haram had not incorporated women and girls into its operations. Between 1990 and 2003, girls were part of fighting forces in more than 50 countries, including 13 African nations.[7] While many of these women were abducted, others were 'socialized, volunteered, or coerced to participate in such acts' in response to the general grievances that animated their male counterparts, as well as to specifically gendered complaints.[8]

As discussed previously, from the early days of Mohammed Yusuf's preaching, there was a strongly gendered element to his rhetoric; under Abubakar Shekau, the group's gender politics have altered, but they remain, in some ways, provocatively pro-woman given the local context. Association with the sect, according to the women who joined of their own volition, often entails better access to education and greater economic security for women, with less physically demanding work. It's worth noting that this was strictly religious education, and that government and religious schools exist throughout the region. However, many of these girls had been prevented from attending by economic or social factors.

At various points in the group's operational experimentations, other opportunities for female advancement have also been identified and exploited. The life stories of women who joined the insurgency at each phase of its evolution illustrate how women were able to use its disruptive nature to advance their own interests and agenda, despite a generally violent and oppressive atmosphere.

A note on the paradoxical characteristics of marriage in Boko Haram

If I saw [the insurgents], I ran; until one time when I entered into them. I entered because I love him.

Hauwa, 14-year-old who married a
Boko Haram insurgent and joined the sect[9]

When you marry Boko Haram, you are free. All you have to do is clean a little.

Halima, 18-year-old who was forcibly
taken as a Boko Haram wife[10]

Marriage into Boko Haram was frequently identified as a conduit into the group for women. Husbands often coerced, cajoled or convinced their wives to join the sect with them, while other girls married into the group. Temporarily setting aside the issue of post-abduction marriage to insurgents, there remains a spectrum of consent to marriage among Boko Haram members; as Zara, a 16-year-old IDP living in Maiduguri, recalled, when Boko Haram entered her town 'some girls married the fighters willingly, some married for food, and some refused and were killed or beaten'.[11] One of the wives then living at the government-run Safe House camp in Maiduguri told me that, 'if my husband came to claim me here, we could stay here together', suggesting a true affinity between spouses. It is also worth noting that Amina Nkeki, the first of the Chibok girls to be rescued, stated publicly in August 2016 that she missed her husband and was still thinking of him.[12]

Two women's experiences help illustrate how marrying a Boko Haram member (regardless of their treatment once they are wives) can either be an exercise in female autonomy or an illustration of the heights of patriarchy. Aisha's and Umi's experiences, collected in interviews conducted in Maiduguri in June and July 2016, are relayed below and help illustrate this spectrum. Their experiences also help demonstrate the structural violence against women that curtails female autonomy and incentivises participation in a disruptive sect such as Boko Haram.

Aisha's least bad option

Aisha was visiting her aunt in Banki when she married a Boko Haram fighter. She had been raised in a town on the Cameroonian side of the Nigerian–Cameroonian border, where she had attended both a government-run school, in which she had learned English and the 'Western' curriculum, and an Islamic school. Her parents, who worked as civil servants in Cameroon, were virulently opposed to her marriage. Aisha recalled: 'My father wanted me to return to Cameroon to get married.' Her father called her aunt to try to get her to intervene. Aisha's aunt tried to convince her not to marry the young man, advising her to return to her family and continue her schooling in Cameroon. Because of her family's strong stance against it, Aisha did not even tell her parents that she was getting married.[13]

The courtship process was accelerated as Aisha's time in Banki was drawing to a close. She knew that, if she returned home, she would likely be married to a man she didn't care for. Given her parents' preferences, her eligibility, and her limited input in the courting process, it seemed likely that she would be married shortly after her return home. She recalled that 'there was a guy in Cameroon who wanted to marry me, but I did not love him, so the man in Banki seemed like a good option'.[14] The marriage between Aisha and the insurgent was completed quickly. They left Banki shortly after the small ceremony.

Aisha realised the implications of marrying a Boko Haram member when 'he took me to a village where I could not see my family or talk to others'. She spent a year with him, kept largely in isolation, in a Boko Haram camp in Walasah. Although she was initially surprised at the conditions she was kept in, she maintained that her husband 'was very kind and generous to me; he gave me lots of gifts and money'.[15] In the spring of 2016, the Nigerian military raided the Boko Haram camp in Walasah. During the fighting, Aisha was separated from her husband and taken into the soldiers' custody.

When she told me her story, she was visibly pregnant underneath her religious covering. Gesturing to her veiled, rounded belly, she said: 'I am sad to give birth to a child that will never know its father.' When asked what she would tell her baby about his father, she said:

> I don't want to hide anything from my child. One day he will get older and ask, so it is better that I tell him the truth than for him to find out from someone else. I won't call his father a good man, because he took me to the forest and didn't let me visit anyone, but I won't tell him lies about our marriage.[16]

Umi: timely intervention by the Nigerian military

While Aisha was concerned about how to appropriately relay her experiences with Boko Haram to her unborn child, Umi was just a child herself. Her cheeks still boasted stores of baby fat. Despite the fact that she was only 11 years old, she had already been 'married' for more than two years. The majority of Umi's young life had been spent under Boko Haram's rule – she grew up as the daughter of insurgents in Walasah. Umi recalled that, even in her earliest memories, she was sent to study the Qur'an. She enjoyed the classes, impelled by her desire to 'study the Qur'an' and 'be a good Muslim'. Unlike her sisters, who were born before Boko Haram made her home into a part of their nascent Islamic state, Umi never hawked fried foods or caps outside the home to help support her family.[17]

When she was just nine years old, an insurgent approached her father about taking Umi as his third wife. Umi's father was enthusiastic about the prospect. Speaking separately from her daughter, Umi's mother confessed to me: 'I did not want her to get married because I thought she was too young.'[18] A bargain was struck between Umi's parents, with her mother recalling that: 'My husband agreed that we can do the ceremony now and then the man can retrieve her later.' 'Retrieving' Umi entailed moving her from her parents' home to her husband's. However, in this instance, the change would be largely irrelevant as Umi's family shared a compound with her future husband. The bargain was probably a euphemistic framing of when Umi would become sexually active.[19]

Umi was not consulted during the negotiation process, although she recalled that she did not want to get married. When I asked if she liked her husband, she merely responded: 'I knew him from before, because he and his wives had lived in the same house as me and my parents.' Asked to describe him, she ambivalently said he was 'nice', and, eventually, 'handsome'. She went so far as to say that he was 'a kind man because he has Qur'anic knowledge', but she emphasised that her marriage was based on her father's consent, not hers. Their wedding was small, according to her mother, and her bride price was paid directly to her parents, apparently because of her youth. Umi was not even aware of how much the bride price had been and was not certain if she would receive whatever sum it was when she was older.

The mechanisms of the bargain struck between Umi's mother and father was tested when, the day after the ceremony, the Nigerian army raided their camp, separating Umi from her father and her new husband and taking her to Maiduguri for de-radicalisation and reintegration. It seems likely, however, that Umi would have moved to her husband's compound soon after their wedding ceremony. She recalled that 'it is common for girls of that age to be married in Walasah to Boko Haram members and to then go live in their husbands' homes'. Umi's recollection matches Abubakar Shekau's declaration, made in a propaganda video released following the abduction of the Chibok girls, that the insurgents 'would marry them out at the age of 9 … we would marry them out at the age of 12'.[20] Umi's account echoes the exchange between a Boko Haram commander and a 15-year-old abductee, in which the girl argued that she was too young to be married, to which the commander 'pointed at his 5-year-old daughter, and said: "If she got married last year, and is just waiting till puberty for its consummation, how can you at your age be too young to marry?"'[21] Reports of very young, pregnant girls in IDP camps are also evidence of the sexual activity of pre-teens and young women in the insurgency.

Living then in a government-run camp for displaced women with her mother, Umi attended both Qur'anic and Western education classes, which are offered at sporadic intervals in the camp. She hopes to remarry one day – once she is 'older and out of this place'.[22]

A woman's place in war

There is considerable heterogeneity among women's experiences with Boko Haram, often depending on the means by which they were brought into the insurgency and the status of the men they are connected to. Four conditions, though, generally characterise life for women in Boko Haram: *purdah* and mandated covering; a strictly enforced rule of law, education and Qur'anic teaching; an emphasis on childbearing and rearing; and a veil of ignorance concerning the violence of the group.

Purdah and covering
As previously discussed, many suggest that *purdah* is a spectrum ranging from complete seclusion to a veiled 'seclusion of the

heart'. Under Boko Haram, strict *purdah* was enforced on nearly all the women. While some have interpreted this as being due to religious reasons, it is possible that it is also informed by local dynamics specific to northern Nigeria. Regardless of whether the inspiration for seclusion is religious or material, under Boko Haram women were expected to limit their activities outside the home to a bare minimum. When they did leave their compounds, they were expected to cover themselves in *hijab* and socks or *niqab*.

Women in the insurgency did not refer to the practice as *purdah* by name, but consistently reported that, under Boko Haram, their movements were largely restricted to the home. Falmata Hassan was just 14 when Boko Haram took over her village, Masa, and she was married to a fighter shortly afterwards. Under the insurgents, she recalled: 'I didn't see any man except my husband for four months.'[23] Her movements were highly restricted, and she reported that the women in Masa 'were only allowed to go from our home to our family's house', a state of affairs she seemed ambivalent about. Other women were more enthusiastic about the limitations on their movements. Falta, a 58-year-old woman who followed her son into Boko Haram, considered it a major improvement in her quality of life. Throughout her marriage to her husband (who refused to join Boko Haram because it would have meant ceding some of his cattle wealth to the insurgents), Falta had helped him work his farm. The effects of the years of labour showed on her lined brow and deeply wrinkled hands; under Boko Haram, however, 'there is no hard work, only cooking and cleaning'. She concluded simply: 'Not going out is best for us [women].'[24]

Boko Haram's insistence on adherence to strict *purdah* was not the first introduction of this concept in the north. Even in pre-Islamic times and in the early years of Islamisation, wife seclusion was practised in one form or another, most often by elites. The nineteenth-century *jihad*, waged by Usman Dan Fodio, marked a transition to 'strict enforcement of seclusion rules' on the basis of Qur'anic mandate.[25] Over subsequent centuries, *purdah* has become a marker of economic and social class in some parts of northern Nigeria. The ability to care for one's wives and children, without depending on a woman's labour in the fields or in the market, was a sign of a well-to-do man, as well as a devout one. Just as the practice of veiling oneself has been cast alternatively as protective and repressive, so too there is confusion about the implications of seclusion for women's well-being. Important in this debate are the often overlooked variations in the functioning of this institution. As Carroll McC. Pastner cautions, 'the existence of national, regional and local variations and, more recently, the factors of social change and westernizing influences, make it difficult to generalize about the ways in which purdah functions'.[26] While Western analysts might consider such restrictions on the freedom of movement to be oppressive, for some women domestic work is more desirable than work outside the home. In this way, religious prohibitions on their movement were considered liberating. For a number of the wives, their seclusion stood in contrast to their mothers' experiences and even their own histories hawking caps or fried food as children. Zainab recalled that she would 'sew caps to sell in Banki as a girl', but confided that 'now I have forgotten how to sew' because of her lack of practice as a wife of an insurgent.[27] A young woman from a remote town outside Maiduguri, recalled that, before Boko Haram invaded her village, instead of attending school she sold the fish that her father caught alongside the fried foods her mother prepared to support their large family.

One of the most significant impacts of seclusion is the reduction in agricultural production. Various sources differ on whether Boko Haram bans farming for all its members, followers and subjects – and, in fact, the practice itself may vary from place to place – but nearly all report that female participation in farming is banned. The resulting food scarcity within some segments of the group has produced an interesting modus operandi, in which some of the insurgents raid villages and towns outside their control to provide for their members. The current food crisis in the Lake Chad Basin is a direct result of the insurgents' raiding; it is worth noting that the number of fatalities from starvation and malnutrition in the region will surely dwarf the number of people Boko Haram has killed directly. Famed economist Mancur Olson's delineation between roving and stationary bandits in 'Dictatorship, Democracy, and Development' becomes less binary when Boko Haram is taken into consideration. Olson, theorising about the rise of modern states, opined that 'roving bandits' had an incentive only to loot and pillage, before moving on to the next village that they could exploit, whereas 'stationary bandits' had an incentive to promote economic growth, which is then siphoned off for their benefit. To grossly over-simplify the case, states come about when bandits stop roaming and start erecting tax infrastructure. Although Boko Haram has shown some interest in providing services to those who submit to the group's will, it extracts little in return (except for commitment to an ideology). Its taxation is levied on surrounding communities, which do not receive any of the services or governing institutions. One man who finally managed to flee his village in Adamawa State reported that he had to continue farming despite knowing that 'when the field produced, Boko Haram would come and steal the crops'. Those who stopped farming were accused of planning to flee and were killed.

The prohibitions against farming (especially against female participation) and the loss of female agricultural labour have also provided the insurgency a certain degree of flexibility that not all rural insurgencies have benefited from. Unlike other groups that are tied to certain geographical areas for their food supply and are thus somewhat stationary, Boko Haram can ostensibly pack up its camp and move anywhere, continuing to raid surrounding villages to provide for its needs. The insurgency's grain stores, as documented in a number of government reports and vigilante descriptions, are considered to be substantial; this is also likely to give the group a way of smoothing consumption in times of scarcity or when raids are unsuccessful, something that few members would have enjoyed prior to their entry into the group.[28]

Another impact of *purdah* is that the women in Boko Haram are entirely dependent on the men in their lives – for necessities such as food to frivolities like makeup, men are the providers. Although some women find some personal liberty in *purdah*, this should not be confused with independence. The women who had lived with the insurgents in Walasah frequently described Boko Haram's raids on surrounding communities as if the men were merely running errands. Falta recalled that she could tell her son: 'I admire that style of dress; go get it for me without any delays.'[29] Zainab took more of a divinely fatalistic view, stating that the insurgents 'came back with whatever Allah gave them' for their wives – but admits that her husband often brought back the sorts of clothes and food she requested.[30] In the event that a raid was unsuccessful, however, women had no means of providing for themselves. This strict gendered division of labour stemming from *purdah* has also given rise to an interesting phenomenon of intra-Boko Haram marriage. Widows of insurgents who die in the *jihad* are frequently married to another fighter. Women emphasised that once you were a part of the sect: 'You are their blood. You are one. They make sure you are taken care of.'[31]

The history of veiling in northern Nigeria

In Nigeria, as elsewhere, female veiling is a politicised religious issue that has been, at various times, both a means of oppressing women and a way for women to assert themselves in the political space. Boko Haram's insistence on a very conservative form of female covering is the latest development in the long-running Nigerian iteration of this debate. Conservative Qur'anic scholars, in Nigeria and elsewhere, have interpreted the verse 'O Prophet! Tell thy wives and daughters, and the believing women, that they should cast their outer garments over their persons (when abroad): that is most convenient, that they should be known (as such) and not molested. And Allah is Oft-Forgiving, Most Merciful' as justification for a variety of veiling practices. Of course, the debate

concerning female covering has expanded beyond scriptural interpretation of the Qur'an into the political realm.

The duality of the role of the *hijab* as a political symbol is captured
well in this contradictory summary: 'The hijab indicates a woman's
persistence of pursuing their right to be in the public space ... the
hijab indicates a step in men's determination to seclude women and
exclude them from the political process.'[32] A brief history of veiling
(and its political implications) in north-east Nigeria is revealing.

Until the mid-1970s, the *hijab* was a rarity among Muslim
women in northern Nigeria. Female members of the 'Yan Izala were
the first adopters of the covering. According to Mahdi, 'in Nigeria
the hijab has its origins in the values of the educated middle class in
urban centers'.[33] She notes that the trend began in Nigerian institutions of higher education, before trickling down to lower classes
and rural Muslim women in the 1980s. In the 1990s, the *hijab*
entered the realm of civil employment and often gained governmental stamps of approval: 'the *hijab* had begun to challenge official
uniforms in the public service sectors such as the nursing profession and secondary schools. With the expansion of Islamic law in
1999, some of the Muslim States began to introduce the *hijab* as a
compulsory part of girls' uniforms in state schools.'[34]

The 'Yan Izala played a significant role in popularising a
conservative veiling practice. Not only were female Izala members
trendsetters in their early adoption, Izala doctrine, which 'declared
many Nigerian "customs and traditions" un-Islamic, among them
the traditional dressing and veils' used by local ethnic groups,
incentivised the abandonment of local forms of dress. As scholar
Elisha Renne notes in *Veiling in Africa*, Izala's denigration of local
styles of covering 'reflects the tendency of religious reformers to
represent themselves as purifying past practices ... in this case, by
ridding Islam of innovations that were not clearly outlined in the
Quran and hadith'.[35]

In addition to serving a doctrinal purpose, the adoption of
the *hijab* allowed Izala women to enter the public sphere, often to

advance the group's cause but also to engage in daily activities, without jeopardising their morality. Gumi, the leader who was perhaps the most important in popularising the Izala, 'saw the return to civilian rule as an opportunity, equating voting to a *jihad*'. Entering the public sphere on behalf of the group risked exposing women to 'men's hostility' and threatened their modesty. However, while potentially liberating women to enter the public sphere, the *hijab* also marked men's claims to women's bodies. Mahdi argues that, particularly in the twenty-first century:

> Wearing the hijab ... is no longer a matter of women wanting to protect themselves against men's hostility, but also of a man's demarcation of his ownership of her body. No other man, who could be a candidate for her hand, should gaze at her. For that ownership to be realized, none of the Nigerian veils, at least not in the way they had been adorned before, would have been adequate, it had to be the hijab.[36]

A further catalyst in the shift towards the *hijab* was the social upheaval in Nigeria during this period. Since the 1970s, Nigerians have witnessed a wholesale restructuring of their country's economy, radical changes in their political system, cycles of economic expansion and contraction, and processes of modernity that call into question foundational identity markers. With these sweeping changes came economic and social insecurity. Renne identifies 'a failing infrastructure, government's inability to provide basic services such as water and electricity, armed robberies, and bombings' as contributing to Nigerians' 'sense of vulnerability "on both a physical and a spiritual plane"', encouraging the adoption of women's veiling and deeper identification with religious groups.[37] Further, modelling itself on the Saudi/Wahhabi model of service provision, Izala often preconditioned social programmes and benefits on the adoption of such covering.[38] Across the north, the result of the debate over the *hijab* and veiling in northern Nigeria is a patchwork of practices: headscarves of all local varieties and the *hijab* are seen frequently.

Unsurprisingly, given Boko Haram's roots as a dissident sect that splintered from the 'Yan Izala, female covering is an important marker of membership in the group. In particular, Falta and others observed that Boko Haram members 'were very focused on covering women and preventing them from farming'.[39] The dictates for coverage were simple, albeit potentially stifling in the heat of the north: women were to cover themselves entirely, including with the *niqab* and socks. The adoption of the *niqab*, which leaves just an opening for the woman's eyes, is a remarkable innovation in the debate over female veiling in northern Nigeria. A 17-year-old who lived under Boko Haram as the wife of an insurgent recalled that she was told: 'Keep yourself sharp, sharp clean and covered, so that the sun cannot touch your hair.'[40] Wife seclusion, prohibitions on farming and female veiling are all deeply intertwined. One of the reasons why the *hijab* was resisted by some in the north was because such a style of dress would make it difficult for women to engage in work outside the home, especially farming.[41] The sect's adoption of the *niqab* and socks is a means of asserting that the proper place for women is within the domestic sphere. Covering ensures that women are literally physically shielded from public spaces when they leave their compounds; it should be noted that some scholars have interpreted strict covering as a means of taking the home into the public sphere. Further, the demand that women wear such clothing is a means of elevating and enforcing the prohibition of female farming, as demanding agricultural labour is not possible in these garments.

Aisha, the commander's wife who abandoned the dress code after being brought to Maiduguri, recalled that her husband told her that: 'My body is *haram* if the world sees me, it is *haram*, so we must cover every part of our bodies except for our eyes.'[42] Underneath their coverings, however, the women delighted in wearing makeup and applying henna. Many of the wives cited makeup as one of the most important gifts that their husbands provided for them – Aisha, the wife of the emir, in particular, had access to 'makeup of every kind, the foundation, the lipstick and the [eye] shadows'.[43] Keeping themselves and their domestic environments clean, beautiful and the purview of their husbands was one of the most critical tasks of women in Boko Haram. According to Aisha, there were also different standards of dress for the married women as opposed to single women. Although all of the women were expected to don the *niqab*, single women were permitted to wear patterned fabrics, whereas married women were expected to wear monochromatic clothing.

Boko Haram's use of the *niqab* and socks suggests that the sect is emulating certain Middle Eastern practices. Although the United States' intelligence agencies declared in the summer of 2016 that there appeared to be no operational connections between Boko Haram and the Islamic State in the Levant (ISIL), despite the Nigerian insurgents' declaration of *bayat* in 2015, some of the women in the sect reported that they were taught that their *jihad* was led by ISIL. Falmata, from Dikwa, recalled that they were shown pictures of ISIL leader Abu Bakr al-Baghdadi and told that the *jihad* is led by him.[44] Other girls, when asked to describe the group's leadership structure, placed al-Baghdadi at the top – superseding Abubakar Shekau. Aisha, the commander's wife who today wears a light headscarf and open-necked dresses in the grounds of the government-run 'Safe House' where she lives, boasted that her husband had travelled to Iraq and even suggested that he was an Arab. Her pride in his purportedly foreign roots seemed undiminished despite the fact they there were quickly debunked; her mother-in-law, who lives in the camp with her, is a Kanuri woman who had a Kanuri husband.[45] The introduction of strict, imported dress codes may be a means through which the cosmopolitan aspirations of the sect manifest themselves.

Education, Qur'anic teaching and the rule of law

For those who consider the sect to be a collection of thugs, loosely united under the banner of Boko Haram, the extent to which the insurgency invests in religious education should come as a surprise. While there is undoubtedly a thuggish and criminal element to Boko Haram, there is also a commitment to Qur'anic education that seems to surpass what would be required for a successful propaganda effort. The insurgency provides regular schooling to both men and women in their insurgency, regardless of whether they joined willingly or by force.

Aisha, the wife of the insurgency's commander in Walasah, recalled that: 'We went for Qur'anic education every day except for Thursday.' Aisha was taught by a female member of Boko Haram and she insists that the *malam* 'taught us the same things as normal Qur'anic school – we learned the Qur'an and the hadiths'. Falta, the mother of the commander, was also given Qur'anic education by the insurgents despite her advanced age; she described it as similar to what she learned when she listened to Izala preachers.

In another Boko Haram camp at Masa, Falmata reported that the insurgency had co-opted local *almajirai* to serve as Qur'anic instructors. She attended the mandatory classes from Saturday to Wednesday for two hours each morning. 'My class was only girls,' she said, reflecting the ubiquitous gender segregation under the sect. She estimates that in her classroom alone there were more than 60 pupils.[46] The *almajiri*-cum-teacher reportedly rotated classrooms. Falmata remembered that, 'when you went into the classroom, you turned your back on your teacher' in an attempt to preserve gender segregation despite the overwhelmingly male demographic of the *malams*. 'You could not tell if your instructor was a man or a woman until they spoke,' she recalled. In addition to the near-daily classes, the women were expected to attend weekly public preaching, often with gender-specific messages.

As one would expect, the women brought into Boko Haram forcibly are considered to be especially in need of Qur'anic education. Reports from across the north-east, collected both from women who joined the sect voluntarily and from those who were abducted, generally paint a similar picture. When Boko Haram invades a town, women who are abducted or captured are rounded up in a single location. Often, they are given a choice of accepting Boko Haram's ideology and joining the sect or being killed. In some instances, they are given the option of fleeing. The experience of Aisha, a middle-aged woman from Marte, is illustrative of the choices given to women. Aisha recalled that the fighters who invaded her town took a softer approach to the one often depicted in the media: 'They told us that if you want to follow our ideology, you should come with us. If not, you should leave.' The insurgents tried to convince Aisha to join them: 'They said that I should leave my mother behind to come with them to do the work of God. But I told them I could not leave her, and if I did, I would not stop thinking of her.' Aisha eventually left Marte, trekking through the bush with her mother (who was very old – Aisha claimed she was '120') curled in a wheelbarrow, to take refuge in Maiduguri.

Those who are neither killed nor able to flee are then typically taken a large building where they are held in isolation from the rest of the insurgency. There, they are given Qur'anic instruction. Aisha, the wife of the commander, explained that the schooling process was essentially a way of preparing the women for marriage to an insurgent. When a fighter sees and 'likes a woman, they take her'.[47] Once she and any others have been captured, they are 'given schooling for three months or so. Particularly if she is older, she must go to school before she is married. If she is young enough, she is married straight away.'[48] Education is not only a means of socialising women into the sect, it is intended to dislodge other interpretations of Islam.

The unmarried women, including those who are abducted and kept by force, who live with Boko Haram are called *mustadafin*. Interestingly, the word *mustadafin* means the weak, or downtrodden. Some Islamic scholars have asserted that the word specifically refers to those who are weakened by external forces, 'such as social structure, corruption, capitalism, etc.'.[49] It is possible that, in using the word *mustadafin*, the insurgents are furthering their claim to be a vanguard for Muslims throughout the country. The transition from *mustadafin* to 'Yan Uwa (a term that is used by a number of groups, not just Boko Haram, and translates as 'brothers') is accomplished through religious training and eventual conversion.

Those who had been kept as *mustadafin* recalled that, although their living conditions were far from luxurious, they were typically fed frequently and entreated to convert to the insurgents' ideology wholeheartedly. One woman who was held by the insurgents while they travelled to towns across Adamawa State recalled that insurgent leadership dictated that 'everyone should be given a chance to convert and Muslims should not be harassed'.[50] This was particularly true for the women the insurgents came across and took as *mustadafin*. Few of the women I spoke with reported any sexual abuse while being held as *mustadafin*, despite the obvious potential for harassment. A woman who was held as a self-described slave (likely considered part of the *mustadafin* by the insurgents) reported that, despite her subordinate position, she was never harmed. 'I do not know what they have done to other people,' she said, 'but to me they have been just fine.'[51] In general, she offered: 'If you are staying with them, they will not touch you.' She concluded simply: 'I would not say that they are bad people.'[52] The lack of sexual abuse against *mustadafin* suggests that insurgents identify their education as a strategic objective – the abducted women are not merely sexual slaves or a means of attracting young men to the insurgency (although this is certainly the case in a handful of cells). By and large, the women in the sect are considered members of a new religious order that is cultivating radical social change.

Other women emphasised that educational services were a means of introducing women to the 'correct path'. Falta recalled that, once women and girls were abducted, the insurgents then 'preached, preached, preached to them to make them understand'.[53] Although the curriculum of the sect's education is largely similar to what students studying under Izala preachers could expect to learn, there are some variations, including the strict prohibition on female farming (except for some older women), the importance of covering, and certain punishments.

Both the marital and the ideological functions of the educational infrastructure allow Boko Haram to justify its governance patterns and introduce the rule of law under its authority. The previously discussed practice of *purdah* is just one of the notable shifts in Qur'anic interpretation with implications for the rule of law under Boko Haram. Amnesty International summarised life under Boko Haram's dictates:

> Boko Haram fighters ruthlessly enforced a common set of rules across towns under their control, which they would announce to the assembled population soon after taking over. Residents were ordered not to sell or consume cigarettes, Indian hemp, or other drugs; men had to let their beards and hair grow and wear trousers that did not touch the floor; women should cover themselves including their faces in public; all transactions had to be conducted directly between producer and consumer – intermediaries were forbidden; women were not allowed to move around outside without a permissible reason, travel between towns required special permission from the Amir and residents were frequently prohibited from leaving Boko Haram territory.[54]

In addition to these regulations on behaviour, the sect has introduced a number of laws and punishments that are foreign to northern Nigeria. Rule of law under Boko Haram was frequently described as consistent and predictable, albeit strict and violent. Most of those who had lived under the sect reported that, after three violations of a rule, the perpetrator would be punished. In Walasah, the group evidently revived practices described in the Qur'an but not practised in northern Nigeria, including *rajumu*, where those found to have committed adultery would be buried alive 'up to their head' and then stoned to death.[55]

In general, the punishment for defying the sect was whipping or beating. Falmata Hassan, a 16-year-old girl from Dikwa, recalled that under the group 'there was a lot of flogging. They would flog the drug users because they believed it would rehabilitate them.'[56] However, one scholar in Adamawa State's Modibbo Adama University of Technology noted that Boko Haram's sharia is far from being derived from scripture, observing that 'every crime in Boko Haram is punished by death. Sharia has levels of punishment, clearly Boko Haram is not Sharia.'[57] While perhaps not every crime was punished by death in Boko Haram, corporal punishment was certainly a feature of life under the group. Falmata recalled that as soon as Boko Haram entered a town, 'they would kill you if you received a government salary', and that as the group consolidated control and expanded its authority, 'informants were taken to the outskirts of the city and shot'.[58]

Given the raiding nature of many Boko Haram cells, there are frequent periods when there is a limited male presence to enforce these changes and regulations. Interestingly, some women who were abducted or held as submissives noted that there were groups of women in the camps tasked with maintaining order among the women, particularly at times when the men left the camps. This class of women was in charge of enforcing the moral and legal restrictions on women and preventing the abducted women from escaping. Accounts from women who had lived with Boko Haram were divided in describing the relationship of these 'enforcers' to the other insurgents. Some of the women claimed that they were the wives of the insurgency's leaders, while others claimed (somewhat unreliably) that it was the 'Chibok girls who were in charge of the camp'.[59] These women were also involved in enforcing attendance at and participation in Qur'anic education. According to IDPs in Yola, 'young girls who couldn't recite were ... flogged by the "Chibok girls"'. These women, regardless of how they were identified in relation to the group, were frequently described as 'violent' and 'ruthless' in their application of the sect's doctrines and rules.[60]

Some more sympathetic women, however, maintained that these women abided by the 'three admonishments prior to physical punishment' that characterise life under Boko Haram's control.

The fact that there is a class of female enforcers of the sect's ideology and rule of law seems in line with what one would expect given the pervasive gender segregation in the camp's operations. More importantly, however, the use of the 'Chibok brand' to instil fear is significant. Conversely, such a class of enforcers might challenge the sect's scriptural interpretation of men being responsible for the monitoring and judgement of female behaviour. Given the heterogeneity of the cells comprising Boko Haram, it is possible that some cells employ this sort of gendered enforcement of norms, while others do not.

Childbearing and child-rearing

Since the Chibok abductions, there have been intermittent reports from human rights groups and news outlets decrying the number of women rescued from the insurgents who discover that they are pregnant with an insurgent's child when they are given a medical assessment at a displacement centre. In the spring of 2015, Borno State Governor Kashim Shettima addressed this phenomenon, asserting that:

> The sect leaders make a very conscious effort to impregnate the women ... Some of them, I was told, even pray before mating, offering supplications for God to make the products of what they are doing become children that will inherit their ideology.[61]

The sect's reported pre-coital prayer has been the subject of much discussion in both the Nigerian and international press. A *Washington Post* article published in April 2016 relayed the story of Hamsatu, a girl who was forcibly abducted into the group and brutally raped. Kevin Sieff reported Hamsatu's account, in which one of her captors 'entered the hut and said a prayer in what sounded to her like Arabic' before raping her. Sieff quoted Governor Shettima, who asserted that members of Boko Haram 'have a certain spiritual conviction that any child they father will grow to inherit their ideology'.[62] The alarm raised about the dangers of the 'children of Boko Haram' reflects some of the country's deep-seated fears and geopolitical biases, while the salaciousness of this reporting decontextualises Boko Haram from the generally pro-natal atmosphere in Nigeria.

What these reports ignore is the simple fact that throughout Nigeria (and much of sub-Saharan Africa) large families are considered desirable – thus, the insurgents' desire to have many children with the women they consider to be their wives is not a deviation from the social norm. Speaking generally about the country, Governor Shettima noted with a sharp wit the challenges presented by the prevalence of underemployed, virile paterfamilias figures in Borno. He identified these men as engaging in 'procreation without responsibility'.[63] The average family size in Nigeria is five people in total, with larger families in the north. Nearly 20 per cent of households in the north-east have nine or more members, according to the Nigeria Demographic and Health Survey.[64] These numbers are often difficult to verify between different surveys, however, as methodologies vary as to whether family size is determined by the number of children born to a woman or fathered by a man. However, it is clear that families in the north are large, even by national standards. Given these characteristics, it would be an anomaly if members of Boko Haram did not seek to have as many children as possible. While it is certainly the case that the sect is engaging in systemic sexual assault and promoting fertile marriages (either voluntary, coerced or forced), the breathless reporting surrounding the desire of Boko Haram members for large families obfuscates the group's cultural context. Particularly when Western media carries such reports, it seems to be a fetishization of the exotic.

Underlying the sensationalist reporting of Boko Haram's procreation is a real, but unsurprising, preference for large families.

Aisha recalled that there was an expectation in her marriage to the commander that they would have 'lots of kids', and that he was going to 'breed them to be Boko Haram'.[65] Within the sect, as in Nigerian society generally, there is a strong preference for sons. Aisha said that, among the sect's elite, the birth of any child was cause for celebration, but 'if you give birth to a girl, they slaughter one goat; if it is a boy, they slaughter two'.[66]

Not unlike life outside the sect, bearing and raising children are central to women's lives as members of Boko Haram. Particularly since the fathers of the children are frequently away on raids in surrounding communities, to obtain resources or to wage war on the Nigerian state, children fit firmly into the domestic sphere – and are thus the responsibility of women. According to the wives of insurgents, until their sons are old enough to be trained as soldiers and their daughters old enough to be married, it is the mother's responsibility to ensure that the child attends the sect's Qur'anic education and, when appropriate, public preaching. Socialisation into the sect begins at home, giving women an unsung role as enforcers of the group's ideology and mission. Leaving aside the combat training adolescents receive, this model is not unlike other strict Salafist interpretations of Islam, in which the mother is responsible for facilitating the moral education of her children.

The operational implications of this practice are unclear. It is possible, however, that it further incentivises the group's tactic of maintaining relatively remote bases and engaging in raids and attacks in neighbouring communities or on government installations. These tactics keep the theatre of operations relatively distant from their own home front, allowing for socialisation into the group's ideology to take place without daily exposure to the destabilising and traumatising violence of the group's *jihad* against non-Muslims, 'fake Muslims' and the government.

Somewhat surprisingly, given the sect's stance on many aspects of Western modernity, a number of women reported that they had access to doctors and relatively advanced medical care when they gave birth. One man who had briefly been captured by Boko Haram recalled: 'They never kill a doctor; if you are a doctor they treat you well and try to convert you.' These doctors are not merely tasked with caring for wounded insurgents, but also with attending to women during childbirth.[67] When Aisha gave birth to her son with the commander, she had a doctor and medicine for the pain, despite delivering the child in the Sambisa Forest. Women with less prominent husbands also reported having some access to medical care. It is worth recalling that, outside Boko Haram, few women in the north-east have any medical assistance at all when they give birth. Although maternal mortality rates in Boko Haram are impossible to discern, one wonders if the insurgency manages to provide mothers with similar (or even better) healthcare compared with the situation in the rest of the north-east.

Despite women's general access to healthcare services under Boko Haram, the tangible threats to women's health posed by early and frequent childbirth are significant. Further, the future of these women is often uncertain when they are widowed or separated from their husbands. Being a single mother is difficult in Nigeria, even without the stigma faced by these women and the children they bear with insurgents. Dr Bulama Gubio notes that the north-east is now grappling with how to deal with what he calls 'kid widows', defined by him as 'girls younger than 15 years old who were forced into marriage and who often have children of their own'.[68]

Veil of ignorance

Although female members of Boko Haram spoke relatively freely about their weddings, children and education, there was often a reticence about admitting that they knew about the violence in which the sect engaged. Hamsatu Allamin recalled that women knew of the violence the insurgents were was involved in, and reported that, 'in Bama, women would sing for these boys when they came back, with their hair very long and grown with lice, but the girls were happy to marry them'.[69] Women themselves frequently bristled at the claims that the insurgents engaged in indiscriminate violence, offering a defence of their actions while simultaneously trying to deny any knowledge of insurgent activities.

A social worker at one of the government-run camps asserted that 'they make these girls swear an oath called *mubaya*', which means that, 'if you join them and then take their secret out, you will be punished by God'.[70] According to this social worker, this vow has created a culture of fear among the women, impeding the de-radicalisation process: 'Their fear is that if they tell us the truth and then return to their place, the other women will reveal who said what and they will be punished.'[71] Reuben, a psychologist with the Neem Foundation who works with radicalised and traumatised women in government-run displacement camps, came to the conclusion that silence during his sessions 'is an indication that they are still holding onto their ideology'.[72] The tactics women adopt to avoid admitting their compliance with the sect's violent campaign generally take three forms: occult explanations, claims of ignorance and normalcy, and deference to a divine force.

Charms and the occult

The women often cite being 'charmed' by the insurgents through drugs or even occult practices, which has led to rumours that consuming the food or tea that Boko Haram gives you will 'change your heart'.[73] Fatima observed that the insurgents frequently brought tea and dates 'to the men and women that they like – even children – to get them to convert to their beliefs'. She believed that 'they spit in the tea and put things in your food that can control your mind'.[74]

When asked if she had pledged *mubaya*, Aisha said that: 'I was asked if I believe in Allah, the Qur'an, and then they gave me dates and tea. I ate and I slept and when I woke my heart was turned to them.'[75] This refrain of losing autonomy after eating Boko Haram's food was widespread, among both sympathisers and detractors of the insurgency. Shettima, the long-haul lorry driver, recalled despondently that: 'I am not sure if my kids joined [the insurgency] because they wanted to, because they were kidnapped, or because of what they ate.'[76] These supernatural explanations for joining the insurgency are often used as a means of deflecting responsibility or to explain away censured behaviour. While it is possible that these ideas have attracted earnest believers, they also are undeniably a means of escaping culpability and an example of coded, deflecting language.

Claims of ignorance

Women also frequently claimed to have no knowledge of the violence perpetrated by the sect. Despite her vivid descriptions of other aspects of life with Boko Haram, Zainab was reserved when discussing violence. Her account frequently contradicted itself, suggesting that she was trying to obscure the extent of her knowledge about the violence. Although she observed that 'our prophet did *jihad*, so Boko Haram is imitating the prophet', she later deflected questions by stating: 'Since I am a woman, I don't know anything about *jihad*.'[77] When pressed about the justification for the insurgency's cause, she irritably waved off the question and insisted: 'They were just killing non-Muslims and military people.'[78]

This was a common pattern – women would deny knowing specifics of the violence, but would then become agitated when Boko Haram was characterised as killing indiscriminately. Sometimes this agitation would result in them revealing the true extent of their knowledge. Some of the female insurgents would even admit that they supported the *jihad*, while suggesting that they knew little of the violence it entailed. Aisha, the commander's wife, admitted at one point that she supported the violence against the *kafirs* and wanted all of Nigeria to be a *daula*.[79] She later relayed an account of a time when she saw her husband kill a Nigerian soldier who had found himself near the settlement in Walasah: 'One day I saw him kill a soldier, and I ran back to our home and I was shaking and scared. My husband came home to find me crying. He explained that if the soldier saw him, he would have been killed.'[80] Aisha said that she then supported her husband's violence and she knew that the soldier would have killed her too.

Many women claimed that they didn't ask their husbands about their activities when they left the camp. Zainab stated that 'the men would leave and we wouldn't ask them what they did'. Pausing thoughtfully, she concluded: 'Anyway, they weren't keen to talk about it even with the wives.'[81] Another wife, Aisha from Cameroon, who lived with her husband in Walasah for a year, echoed Zainab's self-imposed veil of ignorance: 'I wasn't afraid to ask him about what he did, but I never asked.'[82] These claims of ignorance are undermined by reports – frequently from the same women – that their husbands, sons and brothers 'brought back videos of the violence' and shared them with their wives and families.[83]

These claims of ignorance were frequently coupled with assertions that life with Boko Haram was 'normal'. Aisha, the commander's wife, claimed that even Abubakar Shekau was 'just a normal man'; she recalled that, when 'he visited our town two years ago, he told us to be patient and asked the men if they had settled their families'. Zainab summarised her time in Walasah as simply: 'We were living a normal life, doing normal chores.' She claimed that there were 'no guns or aggression' in the camps and that even the Qur'anic education was just 'normal', focusing on scripture and the hadiths.

Divine will

Finally, many of the women denied culpability by attributing their actions and those of fighters in Boko Haram to divine providence. This is perhaps unsurprising, given a broader cultural context in the north-east that attributes nearly all developments to the will and whims of the divine; this is perhaps best illustrated by the prevalence of the phrase *inshallah* (God willing) as a response to nearly any question or observation. Still, it is worth noting as a defensive tactic for women sympathetic to Boko Haram and now under government control. Hauwa, who was married at just 12, defended her husband's actions (and, by implication, her consent to the group's dictates) by saying that 'everything our husbands do is for the sake of Allah, so if they make us do it, it's for the good'.[84] Similarly, when asked about her son's duties as a commander in Boko Haram and how he rose to such a prominent position, Falta responded: 'Allah gave him that power and authority.'[85] This attribution was not only applied at the individual level; it was also deployed to explain the group's successes and setbacks. When asked how Boko Haram came to control Banki and other towns, Zainab responded forcefully: 'Allah gave us the power to hold this place.'[86] When asked how Boko Haram had lost control of territory, she demurred and responded that this was Allah's will as well. She was considerably less enthused about this expression of Allah's will, but resigned nonetheless.

Female fighters and participation in violence

Given the frequent claims of ignorance of the insurgents' violence made by women in the sect, it is unsurprising that female fighters are not a defining feature of Boko Haram. Among vigilante groups and members of the military posted in the region, there are a number of apocryphal tales of 'women in *burkas* with AK-47s'. Amnesty International recounted the story of Aisha, who was kidnapped from a wedding and taken with her sister to one of the insurgency's bases in Gulak, Adamawa. In Gulak, Aisha and the other 100 or so abducted girls who lived there were forced into marriages and taught to fight. Aisha recalled:

> They used to train girls how to shoot guns. I was among the girls trained to shoot. I was also trained how to use bombs and how to attack a village. This training went on for three weeks after we arrived. Then they started sending some of us to operations. I went on one operation to my own village.[87]

Soldiers manning a checkpoint at the 7th Division garrison in Maiduguri excitedly talked of seeing women on the field of battle, but were vague about the details of when and where, giving the stories of female fighters an aura of myth.[88] Elder, a top commander in the CJTF in Borno State, who boasted of his time spent fighting the sect on the front lines, insisted that there are female fighters. 'They are not many, but they are there. I have even seen one using an RPG [rocket-propelled grenade],' he said confidently, before opining that 'the women fighters are even more dangerous than the men fighters' because they seem even more fearless than their male counterparts.[89]

These rare female fighters have acquired regional reputations. Bulus Mungopark, a vigilante from Chibok living as an IDP in Maiduguri, recalled seeing one female fighter a number of times. He claimed that at first she was just a sympathiser who helped cook for the insurgents. Over time, Bulus said, she was brought into the sect as a fighter when she demonstrated her grit and strength.[90] Alhassan, the state security intelligence head for the CJTF, said that these female fighters are typically older than the male fighters in the sect, but he was unable to provide an estimate of the number of female fighters.[91]

The motivations of these female fighters are likely to reflect the motivations identified by scholars of female participants in other insurgencies. Mia Bloom, a noted scholar on women in violent conflict globally, classifies these motivations as 'the four Rs plus one': revenge, redemption, relationships, respect and rape.[92] While each one is a powerful force in its own right, Bloom identifies relationships as the 'best predictor of a woman's involvement in terrorism'; whether the relationship is with 'her father, brother, husband or even her son', a sense of connection creates conditions in which 'terrorism becomes a bit of a family business'.[93] Particularly in the Nigerian context, where state security representatives are often abusive and predatory, revenge probably also plays an important role in mobilising women. Another possibility, given the widespread reports of sexual harassment by the Nigerian security sector, is that Bloom's rape (a category here that includes other forms of sexual assault) is a motivating factor. Recalling the Tamil Tigers insurgency, Bloom states that 'there were editorials in the paper saying that soldiers really had to stop raping Tamil women at checkpoints because they were just creating more operatives. The [Tigers] were cognizant of this and exploited it: "Don't be a victim, join the movement."'[94] These factors may well be at play in northern Nigeria. It is difficult to discern the motivations of female fighters, since they are suspected of being a rarity and women 'liberated' by the insurgents are assumed to be wives – even if they are potentially fighters.

The women who joined Boko Haram willingly seemed confused by the concept of female fighters. Most said that they had never seen female fighters in the sense of women taking up arms and participating in combat. A few identified individual female fighters, but emphasised that these women were not the norm. Far more common were reports of female suicide bombers. Although infrequently analysed, female suicide bombers have become an integral part of Boko Haram's campaign. In fact, no other insurgency in history has had so many female suicide bombers. The Tamil Tigers, previously the holder of the dubious honour of the most female suicide bombers, deployed 46 women over the course of a decade of suicide missions. Within just two years, Boko Haram has been identified as being responsible for more than 100 female suicide bombers.

Angela Dalton and Victor Asal have outlined some of the general tactical benefits of using female suicide bombers, observing that:

> the very fact of being female is proven to enjoy several tactical advantages. First, women suicide terrorists capitalize and thrive on the 'element of surprise.' They can take advantage of cultural reluctance toward physical searches to evade detection. Given their seemingly feminine facade, they are categorically perceived as gentle and non-threatening.[95]

Female suicide bombers are a relatively recent innovation in the sect's operational portfolio, beginning in mid-2014. As discussed previously, this time period was characterised by a renewed military effort against the sect and an increase in the presence of the military and police in urban centres across the north. Boko Haram's female suicide bombers have largely been deployed against soft targets such as markets and bus depots in urban centres. It appears that 'since Nigerian counterterrorism efforts increased in urban centers as a part of the State of Emergency and Multi National Joint Task Force, women have become tactically important for the group to maintain an urban presence'.[96] The symbolic value of using women as weapons, including the ability of this tactic to cultivate an aura of fear in local populations by upending gender norms and expectations, should not be underestimated. As the Chibok girls have demonstrated, the symbolic value of women and girls can be critical strategically. As Andrew Walker notes in *Eat the Heart of the Infidel*: 'the stream of female suicide bombers contained a potent propaganda message: that Boko Haram is prepared to destroy the things the West holds most valuable.'[97]

It should be noted that it is unclear if all (or any) of these attacks can rightly be described as 'suicide bombings'. The phrase implies that the 'decision to martyr oneself is made of ... her own volition'. However, media reports of girls of nine years old being used as 'suicide' bombers calls into question the girls' agency in such cases.[98] According to a military source quoted in the Nigerian press, 'some of those girls might not really know they were strapped'.[99] Other sources have suggested that family members coerce their children into engaging in such acts. A young woman from Borno who fled to Abuja after being abducted and held by the insurgents claimed that, once a week, all of the abducted women were gathered together and told that, if they 'volunteered' to undertake a suicide bombing, they would be given better food and lodging while they trained to complete their mission.[100] One should be careful, however, not to remove *all* agency from female bombers. As Dorit Naaman notes: 'the figure of the female suicide bomber is always already determined as damaged, deranged, or deluded ... [They] are not

understood as agents, committed to fighting oppression and participating in armed struggle.'[101]

The wives of Boko Haram insurgents insisted, when asked, that
the female suicide bombers were all volunteers. Aisha claimed that
they go to the leader and volunteer, and then the sect gives them 'three
months training, so that they can see your mind', before sending them
out on a mission.[102] As for the motivations of these women, Aisha
said that 'some of those who go are widows and some are married
and go with their husband' on joint missions. Adam Higazi's broader
study of the phenomenon confirms Aisha's and other wives' claims
that many of the female suicide bombers volunteer to undertake such
a mission.[103] The role of revenge in motivating female participation
in violence has been well documented, often focusing on the frustrations and vulnerability of widows. Hauwa, however, also claimed
that revenge (rather than coercion) was a motivating factor for child
suicide bombers. When asked about the reports of a particularly young
girl who had been a bomber, she explained: 'It's done as revenge. If a
seven-year-old girl is a bomber, it is probably because her mother has
died, so she is sent out to take revenge on the Nigerian military.'

The training that coerced or voluntary suicide bombers undergo
is likely to include a misinformation campaign, sometimes coupled
with additional religious indoctrination. Dionne Searcey, the *New
York Times* West Africa bureau chief, claimed that female bombers,
particularly younger ones, are told that the only pain they will feel
is 'like a mosquito bite'.[104] Bloom asserts that this is common,
observing that many of the women sent on suicide bombing
missions around the world are made fantastical promises, such as
'You'll have the perfect husband, you'll be restored if there's been
any illness or disfigurement, and not only are you going to be with
Allah, but 70 of your relatives are going directly to heaven' in order
to steel their will to complete their assignment.[105] Other women,
however, are convinced that their actions are religiously justified, or
consider their actions to be a strike against an abusive or predatory
state, and do not need much cajoling.

A note on divorce in Boko Haram

Somewhat unexpectedly, divorce appears to be relatively common in Boko Haram – and can be initiated by women. Interestingly, even after a man demands (or grants) a divorce, he is still responsible for the well-being of his ex-wife until she is remarried. Talking of her first husband, Zainab recalled that, even after she divorced him, he had to take care of her. That was custom. She lived in his house and he gave her food and money, even after he accepted that she was going through with the divorce. While she was observing a period of isolation called *iddah* prior to re-entering the marriage market, Zainab mobilised her female friends to help her find a new partner. She remembered: 'I told my friends, "I am beginning *iddah*, you need to spread the word that I am looking for a new husband."' Thanks to her friends' efforts, 'three or four men were waiting for me immediately after I finished *iddah*'. Zainab remembered that: 'I picked the one who gave me the best gifts.'[106] Only then was the husband that she had left relieved of his burden to provide for her.

Fati Abubakar, a humanitarian worker, writer and the photojournalist behind the *Bits of Borno* project from Maiduguri, asserts that these practices 'seem like a throwback to Kanuri culture', perhaps reflecting the overrepresentation of the Kanuri in the insurgency's leadership and early membership.[107] The Kanuri are a largely Muslim ethnic group concentrated in the area around Lake Chad, with members in Chad, Niger and Cameroon as well as Nigeria. Early anthropological work done by Ronald Cohen confirms Abubakar's observation; in 'Marriage Instability among the Kanuri of Northern Nigeria', Cohen observes that 'divorce is looked upon as an unfortunate break-down in inter-personal relations', but also that 'all informants feel that the institution of divorce is a good and desirable practice. They laughed at and decried any hypothetical situation in which divorce is not a practicable possibility in marriage.'[108] The practice of actively seeking a husband following a divorce is also observed in Cohen's review of Kanuri marital practices, in which he observes that 'a divorced woman ought to be looking for a husband. If she is obviously not doing so and publicly states her desire to remain singly, she is looked upon as a loose woman or a prostitute.'[109] Although this similarity between Kanuri practices and Boko Haram operational character- istics might be coincidental, it is worth noting that it is not the only such similarity. Wife seclusion, called *nyia kule* (in Kanuri), was also practised by the Kanuri. On the issue of wife seclusion, Cohen notes that: '[W]hether or not he can do without his wife's labor outside the compound on his farm plots, or at the well obtaining water, every Kanuri man expects and hopes that his wife or wives will leave the compound as little as possible.'[110]

Variations on the theme

Having discussed the points of commonality among women who join Boko Haram voluntarily, we should also address the points of variation between different women's experiences. Many of these differences are ultimately a result of the hierarchy within Boko Haram.

Life at the top
Despite being in many ways a revolt from the margins, Boko Haram sometimes reproduces the sorts of hierarchy that aggrieved its initial followers.[111] Wives of the sect's leadership reportedly have a number of servants to assist them with their household duties. Aisha laughed, revealing that she had servants but did not use them, because she wanted to be the one attending to her husband's needs.

One of the most visible class markers within Boko Haram involves weddings within the sect. Although 'bride price inflation' can be considered a factor that limited marriage prospects and primed the area for conflict, commanders, leaders and elite members of the sect typically pay a higher bride price than their subordi- nates. In the early 2000s, this higher bride price was reported to be 100,000 naira by a handful of women.[112] Such a sum is notably lower than what elites outside Boko Haram may pay – which can be millions of naira[113] – but it is still many times what most women who married foot soldiers in the insurgency claimed to have received as bride price (usually around 5,000 naira).

Despite the sect's leadership having the largest, most lavish weddings of any members of the insurgency, it is worth noting that these affairs are still markedly smaller than traditional marriages outside the sect. Falta recalled that her son's first wedding, which happened before he joined Boko Haram, 'was a big occasion that took two days'.[114] The cost of the ceremony required that Falta and her husband contribute to the bride price and wedding budget. After her son's entrance into the sect, however, she reported that his weddings 'were done on his own, with no help from us, his parents'. The events were smaller, quicker, and involved less parental consultation, in addition to occurring without any familial financial assistance.

Again, mirroring the norms of the society from which the sect emerged, the number of wives an insurgent has is a marker of his position within Boko Haram. Aisha, the commander's wife, was either his third or fourth wife (the number varied, depending on whether it was Aisha, her mother-in-law, or one of the other women who lived under her husband's rule relaying the tale). It also appears that women related to or married to leaders of the insurgency had a role in organising the operations and management of the camp's social services. Aisha recalled that, 'as *amira*, I went door to door to give gifts' to the group's members.[115] The gifts she gave were typically food or a few thousand naira. This presence was important in cultivating the loyalty of Boko Haram members and submissives, as Aisha's mother-in-law Falta explained: 'So long as he is giving away food and items, whatever he says we will follow.'[116]

The extent of Aisha's reputation as a powerful woman is clear from the continued deference she received from the women at Safe House. Before talking with social workers or other government representatives, the other women looked to Aisha for her approval. A click of Aisha's tongue or a pointed look still had the capacity to silence the women mid-sentence. Fatima, a social worker in the camp, observed that this fear was related to the authority Aisha would have to order their punishment if they were seen to violate the group's code of secrecy.[117] Fatima suggested that this fear is part of the reason why the process of de-radicalising the women has been slower than anticipated; however, there is not yet a compelling body of literature regarding successful so-called 'de-radicalisation'.

Soldier's wives

Wives of soldiers who have not climbed the ranks of the insurgency have fewer privileges than the wives of the sect's leadership. The routine weddings of foot soldiers to their wives are generally small affairs. Falmata, who was first married at 12 years old, observed that Boko Haram weddings 'were different' from traditional weddings 'because they did not give the big boxes of clothes or a dowry to the parents'. Women reported that these weddings were gender segregated, and at times they did not have dancing, or traditional ceremonies, or accoutrements such as henna.[118]

In addition to keeping house and rearing children, the wives of foot soldiers were also sometimes responsible for carrying their husband's weapons. This has two implications: first, the veil of ignorance adopted by many women about the sect's violent activities is, to some degree, a charade; and second, the reports from military and vigilante groups of women in conservative veils carrying weapons may not refer to female fighters, but rather to helpers of the soldiers.

Other wives of foot soldiers reported that their husbands were not wealthy enough or high-ranking enough to have 'real' weapons, instead taking handmade or crude weapons into battle. These women were thus relieved of the duty to carry their husbands' weapons into war. The assertions of these women that their husbands go to battle out-gunned to such an extent suggest a number of possibilities about the functioning of Boko Haram: that there is a stark hierarchy within the sect, that this is an alternative version of the 'veil of ignorance' discussed earlier, or that the media's portrayal of the strength of the insurgency is overblown.

Slaves or submissives

Among many of the women, the terms 'slave' and 'submissives' were used interchangeably to refer to non-fighting members of the sect who still abided by the group's ideology and dictates. Those who refused to submit to the will of the insurgents were considered non-Muslims and killed. There is a fine line between those abducted into the sect and submissives, particularly since there is a possibility of movement between the two classifications – and, indeed, into the sect itself. Among the women, the line between the insurgency's submissives and the wives of low-level insurgents is a particularly thin one. Aisha, the commander's wife, asserted that, during raids, 'if you are praying before you are caught then you are a wife; if you are not praying, you are taken as a slave but you can be made into a wife'.[119] Conversion and adherence to Boko Haram's ideology are means of making oneself eligible for marriage.

Although the submissives in Boko Haram are expected to attend schooling and abide by the restrictions on dress and activities that other women are subjected to, there are (at times) some exceptions made for slaves and submissives concerning other parts of the group's rule of law. According to one woman who lived under Boko Haram's rule, her husband was allowed to continue farming. She observed that 'the rich and powerful do not till the land, but some of the poor and the slaves do'; however, she was quick to note that even slave women were not permitted to farm.[120] The categories of gender and class are as powerful within the sect as they are outside it.

Contextualising Boko Haram's use and abuse of women and girls

While Boko Haram is often discussed as part of the 'Global War on Terror' and considered an expansion of the Salafi-Jihadi threat in sub-Saharan Africa, joining the ranks of terrorist groups such as Al Qaeda in the Maghreb (AQIM) and Al Shabaab, it is important not to overlook the similarities that the group has with other rebel movements and non-jihadist armed insurgencies across sub-Saharan Africa. Boko Haram's relationship with women and girls resembles those of rebel movements across sub-Saharan Africa, where female participation (both coerced and voluntary) is important but understudied. Women, when they are considered in assessments of African conflicts, are often portrayed entirely as victims. A few examples are illustrative of the ways in which Boko Haram's gender politics reflect its regional context.

As in Boko Haram, having a number of wives and girlfriends was a sign of status among Liberian insurgents in the 1990s. Mats Utas observes that, among these rebels:

> Girlfriends were not only picked up for the pleasure of the soldier, but also for the status he obtained by being able to cater for them. Often the presence of 'wives' gave the soldier his status as a senior man in the same fashion as in 'traditional' polygamous households. In the eyes of many urbanites in Monrovia, polygamy was hopelessly backward but as most of the rebels had their roots in the countryside, they were merely mimicking strongmen in their villages.[121]

In the LRA, women and girls have been active participants.[122] Jeannie Annan, Christopher Blattman, Dyan Mazurana and Khristopher Carlson concluded that 'women and girls ... play active roles and are not passive victims'.[123] Interestingly, although a number of the female fighters in the LRA were abducted, as in Boko Haram, 'LRA treatment of females – especially strict rules against civilian rape and the use of forced marriage – serves an instrumental purpose, enhancing control of the forces and protection from HIV.' It also incentivises female loyalty to the group and reduces defection.[124]

The comparison between the LRA and Boko Haram is an especially valuable one for understanding the role of women and girls in African insurgencies and dispelling the myth of 'terrorist exceptionalism' that often taints analysis of Boko Haram. Despite their ideological incongruity, the two groups have demonstrated remarkable similarities. Consider the incentives (declining public support and increased government security presence) that have prompted both groups to rely more heavily on abductions and conscription to fill their ranks. Like Boko Haram, 'the LRA took to looting homes for supplies and abducting youth to serve as fighters, servants and 'wives'.[125] Annan *et al.* found that the forced marriages between LRA soldiers and abducted girls are 'highly regulated and controlled by the LRA's top leadership, with females being distributed to males based on the males' rank'.[126] The LRA's strategic use of marriage mirrors Boko Haram's 'rewarding' of foot soldiers with wives.

As in Boko Haram, the LRA seems to have a sorting mechanism for the women within its ranks. Annan *et al.* report that:

> Our interviews suggest that rebels divided females into three groups: prepubescent girls, young adolescents, and those thought to have had prior sexual relationships. Prepubescent girls were kept as babysitters to be given later as 'wives', while young adolescents were kept to be forcibly married as soon as possible. Older adolescents and young women, seen as potential carriers of sexually transmitted infections and HIV, were more seldom given as 'wives' and were more often released.[127]

Although Boko Haram's sorting mechanisms are less concerned with sexually transmitted diseases and more concerned with ideological indoctrination, both groups' categorisation of the women reflects the strategic value of the women in their ranks.

Unlike in Boko Haram, however, rebel marriages in the LRA are generally conducted without a ceremony and never included 'rituals resembling traditional marriage practices'.[128] Another potential difference, that only time will illuminate, is that fewer than 5 per cent of all forced wives stayed with their LRA husbands in the post-conflict era. At the time of writing, a number of Boko Haram women (including the first Chibok girl rescued) have expressed interest in maintaining their marriages after the conflict and consider them to be legitimate.[129]

Frelimo, now a dominant political party, which began as a nationalist armed group in the war in Mozambique that raged between 1976 and 1992, adopted a tactic that blurred the line between recruitment and abduction. So-called 'press-ganging' bears a striking similarity to Boko Haram's tactic of abductions followed by indoctrination. Press-ganging has been described as such:

> Frelimo recruiters arrived with buses at schools where they asked girls to volunteer for the military. When few agreed, girls were forced onto buses and taken to a military base where they met with other 'recruited' girls and began military training.[130]

It is important to recognise that, while press-ganging was certainly a coercive mechanism that brought a number of women into the rebel group, some women also joined Frelimo because of 'the promise of new and emancipatory roles, to escape rural areas and expand traditional gender roles, and in hopes of improving their educational and career opportunities'.[131] Like the women who joined Boko Haram in order to improve their standard of living or social status, some female members of Frelimo joined in order to improve their lot.

Susan McKay, discussing female participation in the Revolutionary United Front (RUF) in Sierra Leone and in the LRA, characterises women's participation in rebel groups as a response to violence specifically targeting women and girls. Frequently, 'victims of terrorist violence subsequently become perpetrators of similar violence'.[132] The similarities between the RUF's and Boko Haram's use of women and girls underlines the characteristics of

Boko Haram that make it more akin to an African insurgency than a terrorist group with transnational influences and aspirations. An important difference between the treatment of women by the RUF and LRA and that of Boko Haram is the military training women received in Sierra Leone and Uganda. In the RUF, women and girls not only 'cared for the sick and wounded, passed messages between rebel camps, served as spies, and some worked in diamond mining for their commanders', but they also 'killed people, stole property, and looted and burned houses'.[133] Similarly, in the LRA, not only were girls responsible for 'raising crops, selling goods, preparing food, carrying loot, [and] moving weapons', but they were also given military training and participated in front-line combat.[134] Their participation could be rewarded through promotion within the rebellion's ranks; over the course of the insurgency, a number of women obtained command positions. While women in Boko Haram do not appear to have received the same sort of extensive military training that females in the RUF and LRA obtained, their motivations, domestic responsibilities and limited agencies are all similar.

Another potential difference in the ways in which Boko Haram uses women, compared with other African insurgencies, can be extrapolated from the dearth of reports of gang rape of women and girls abducted into Boko Haram. Dara Kay Cohen's work on sexual abuse against women and girls by insurgencies during civil war suggests that the reason why gang rape is engaged in disproportionately is to cultivate social bonds between fighters. The lack of reports of gang rape by Boko Haram members may be a function of the lack of media access; however, it may also suggest stronger initial social cohesion between insurgents than in other African insurgencies.[135]

According to McKay, the very process of 'discrete categorization as "victim" or "perpetrator"' fails to understand the complexities of shifting roles and experiences, such as the seeming paradox of girls becoming allies with individuals who were responsible for abducting and victimising them and who continue to sexually abuse them. Just as structural violence in northern Nigeria was both a powerful force in recruiting women and also replicated in the hierarchy of Boko Haram, so too have 'girls in the northern Ugandan and Sierra Leonean rebel forces … been victimized because they have been forced, at the threat of their lives, to participate in terrorist acts such as killing friends or family members and torching homes', while also demonstrating 'resiliency, agency, and ability to resist – although usually not successfully – their oppressors'.[136] Across these conflicts, women's and girls' 'experiences are poorly understood and only occasionally acknowledged'.[137] This oversight not only prevents effective counter-insurgency strategy, but also puts women at a disadvantage in the post-conflict era of demobilisation and reintegration. These three brief regional comparisons illustrate that Boko Haram's treatment of women and girls is not unlike their treatment by other African insurgencies. Although many have framed Boko Haram's practices in relation to the abductions of Yazidi women by the Islamic State, this comparison may not be the most revealing.

Although the atrocities that communities living under Boko Haram have suffered are breathtaking, the humanitarian crisis unfolding across the Lake Chad Basin means that escape from the insurgents is often followed by a gauntlet of struggles to survive. From the initial 'rescue' of communities from Boko Haram by Nigerian (or Chadian or Cameroonian) soldiers, to their screening, to their lives as IDPs in camps and host communities, those affected by the Boko Haram insurgency are truly beset on all sides. The problems surrounding 'rescue' and the challenges faced by those living as IDPs are the subjects of the following chapter.

Chapter 6

RESCUED TO WHAT? DISPLACEMENT, VULNERABILITY, AND THE DARK SIDE OF 'HEROISM'

Our remorse will always be manifest when we ask for coal and
we are offered cinders.

Nigerian Tribune, 29 November 1979

The humanitarian situation in the Lake Chad Basin, a result of the
insurgency's violence and decimation of regional trade routes and
agriculture, is one of the worst in the world – although it has failed
to receive the same sort of international attention that similar crises
in Syria and South Sudan garnered – and appears to be growing ever
more dire. A crisis of this scope and scale will be a feature of the
region's socio-economic landscape and social memory for generations to come. Women are at the heart of the crisis simply because
they are the demographic that remains. In IDP camps across the
region, one is hard pressed to find able-bodied men between
adolescence and old age. This chapter documents the scope and
implications of the humanitarian crisis through the experiences
of those who are liberated from insurgent control by the Nigerian
military, those living in official camps and informal settlements and
those impacted by the government's clumsy demobilisation efforts,
as well as the challenges for those seeking to return to their commu-

nities and rebuild the north. It also discusses the international community's complicity in the shortcomings of the existing efforts.

A quiet crisis

An activist in Maiduguri lamented that the humanitarian situation in the Lake Chad Basin is 'not like the crisis in Syria or Afghanistan. It's not been ten years with foreign fighters and a big war with just 50,000 dead.' He sighed and continued, gesturing emphatically: 'Here, we lose entire communities in the blink of an eye and people do not seem to look.'[1] In an interview that I conducted with a handful of UNHCR staff in Maiduguri, one opined that: 'If nothing is done, we will have a humanitarian crisis that nobody can contain.' His colleague, seated beside him at a small table, quickly responded: 'I think we already have it.'[2]

Even devoid of global or regional context, the sheer statistics of the crisis are shocking. At the time of writing, more than 2.8 million have been displaced, and more than 4.4 million people face 'severe food insecurity' and are at risk of starvation and malnutrition as a result of the insurgency. In total, the United Nations (UN) has estimated that more than 14 million people in the region have been touched by the crisis.[3] Hundreds of thousands of children throughout the Lake Chad Basin are considered to be 'severely acutely malnourished'. The UN has warned that this level of malnutrition results in death within weeks if people don't receive assistance.[4] Tens of thousands of people in Borno State alone have been classified as 'Phase 5, the highest level of food insecurity' in the predominant assessment system; between June 2015 and June 2016, the people in need of 'immediate food assistance' increased by 400 per cent.[5] The humanitarian disaster, like Boko Haram's violence, is primarily concentrated in north-eastern Nigeria, but it has also affected communities in Chad, Cameroon and Niger.

Throughout the region, the majority of the displaced are women and children, creating a specific set of humanitarian needs and considerations. Women's health programmes, including provisions for safe labour and delivery, are a pressing need. Beyond the immediate threat that the violence and food crisis present, displaced people across the region are grappling with a multitude of long-term issues. With more than 1 million out of school in Nigeria alone due to Boko Haram's insurgency, children are being robbed of their education, threatening the future development and stability of the region.[6]

Bama, a large city in Borno State that has been ravaged by the insurgency, provides an almost allegorical example of the state of affairs across the Lake Chad Basin. According to Adam Higazi, Bama used to be a relatively bustling city with a population of close to 250,000 people. As a result of the Boko Haram crisis, by July 2016 a mere 25,000 people remained in Bama – the rest had been either killed or displaced by the insurgency. As is the case for many communities outside Maiduguri, the government and aid agencies have struggled to provide assistance to the besieged population. In June 2016, nearly 1,200 people were evacuated from a government-run IDP camp for emergency medical care in Maiduguri's hospital.[7] When Médecins Sans Frontières (MSF) was granted access to the camp nearly a week after the evacuation, they reported that nearly a fifth of the 800 children who underwent a rapid nutritional screening were suffering from 'severe acute malnutrition – the deadliest form of malnutrition'. In the few hours during which MSF was granted access to the camp by the state government, it became clear that the crisis in the community was long-standing and lethal. The team observed more than 1,200 graves dug in the last year, more than a third of which were for children.[8] The evacuation was well publicised, with the Borno State government's public relations team circulating photographs of the malnourished IDPs receiving treatment and commending the government's generosity on social media.

Despite this public relations push, behind closed doors, Nigerian politicians were embarrassed and frustrated by the government's inability to provide for those affected by the insurgency. In these closed-door meetings, there was a persistent curiosity as to where the billions of naira allocated by the government and the millions of dollars promised by the international community for humanitarian aid were going.[9] In Maiduguri at the time of MSF's intervention in Bama, government employees of Borno State stated freely that those media outlets that did not toe the government's line would have their access curtailed or revoked outright.[10] A cynical interpretation of the situation is that human suffering of the highest order is being compounded by governmental incapacity and corruption, then churned into political fodder and PR material by politicians who also crush the critical independent press. Even a more generous assessment of the government's efforts would struggle to explain the government's relationship with traditional and social media, which is contentious at best. When the media has been given access, reports of corruption have surfaced, often resulting in denunciations and, consequently, less transparency. Despite the limited ability of the media to investigate, intrepid reporters have constructed credible narratives about the diversion of aid. In December 2016, suspicions over corruption in the humanitarian sector finally resulted in calls by the Nigerian senate for Babachir Lawal, the Secretary to the Government of the Federation, to resign over his contracting practices that diverted money intended to benefit IDPs in the north-east to companies he was involved in.[11] It seems likely that other politicians will be accused as this investigation progresses.

Despite the pressing need for well-coordinated and robustly funded humanitarian interventions, in north-east Nigeria the necessary bureaucratic capacity is lacking, resources are scarce, and – perhaps most damningly – the government agencies tasked with caring for these vulnerable populations are often abusive and predatory.

A hero narrative and dubious rescues: abuse by the security sector

The challenges facing displaced communities often begin before they have fled their homes. Interviews with displaced communities across the north reveal abuse and harassment of civilians by the security sector during their operations and routine patrols. 'They told us to follow them and we followed the military vehicles to Cameroon. As we left, they burned down our houses so that Boko Haram could not loot them,' Muhammed recounted from his seat on the steps of an official-looking building repurposed to hold IDPs in the Fufore camp in Adamawa State. When Muhammed and the other 1,500 people – according to his estimate – fled Bama behind their Cameroonian guides, he had no idea what the future held and had only the possessions he had on his person when Boko Haram invaded his village. For a few months, he and his neighbours settled in a camp in Cameroon. Some of the men were able to find some 'small work', and families worked hard to adjust to their new lives.

One day, the Cameroonian military came to the camp and demanded they once again follow the soldiers without question. Mohammed and others from Bama were led to the camp in Fufore, where they joined the ranks of the thousands of Nigerians forcibly returned to their home country.[12] Other IDPs, then based in a small transit camp in Mubi, a town in northern Adamawa State on the Nigerian side of the border with Cameroon, reported that they were not only forcibly returned to Nigeria; they also had to pay to have their fundamental rights violated. These IDPs reported that they were forced to pay the soldiers 12,000 naira (then about $60) for 'safe passage'.[13] This forcible return, whether coupled with extortion or not, is called refoulement. It is a major violation of international human rights law that was established at the 1951 Refugee Convention.[14] The Organisation of African Unity (now the African Union) reaffirmed the principle in the 1974 Convention Governing the Specific Aspects of Refugee Problems in Africa.[15] Both Nigeria and Cameroon are parties to this convention, which unequivocally declares that 'no person shall be subjected by a Member State to measures such as rejection at the frontier, return or expulsion, which would compel him to return to or remain in a territory where his life, physical integrity or liberty would be threatened'.[16] Unfortunately, the aspirations of international and regional treaties are nowhere to be found on the ground, as thousands have been forcibly returned to Nigeria.

Cameroonian troops are not alone in perpetrating gross human rights abuses under the pretence of 'rescuing' communities from the scourge of Boko Haram. A woman in Fufore IDP camp who had lived under periodic Boko Haram attacks in Damboa (southern Borno State) was able to flee when the Nigerian military came to her town to liberate it. 'My town was along the Boko Haram route, so they attacked us regularly but never ruled over us. We were just trapped in our town,' she recalled.[17] When the Nigerian soldiers came to her town, they 'burned all of our houses and our fields'.[18] She reported that the inferno was supposed to prevent looting by Boko Haram, but that she had no time to collect her possessions before the fire began.

The end result of villages burned by the government and villages looted by the insurgents is often the same for those who used to live there: they are left without their livelihoods and property, with an uncertain future. When asked to give an official comment, the Nigerian military often claims that the fires are set by Boko Haram; however, displaced people, military personnel requesting anonymity, and journalists from communities across the north have all reported the systematic burning of fields and homes by the military in pursuit of Boko Haram.[19] A woman who had lived with Boko Haram in Walasah, before being rescued by the Nigerian military, recalled that when the Nigerian army entered her community 'they did not stop to ask who was Boko Haram; they just burned down the whole village'.[20]

When vigilantes and soldiers – and, at times, IDPs themselves – defend the military's practice of burning villages as part of the liberation process, they often cite the importance of depriving Boko Haram of the opportunity to loot resources.[21] However, not all of the army's abuses can be attributed to strategy. In fact, some of the military's abuses are as victimising as the offences committed by the insurgents. A UNICEF employee who has worked on protection issues throughout northern Nigeria reported that, when Nigerian soldiers entered communities in northern Adamawa to liberate them from Boko Haram's rule in March 2016, they would 'kill local men and take their wives'.[22] With a resigned shrug, he said: 'You can never have security forces acting to code 100 per cent of the time anywhere.'[23] When your husband has been killed, your home burned, and your marital ties forcibly grafted on to a new partnership, whether the source of these changes is wearing a uniform or is an insurgent seems insignificant. The persistent abuses by the security sector have hampered counter-insurgency efforts by reducing citizens' trust in the military.

The extent of the abuses committed in the fight against Boko Haram and the liberation efforts of the Nigerian military has warranted investigation by the International Criminal Court.[24] The court is investigating claims of extrajudicial killings and illegal detention practices, which were highlighted in a number of reports by activist groups such as Amnesty International and Human Rights Watch. Among the most comprehensive and distressing of the accounts was the 2015 *Stars on their Shoulders, Blood on their Hands*, an Amnesty International report that reached a tally of more than 7,000 deaths in government detention centres, 1,200 additional extrajudicial killings, and the 'arbitrary arrest' of more than 20,000 people in the course of the counter-terrorism campaign.[25] Amnesty claimed that 'the military extra-judicially executed people after they had been captured and when they presented no danger ... many were shot dead inside detention facilities, while others were either shot or had their throats cut after being captured during cordon-and-search operations'. The advocates documented a 'mop-up' operation in Baga in April 2013, in which nearly 200 people were killed by the military, who had come in response to an attack by the insurgents.[26]

These fatalities are largely a result of the operational style of the Nigerian counter-insurgency – a 'cast a wide net' approach that involves 'house-to-house raids' and the use of frequent security checkpoints along roads. Amnesty's report concluded that 'on numerous occasions, particularly following Boko Haram raids, soldiers have gone to the town or village, rounded up hundreds of men and boys and taken into custody those identified as Boko Haram by paid informants'.[27] Those rounded up have included boys as young as nine years old and at least 30 women and girls. Regardless of gender, the 'vast majority of arrests carried out by the military appear to be entirely arbitrary'.[28] One man I spoke with in Maiduguri recalled: 'When the military first came, they thought everyone was Boko Haram. We were like Tom and Jerry [the cartoon].'[29] The military's reliance on 'local informants' and vigilantes (who themselves are dependent on payments from the military to make ends meet) further undermines the legitimacy of the military's operations. The lack of transparency about the status and location of those detained by the Nigerian military helps cultivate an aura of fear and insecurity in the country.[30]

However, the military abuses these communities have suffered are all the more disturbing because they are presented within the context of a hero narrative. Since President Buhari took office, the military's public relations team has gone on the offensive, relaying details of military victories, 'rescues' and 'liberations' on a seemingly daily basis. It is worth noting that, even in instances where the military have not engaged in predatory and abusive behaviour against residents, there are reports of less-than-heroic conduct. According to some, when confronted by well-armed Boko Haram insurgents, the Nigerian 'soldiers would take the *hijabs* of the local women to dress as women to flee'.[31] In my interviews, members of the community rarely commented on the valour of the military, creating a stark contrast between oral accounts of the conflict that emerge from the communities most affected and the government's official accounts published in newspapers and press releases. This is not to say that the Nigerian military has not improved in its counter-insurgency efforts over time, or that they are a universally predatory force, but rather to convey the perception of their activities by many in the community.

The Nigerian press – whether due to sympathy, a lack of training, or coercion – often relays the government's reports (and heroic framing) without question. Consider the 26 June 2016 statement from army spokesman Sani Usman that Nigerian troops 'liberated over 5,000 persons held hostages by Boko Haram terrorists and recovered 5 motorcycles and similar number of bicycles'.[32] The status of those rescued, where they were taken and their demographic profiles were not given, and the number of reported injuries and fatalities sustained by the Nigerian troops seemed almost unbelievably low.[33] In March 2016, Usman claimed that the military had rescued more than 11,000 people, a number that was reported in the press with neither independent verification nor scepticism.[34]

This constructed hero narrative is not unique to the Nigerian military's response to Boko Haram – it was deployed by the United States in the war in Iraq to bolster public support. This narrative is useful, serving to improve the military's self-perception and civil–military relations. As Kumar observes, it acts 'as the means by which a controversial war [can] be talked about in emotional rather than rational terms'.[35] Framing the Nigerian military's (often predatory and abusive) counter-insurgency campaign as the liberation of thousands of Nigerians from an oppressive and backward sect forces the public to assess the army's intervention in relation to the activities of Boko Haram, rather than measuring it by an objective standard.

These dispatches, in which military officials usually claim that soldiers have liberated a few hundred Nigerians, are released so regularly that it was surprising that most people I encountered in official displacement camps and host communities reported that they had escaped from the insurgents on their own. Indeed, if government accounts are credible, everyone rescued by the military is taken to an IDP camp (following 'screening', a process described later), yet approximately only one in ten IDPs live in such camps. If my interviews were representative of the general population in the north, this suggests that the majority of IDPs are freeing themselves. However, this community is rarely considered to be heroic and their incredible efforts to liberate themselves and their families are not frequently discussed. In no small part because the displaced are overwhelmingly female or children, this population is not considered heroic. As Lori Handrahan noted, in post-conflict situations: 'The woman was not a fighter, and hence is not a hero. She can expect little comfort or recognition after the war.'[36] Although not widely recognised, these women's stories are an incredible testament to human resilience and will – as well as a startling condemnation of the government's ability to provide services or security. Aisha, from Baga, is now living as an IDP in Maiduguri. When Boko Haram entered her village in February 2015, she fled from the insurgents, 'but then I realised that they had taken one of my sons'.[37] She recalls that she 'followed Boko Haram to recapture him' and that she and her other children followed the insurgents for five days back to their camp. 'My son was 12 years old then,' she said, so when he arrived at the camp 'Boko Haram told him that they wanted to put him in a school'.[38] Watching from her hiding place, Aisha waited until her son and the other abducted boys were being watched by only two guards and then approached them, saying she 'would get him clothes and food and then would take him to the Boko Haram school'. Reunited with her son, Aisha and her family fled through the bush, but 'when Boko Haram realised we had taken him, they pursued us back to another village, through the bush, for days. We arrived and thought that we were safe, but then they set the village on fire.' Running from the inferno and the insurgents, Aisha and her family finally made it to Maiduguri together.[39]

After the rescue: detention and deliberation in a broken system

After the military's 'rescue missions' are conducted, those who have been identified as potential members of Boko Haram or sympathetic to their cause are subject to a process called 'screening', in which the military attempts to discern individuals' levels of involvement with the insurgency. The process is deliberately opaque. Hamsatu Allamin stated that 'the NGO world is not privy to screening practices', despite the obvious interest of human rights activists in monitoring this process.[40] A report by UN relief agencies summarised that, 'even if the Nigerian military appeared disciplined and benevolent towards the IDPs, without a follow-up or transparency in this process, violations of human rights may exist as individuals may by falsely accused due to lack of documentation'.[41] Even UNHCR employees engaged in protection practices reported that, 'when people are rescued, they go through a military screening. This is a no-go zone for NGOs; we are not invited. Only after they are screened do we get access to these people.'[42]

The information that has trickled out about the military's rescue practices reveals a general pattern: immediately following the rescue, those who have not fled or been killed in the crossfire are taken to military barracks to be screened. During screening, those who have been rescued 'are immediately separated by gender', according to a brigade commander; from there, the military tries 'to determine their level of support and involvement'. This screening often relies on vigilantes who are from the same community as the suspects; these vigilantes are often tasked with reporting whether or not the detainees joined the insurgency by force or voluntarily.[43]

The reliance on violence and vigilante screening is deeply problematic – and likely counterproductive as the military tries to garner trust from communities across the north-east.[44] Those who are suspected of supporting the sect or who have been identified by vigilantes are subjected to indefinite detention and, frequently, gross human rights abuses. In theory, those detained have charges brought against them and a court determines their guilt or innocence. However, as one soldier noted, 'prosecution is a long process, so many of them are just awaiting trial' in detention centres.[45] To give a sense of how long cases may take to reach a sentence, it is worth noting that those suspected of being involved in the Abuja bombings of 2011 have still not received a verdict.[46]

Disturbingly, there seems to be no standard screening procedure across commands, and there is no standard set of questions or metrics to gauge the level of support or involvement. 'We often ask them what their names are and where they were abducted,' one soldier reported. 'Even though we know they were not all kidnapped, we still often phrase it that way.'[47] This sort of priming inevitably has an impact on the interrogation process. A variety of military men, vigilantes and local politicians all admitted that screening was conducted largely on a case-by-case basis, in which the soldiers involved had wide discretion but not necessarily the sort of training necessary to conduct these interviews. Some of the girls who had been 'rescued' by the military reported being traumatised by their experiences with the soldiers. A 20-year-old girl from Bama, currently living in Dalori IDP camp in Maiduguri, recalled that after the military raided the Boko Haram camp, she was kept in the military barracks for ten days. During those ten days, 'I didn't sleep very much – there was always *boom boom*,' she said, imitating gunfire and shaking her head. 'They [the military] asked me what I knew about the bombings and all of the weapons. They asked me about my village and my body.'[48]

There is no recourse for those who have been falsely accused or identified by vigilantes. Amnesty International notes that:

> internal military reports examined by Amnesty International also show that field commanders regularly informed Defense Headquarters and Army Headquarters how many people had been arrested during cordon-and-search operations. The reports usually label those arrested as 'confirmed Boko Haram members' or 'confirmed Boko Haram terrorists,' but do not reference any evidence against them and at times indicate, on the contrary, that no evidence was found. The reports do not specify whether any of the detainees were later released, handed over for investigation or charged.[49]

The mix of the military's incentives to present a heroic narrative and vigilantes' self-interest in proving their worth by identifying lots of insurgents means that the official record of who is an insurgent and who is not is unreliable.

The Giwa example

One of the centres where those suspected of being members of Boko Haram or sympathetic to the sect are kept is the Giwa Barracks in Maiduguri. Giwa is notorious for the abusive practices that go on behind its gates. In May 2016, Amnesty International released another damning report, titled *'If You See It You Will Cry': Life and Death in Giwa Barracks*, documenting how the conditions at the barracks have deteriorated under the additional pressure that the counter-insurgency campaign has placed upon them. The group concluded that, although they are unable to say with certainty what has caused the surge in deaths in military custody at Giwa, 'it is likely that starvation, dehydration and disease, all linked to over-crowding at the detention cells in Giwa Barracks' are to blame.[50] The number of people being held at Giwa is not made public, but Amnesty believes that in March 2016 there were at least 1,200 people being held at these barracks. Even high-ranking military officials were uncertain as to how many people were being held at Giwa, but the 'rescue operations' have clearly swelled the ranks of those confined there. As one brigade commander revealed: 'It is difficult to give numbers [of people detained in Giwa], because only those at the barracks have the full numbers. All of the different divisions are contributing.'[51]

Amnesty International documented nearly 150 deaths in the barracks between January and May 2016, a tally that included 'at least 12 children and babies, including two girls of approximately two and five years old' and ten boys, including some as young as five months.[52] At least 250 women and teenage girls were being held at the barracks, along with 'many small children', who were frequently detained with their mothers.[53] The government has not demonstrated any significant change in Giwa's management, suggesting that the death toll has only increased since the report's publication.

Conditions in Giwa are wretched. According to Amnesty International, 'witnesses describe cells too crowded to lie down properly and that they were provided with insufficient amounts of food and water'.[54] The testimonies of those who have been held in these cells are harrowing and straightforward. One told the researchers:

> The cells were never cleaned while we were in there. The place is unhygienic. There was no washing, no sweeping and no ventilation. It is very smelly. If you see it, you will cry. You are making stool and urine in the same place you are in for 24 hours. There is no cleaning, so you live in disease. It is like a toilet.[55]

A teenage girl who had been held in the women's section of Giwa for more than two months reported that 'the cell is overcrowded with children and elderly. There are many children with us in the cell, [aged] between one month and one year. The cell is too congested; you can't turn from right to left when you sleep. In the night the chairman arranges you in lines for sleeping. There will be arguments because of space.'[56]

Across the gender and age spectrum, detainees reported that food in Giwa was scarce.[57] A man held at the barracks for three months observed that:

> This is the first punishment – hunger and thirst. People were losing weight terribly. They will arrive normal, then after some days they will become hungry and thirsty. It is mostly the elderly that were dying due to the hunger. They cannot stand up. No one has a shirt, so you can count the ribs of their body.[58]

In addition to the inadequate nutritional, sanitary and health conditions in the detention centres, there are reports of continued, regularised violence at Giwa Barracks. Although the military is aware of the issues in the camps, rights groups assert that none of the incidents have been 'meaningfully investigated'.[59]

One girl in Maiduguri who had been held by the insurgents and then detained in Giwa Barracks for six months recalled that she had been arrested after she had fled from Boko Haram and had been living with her parents for a number of months. She recounted: 'I was staying in my parents' home when they came in and arrested me. They did not tell me anything of the charges against me – they just took me to Giwa. It was after a long time that I found out why I was picked.'[60] A vigilante from her community had accused her of being sympathetic to the sect; her family had no means to appeal her arrest. When she was brought to Giwa, soldiers berated her and accused her of being in Boko Haram: 'They kept telling me, "You must be in Boko Haram, you must have witnessed, you must have wanted to join."'[61] Eventually, she was released from detention – but she was then treated with suspicion by her neighbours. These arrests and practices contribute to a culture of fear, characterised by unaccountable security forces, 'secret police' and vigilante groups, which heightens tensions and makes communities less secure. These suspicions have also contributed to the militarisation of the humanitarian system in northern Nigeria.

Demobilising fighters

It is worth observing here that it is not only those who are 'liberated' from insurgent control who are subject to the screening and detention process. Fighters who are captured, rather than killed, are also screened to determine whether or not they joined voluntarily and to gain information about the ways in which the sect operates. Although the violence in north-east Nigeria is ongoing, some tentative plans for disarmament, demobilisation, de-radicalisation and reintegration of fighters (both male and female) are taking shape. These plans will be further addressed in the next chapter, but they are worth addressing here, considering how closely they are tied to the imperfect screening process. In April 2016, the Nigerian military announced the launch of Operation Safe Corridor to encourage insurgents to defect from Boko Haram. Complementing the military offensive against Boko Haram, Operation Safe Corridor was intended to provide an officially sanctioned way for militants to escape the insurgency and begin the process of reintegrating into society. Although, on occasion, the Nigerian political elite had paid lip service to the idea that there was 'not a military solution to Boko Haram', Operation Safe Corridor was one of the first tangible examples of a softer approach to counter-insurgency by the Nigerian government. Particularly following the Buhari administration's shutting down of a countering violent extremism (CVE) and de-radicalisation programme that had started under his predecessor, Goodluck Jonathan, the launch of an avenue for demobilisation and reintegration was considered an encouraging sign.[62]

The programme was announced by Brigadier General Rabe Abubakar, who stated that 'the Defence Headquarters ... wishes to appeal to other recalcitrant terrorist members ... still carrying arms against their fellow citizens in our nation to repent today and benefit from numerous opportunities offered by the Camp', the location and benefits of which would be disclosed at a later date.[63] Abubakar's press release also promised that the military offensive would continue and encouraged 'reluctant Boko Haram members' to 'see wisdom in surrendering now ... saving themselves from imminent calamity that is about to fall on them'.[64]

Details about the programme were scant, however. The link that the Nigerian military's official Twitter account provided led to an error page; further, it was unclear who would be providing the programme with funding or technical support. The days and weeks after the announcement did not see the release of any additional information. Despite the ostensible launch of the programme, it was unclear how the military would manage defectors, how the pro-defection message would be disseminated into the insurgents' territory, what sorts of de-radicalisation and reintegration programmes would be available, or where the programmes would be run. These 'known unknowns' became all the more pressing when the government announced that 800 members of the insurgents had surrendered to the Nigerian military in the month that Operation Safe Corridor was launched.[65]

Finally, on 16 June 2016, Brigadier General Rabe Abubakar announced a few more details, stating that, 'very soon, we will have a camp somewhere in the Northeast where they will be kept for empowering and reintegrating and de-radicalizing them'.[66] According to military officials in Maiduguri who requested anonymity, however, Operation Safe Corridor had been enacted despite the lack of a holding area, operational framework, or programmatic agenda. 'There was supposed to be a centre in Gombe, but it is not yet ready,' one high-ranking military officer said with a shrug, months after the programme had been announced.[67] He reported sheepishly that those who surrendered were taken to Giwa Barracks – the same place that unrepentant militants captured by the military are taken. The same over-crowded, opaquely managed Giwa Barracks, derided as the site of gross human rights violations, was now the focus of the supposed 'softer side' of Nigerian counter-insurgency.

This fatal error was compounded by the fact that there seemed to be no centralised list of those who defected from the insurgency – meaning that, even if Operation Safe Corridor were to be under-taken in earnest, it would be nearly impossible to identify who in Giwa qualified for the programme. One military official remarked that 'it is difficult to give numbers' for the total figure of combatants who have surrendered since the programme was enacted, 'because all of the different divisions are contributing [defectors]' but no one is privy to what happens once they turn themselves in. Although a total is difficult to come by, it is suggestive that more than 300 people surrendered to one division in less than three months. Unsurpris-ingly, given the generally clumsy approach of this programme, there is not a nuanced gender policy for female defectors.[68]

Hamsatu Allamin expressed frustration about the way in which the government treats combatants who surrender, arguing that the programme is more a continuation of war than an attempt at reintegration or rehabilitation. As evidenced by the detention of defectors with captured militants in Giwa Barracks, Allamin observes that there is no incentive to demobilise, since 'admitting involvement [with the insurgency] invites government abuses'.[69] Given that thousands of young men are suspected of having been forced into the sect, the Nigerian government's approach is particularly counterproductive. While the rescue and family reunion of Chibok girl Amina Nkeki was widely publicised, there is hardly any information available about what has happened to her insurgent husband, who helped orchestrate their joint escape. Allamin asserts that, if Nkeki's husband had been publicly treated well, 'we would already have hundreds of defectors'.[70] Her opinion that defectors should be considered 'heroes, because they are helping bring back abducted girls' and that the government should 'broadcast to those in the bush that they can defect safely' is controversial in north-east Nigeria, to say the least.[71] The topic of amnesty for militants is rapidly becoming a political 'third rail' in the region. While international donors are enthusiastic about the softer aspects of counter-terrorism and counter-insurgency, communities whose lives have been upended by the insurgency resist the idea of providing state services to the sources of such destruction.

Life as an IDP in a government camp

Those who the government screens and determines are not members of the insurgency are taken to official, government-run IDP camps, which depend on support from every level of government, international partners, and the national security sector. A significant proportion of the displaced come to Maiduguri, the capital of Borno State, which is considered one of the few safe havens in the northeast and has a number of official displacement camps. Governor

Kashim Shettima's desk is dotted with stacks of papers and folders, paperweights given as tokens of appreciation from heads of state and multinational organisations, and a large bowl of hard candy. Leaning forward to address the three journalists in front of him, he stated with characteristic eloquence and confidence: 'IDP camps come with problems, like child marriage, prostitution, and drug abuse.'[72] With a flick of his hand, he asked if we were familiar with Dabaab, the world's largest IDP camp holding nearly 500,000 people, based in Kenya.[73] Assured that his reference will be understood, Shettima opined: 'The problems of Dabaab have proliferated across every IDP camp ... even here to Nigeria.'[74] The Governor's comments came shortly after the Kenyan government had announced that it would be closing the camp and returning or resettling its population, a move that Shettima praised as the government 'finding the political will' to resolve the issue.[75] The violation of human rights that this resettlement would require was brushed aside, apparently secondary to the burden that IDP camps constitute for the state.

Of the millions displaced throughout the country's north, roughly one in ten have sought refuge in an official government camp. Despite being responsible for a small minority of the total displaced population, the government struggles to provide adequate resources to those in the IDP camps and conditions are dire. In addition to inadequate food and shelter, a variety of rights violations and unconscionable abuses are occurring in the camps. According to international norms and standards, IDPs enjoy the right to 'basic humanitarian assistance (such as food, medicine, shelter), the right to be protected from physical violence, the right to education, freedom of movement and residence, political rights such as the right to participate in public affairs and the right to participate in economic activities'.[76] Even these bare necessities have not been provided for many in Nigeria's IDP camps. Although the government was able to push through a plan that allowed IDPs to exercise their right to vote in the 2015 elections, despite many lacking the required voter ID cards, scarce food, inadequate care and rights abuses characterise life as an IDP in a government camp.[77] The rampant violation of their rights in northern Nigeria is a product of both the lack of funds and the lack of will to protect them.

According to Governor Shettima, 'it's just a frenzy of trying to get money' to provide for services in the camps. The Governor admitted that he did 'not know the exact numbers' but estimated that the state was spending 'at least half of the state budget on IDPs'. These efforts, while fuelled by noble intentions, are insufficient. MSF has responded to multiple outbreaks of cholera in IDP camps in the state; the emergency projects manager for MSF observed that 'the living and hygienic conditions in the camps were and remain ripe for the outbreak of this type of epidemic'.[78]

In February 2016, conditions were so bad that IDPs at the large Dalori II camp in Maiduguri staged a protest. Their descriptions of life in the camps warrant extended quotation. The women's leader in the camp, Hussina Usman, reported that some days the camp residents did not eat until 6pm. On normal days, 'we eat once a day and it's always rice, sometimes mixed with beans', but on the day when she spoke with the press, she hadn't yet had a meal 'because there's nothing to cook'.[79] Cooking food in the camp is the responsibility of the women, often delegated to the household level rather than being centralised at the camp level and distributed to households. This increases the burdens on the women in the camp, as they are often hard-pressed to find firewood, matches, salt, pots or cooking oil. Malam Abatcha Ali, the men's representative in Dalori II camp who acted as an IDP spokesman, agreed that the lack of reliable food in the camps was the most pressing concern, but he also observed that there were 'inadequate bed spaces in the camps'.[80] Many in the camp were 'exposed to mosquitos' because of the poor quality and scarcity of mosquitos nets, raising the risk of malaria. The health services in the camps are placed under strain, subject to increasing demands from a growing IDP population in unsanitary conditions as well as a limited supply of drugs and funding. At the camp's medical facilities, 'no matter the complaints, all you get is paracetamol [acetaminophen, used to treat fever and mild pain], and when we go to hospitals in the town, they ask for money, which we don't have', he explained.[81]

Such conditions in Dalori are typical of camps across the north-east. In camps in Borno and Adamawa States, the people I spoke to complained frequently of a lack of adequate food and health services, in addition to the general shortage of social services such as education and mental health support. In Dalori I, residents reported that, although they might eat twice a day, both meals were 'small bowls of rice'.[82] The lack of livelihood support programmes was also a frequent complaint – women in particular were frustrated that they were unable to engage in the sorts of petty trade that they had conducted prior to the insurgency. A young woman in Dalori I camp in Maiduguri said: 'We do very little here; I sometimes go to school, sometimes I sew caps or cook a little food to sell to other IDPs and the soldiers [guarding the camps].'[83] The camp organisers often claim that they have no budget to provide raw materials to would-be entrepreneurs and few IDPs manage to arrive at displacement camps with any capital to speak of. Schools are often half-built in the camps, or they lack teachers and necessary items such as books and writing materials.[84] The dearth of opportunities to earn a living or advance one's education, coupled with the inability to move freely, has particularly dire consequences for women.

In addition to the issues that stem from a shortage of funds, there are also a number of rights violations in the camps that are a matter of ill intent rather than a lack of capacity. IDPs across the region frequently complain that there is no freedom of movement for camp residents. In Fufore, Adamawa State, camp organisers said that the IDPs could apply for passes to leave the camps if they wished to go into town. No one to whom an OCHA (UN Office for the Coordination of Humanitarian Affairs) employee spoke during a routine visit to the Fufore camp in December 2015 had managed to successfully apply for a pass. When asked, many shrugged and said that they had never seen anyone be granted a pass, so they had not bothered to waste their time.[85] 'Soldiers here prevent us from leaving,' another girl in Dalori I, in Maiduguri, explained. 'I tried to leave once to visit my mother in Cameroon and [the camp guards] beat me.'[86]

Sexual abuse in the camps is also a serious issue, but is largely unaddressed. A young woman in Dalori I reported that the 'soldiers sometimes want to marry the girls here; some just pay them to stay with them'.[87] In a poll of hundreds of IDPs across the three most affected states, 66 per cent reported that camp officials were engaging in sexual abuse against residents.[88] UNHCR employees described sexual exploitation as an invisible menace: 'the soldiers and vigilantes harass the women in places where you cannot see it, but we have heard reports. When they want to go out, access food or get help, they are forced to give sex.'[89] According to activists and aid workers throughout the north-east, some women leave the camps and seek accommodation in host communities to avoid the sexual harassment – despite the fact that those living among host communities receive even less government support than those people living in camps. The effect has been so great as to disrupt the prostitution markets in cities hosting a large number of IDPs; an NGO worker based in Maiduguri noted that the going rate for a woman used to be 5,000 naira, 'and now it is as low as 1,000'.[90] Another NGO employee in Maiduguri revealed that 'young girls sneak out of the camps to sell themselves ... they say that they don't see much government support or good, so they sell themselves to survive'.[91]

The government recognises the vulnerability of IDPs and is aware of the issue of sexual assault. One of the remedies implemented by Governor Shettima was a strict curfew in the camps to prevent girls from leaving to sell themselves. Although well-intentioned, this policy is counterproductive, as it restricts the mobility of camp residents and further subjects them to the authority of a population that has been accused of pervasive abuse. A sight at Dalori I camp in Maiduguri served as a tragic metaphor for the women's situation in the camps: a bright yellow tent declaring the area a 'Safe Space for Women and Girls' was empty, save for scattered boards of wood, a long table with a male guard asleep on top of it, and fading posters proclaiming the importance of valuing and respecting women.[92]

Who's in charge?

Although the problems of displacement camps that the Governor identified have certainly developed around the IDP camps in Nigeria, the military's central role in the management and operations of the camps has created another host of issues. The militarisation of the humanitarian response in northern Nigeria compounds the typical displacement issues by blurring the line between civilians and combatants, adding an additional source of vulnerability for camp residents, and obfuscating chains of command in camp management.

The UN's Guiding Principles on Internal Displacement require that the host country take responsibility for displacement camps – management is usually delegated to 'existing government agencies with relevant mandates'.[93] Nigeria has such agencies – at both state and federal level – in its National Emergency Management Agency (NEMA) and its state-level counterparts (SEMA). Yet these organisations are only one contingent in camp management; the security sector plays a much more prominent role in managing and operating the camps than NEMA and SEMA. The practical difficulties introduced by so many cooks in the kitchen are clear at the entrances to government camps. Documentation from SEMA (the ostensible managers of the camps) granting access, even coupled with an affiliation with an NGO operating within the camp, does not guarantee access. At Dalori II, I was told that approval must come from a garrison commander.

A security sector coalition – comprised of the military, the police and vigilante groups – was given responsibility for ensuring security in the camps, in addition to distributing and managing relief materials. It seems that the security sector's mandate has expanded, so that now this coalition is in charge of the management of IDPs. The security sector's outsized role provides ample opportunity for abuse of power. Aside from the predatory actions previously discussed, soldiers have also been implicated in the theft of relief intended for the displaced.[94] Outside the gates at Dalori I, I witnessed a 'group of men in a mixture of civilian and military outfits … shovelling bags of blankets and plastic goods into an auto rickshaw, known in Nigeria as a "keke" … Kick-started into life by a nearly invisible driver, the keke struggled up a small embankment onto the pot-holed road and was gone.'[95] Apocryphal stories of looting by soldiers, police and vigilantes are often repeated when NGO workers convene in the north. A prominent activist in Maiduguri stated plainly that the camp guards, and even some NEMA and SEMA employees, 'sell the food and goods in order to buy diesel or to line their own pockets'.[96] One UN official relayed to me that an ambulance was brought to an IDP camp, packed with relief supplies, 'packed up in the night and taken away'.[97] A police officer at Dalori told an aid worker that 'taking from these people is like stealing from a corpse', but admitted that such grave robbery is common.[98]

The extent of these abuses of power is made all the more problematic because of the impunity with which the security sector seems to act. A UN official explained that 'reports [of problems in the camps] would have to go to the security officials, but they are the ones most often committing the abuses'.[99] At present, the military seems to be largely uninterested in addressing the abuses committed by its forces or to cede the authority that it has been given at the camps to an organisation with clearer accountability mechanisms.

Further, the presence of the security sector blurs the line between humanitarian intervention and military operations. The military's very presence may make IDP camps into a target for Boko Haram's attacks.[100] In general, attacks on displacement centres are strikingly uncommon in conflicts in sub-Saharan Africa. However, the exception to this pattern is the most glaring and the most relevant for the Nigerian case. According to the Armed Conflict Location & Event Data Project (ACLED), the LRA had launched at least 50 attacks on government-run Acholi displacement centres in northern Uganda between 1998 and 2010. During these attacks, the LRA looted supplies, abducted residents, and (importantly) engaged in offensives against the military installations at the centre of the camps' operations. The military installations at Nigerian IDP camps risk subjecting residents to the same sort of targeting. In September 2015, Malkohi camp in Yola was bombed and in February 2016 a suicide bomber detonated inside an IDP camp in Dikwa during food distribution, killing at least 58 people and wounding more than 70.[101] Given the similarities between Boko Haram and the LRA in a number of their tactics, the possibility of the Nigerian insurgency targeting displacement camps should not be taken lightly.

Silence on this issue not only leaves communities more vulnerable and complicates future international interventions, it also threatens the well-being of aid workers and the reputation of the humanitarian system as a whole. As Pierre Krähenbühl wrote on behalf of the International Committee of the Red Cross, 'over the past decade, deliberate attacks against humanitarian personnel have become commonplace. They are clearly illegal and unacceptable ... the rejection of humanitarians is, however, also the by-product of policies that integrate humanitarian aid into political and military strategies.'[102] Recognising that conducting humanitarian operations in conflict zones is difficult and that the very nature of modern conflicts has undergone a radical shift, he observes: 'some may question the value of independent, neutral, and impartial humanitarianism in today's wars. However ... [w]e know that these very principles enable us to reach, assist, and seek to protect those caught in armed conflict.'[103] Part of the reason for this silence is political: by offending the Nigerian government by criticising it too harshly, the international community risks losing the access it has gained. A former OCHA employee noted that 'the UN haven't been given a choice' about the military's involvement in camp management, despite global regulations, 'and neither UN nor donors feel that there is any room for manoeuvre on it'.[104]

NGOs and humanitarian agencies also risk increased scrutiny concerning their lack of involvement. However, the Nigerian government's politics have also reduced the ability of the international community to intervene. Nigeria's history of interventions in the region, including the provision of peacekeeping troops to civil conflicts in Liberia and Sierra Leone in the 1990s, allowed it to cultivate a reputation as a regional powerhouse.[105] Trading in this reputation in order to receive international humanitarian aid would be a blow to national pride – particularly since few citizens outside the north-east have been affected first-hand by the insurgency. Further, as Governor Shettima's comments about the Dabaab refugee camp reveal, the will to establish the sort of displacement-related infrastructure that comes with robust humanitarian systems is in short supply.

Governor Shettima acknowledged that the militarisation of the camps is a serious issue, and argued that the government has 'done as much as possible to secure the camps, but also to demilitarise them'. He also reported that the state has 'increased the presence of the police, the Nigerian civil defence corps, and the Civilian Joint Task Force'.[106] However, the military remains the most central agency in the operations of the camps – despite the fact that its presence in them not only poses a threat to the residents of the camps, but also reduces the manpower available on the front lines of the insurgency.

Although the residents of official camps are under-served and potentially imperilled by their government, the vast majority of the displaced population living among host communities lead, in many ways, an even more precarious existence.

Burdened neighbours: life in host communities

Those who live outside the official government camps, in a mixture of informal settlements, rented domiciles and the homes of their extended families or kin networks, face an additional set of challenges. This population receives next to no government services or international aid and relies on its own ability to make money, find food, and cultivate the sympathy of the host community. In large part because of the influx of informally settled IDPs, the capital of Borno State is widely estimated to have doubled in size as a result of displacement-related migration. Dr Gubio thinks that the population growth has been even starker. He stated that 'the census said in 2006 that there were 1.8 million people in Maiduguri, projected to have grown to 2.1 million in reality. In Borno's total, there were 4.6 million people, with a lot of population growth ... Since everyone in Borno is now here in Maiduguri,' he concluded his calculations thoughtfully, 'I think we have 6 million people here.'[107] The vast majority of the displaced live among host communities, rather than in official IDP camps.

To accommodate this population surge, much of the city's land and empty buildings have been repurposed to host these communities. The streets have swelled with beggars, who surround cars at traffic lights with outstretched hands. Reports from NGOs in the region sometimes euphemise the practice as a 'negative coping strategy'. Efforts have been made by a handful of international NGOs to penetrate into host communities to provide services. However, these endeavours have all been sadly insufficient and much of the burden is falling on the shoulders of already impoverished communities throughout the north-east.

The Madina mosque example

The settlement at Madina mosque in Maiduguri is illustrative of the plight of informally settled IDPs. The settlement houses an estimated 2,000 people, but even the mosque's leadership – who granted permission for IDPs to settle on their grounds – cannot give an accurate headcount. The people living at Madina mosque are from communities all across the north-east – those who fled from the same community typically cluster in compounds and huts, creating a sea of settlements that subdivide the land ceded to the IDPs. The advantage of living in the official camps is particularly evident when you compare the physical infrastructure of official camps with what exists in their informal counterparts. Housing at Madina is largely hand-built by residents; thatched, often roofless, structures are common. These structures provide little protection from the elements, a particular issue in the rainy season. Although some IDPs have been able to settle in empty buildings in the mosque's grounds, they are overcrowded.[108]

Because of its considerable size, the Madina settlement has attracted some attention from international NGOs. In some areas, it feels like the whole of the north-east has been miniaturised for display in the mosque's grounds – a diverse set of ethnic groups and communities is represented. A coalition of international NGOs provided a water pump and some latrines. In June 2016, residents reported with relief that Save the Children had begun food distributions there on occasion, but also that they were receiving assistance from NGOs or government agencies only once every six weeks or so and that the distribution of aid was difficult to predict. According to one of the mosque's leaders involved with the IDPs, 'NEMA used to bring an ambulance once a week, but for the past three months we have not seen them.'[109] Even when the ambulance came, their advice to seek care in a local hospital was largely unhelpful, as 'people cannot afford medicine, so being referred to the hospital is no use'.[110] The limited aid distribution and its sporadic nature result in profound insecurity for the residents of the Madina settlement.

Schooling in the settlement is minimal. Although the mosque leadership proudly reported that Save the Children was implementing an education intervention in the settlement, none of the women I spoke to sent their children to the classes.[111] Some sent their children to the Qur'anic lessons that spontaneously emerged in the camp, usually led by a displaced religious leader, but even that was rare. Children's education is a luxury many in the settlements cannot afford – even when it is provided free of charge. For many, begging has become the family's only means of livelihood, demanding input from even the youngest of family members. A Shuwa Arab girl living with 20 to 30 members of her displaced community in the camp remarked sadly: 'If the government gives food, then we get food, but if not we hope that our men can take small work or that we can beg.'[112] Work is not readily available for the few men in the camps, however, meaning that they often join their families in begging.

The collapse of the industries that contributed to trade in Maiduguri (among them farming and fishing) has reduced the number of jobs at a time of breakneck population growth. Dr Gubio noted that, because of the conflict, 'the state [of Borno] has not seen tilled land for three or four years and all trade has been stopped for the last two or three years. All of the small businesses and industries have died.'[113] Unemployment figures are unavailable, but would likely be staggeringly high. The simplicity of this statement from Hassana, a 25-year-old IDP from Baga – previously a thriving fishing and farming community near the shores of Lake Chad – is heartbreaking: 'All of our children go to beg, that is how we buy food here.' As is to be expected, begging is a precarious source of income that leaves families almost entirely dependent on the assistance they receive from host communities. A UNHCR employee noted that although 'the food in camps is bad ... the food that the host communities provide is even worse'.[114] He continued thoughtfully: 'Sometimes you see what these people eat and you think even a dog could not eat what these IDPs are eating.'[115]

For most of the people settled at Madina, the lack of attention from the government and the international community is merely a continuation and intensification of the marginalisation they have experienced for years. Although they are now physically safe, life in Madina is still a struggle for those in the settlement. An IDP from Baga explained, as her compound neighbours nodded, that 'there is a big difference between life in Baga and life here. There is no trading here for us to do. In Baga we could sell food and snacks and our husbands had jobs.'[116] She and the other women from Baga, much like those in official camps, concluded that: 'The lack of food here is the biggest problem, then the lack of medicine.'[117]

Births happen fairly frequently in Madina, but unlike in the official camps, there is no infirmary or even the chance of a doctor being on call to offer assistance. Miriam, a young woman living at Madina with her co-wife, gave birth in the camp and was afforded the luxury of a local midwife. Payment was given in the form of whatever money her family managed to scrounge and 'what little property we have here'.[118] Miriam's child is healthy, happily gurgling and tottering about the thatched hut in which Miriam, her two children and husband live. However, the family is now even more financially unstable than it was before and struggles to feed all of its members.

Not all of the mothers at Madina are lucky enough to have healthy children. I spoke with Fatima, a 20-year-old Shuwa Arab, as she held her clearly undernourished three-month-old child in her lap.[119] The pleasant roundness of baby arms was absent in her child; that sign of health was replaced by sagging, loose skin and small, bony biceps. Despite Fatima's young age, this was her fifth child – her eldest was eight years old. Fatima knew that her child was sick, but she admitted that she could not afford medicine or food. When Fatima and her family fled Boko Haram after spending a week under the insurgents, they were unable to bring much of their property and only a little money. They bounced from town to town, seeking safety, before eventually arriving at Madina. Fatima recalled that she and her family met a number of soldiers during this ordeal, and remarked that 'the army could have provided some help, but they demanded money for protection'.[120]

Although the physical conditions in the informal settlements are worse than in the camps, a number of people in the settlements chose not to seek refuge in the government camps. Many of those living in the settlements told me that they feared the conditions and abuse in government-run IDP camps. The prospect of giving up their freedom of movement and being segregated by gender (as is common in the camps), and, for women, of being subjected to frequent sexual harassment by the camp's security personnel, was simply not a trade-off they were willing to make.

While the settlement at Madina has a friendly relationship with its host community, this is not necessarily the norm for host community-IDP relationships through the region. Even prior to the insurgency, the food crisis and the growth in the displaced population, most communities in north-east Nigeria did not have significant savings or financial security. The strain that caring for extended family and competing with other IDPs for limited work has placed on host communities should not be underestimated. Informal settlements in Abuja have already been attacked by impoverished host communities for the donations they have received from local NGOs.[121] Elsewhere, there are reports of sexual harassment and exploitation of displaced women by host communities. The social taboo surrounding sexual assault and the lack of a reporting mechanism for abused women makes it difficult to estimate how widespread this problem is. NGO workers, however, expressed concern about the increasing anecdotal evidence of widespread abuse in host communities.[122]

The Borno State government has attempted to provide support to host communities supporting IDPs. During Ramadan 2016, the Governor instituted a programme in which 1,000 families across 28 wards were chosen to receive food aid. Dr Bulama Gubio explained that, since the household size was calculated based on the male, the average family size was 20 people. A list was drawn up and announcements were sent to the households about how and where they could receive their food aid. News of the programme spread quickly – Dr Gubio reported that, even on the first day of the food aid programme, 'those who were not on the list also came in the hope of receiving help, making it hard to give aid to the genuine beneficiaries'.[123] The distribution took place near the gates of the Governor's mansion, and the thousands of people who flocked to the site disrupted traffic in the city. The crowd spread along the roads leading to the gate, resulting in the police and military tasked with distributing the aid and maintaining order being overrun by swarms of people. It was anyone's guess if the men walking proudly away with sacks of rice emblazoned with Governor Shettima's and President Buhari's faces were the intended recipients.

As difficult as life is in the city's camps and settlements, many believe it is still an improvement on the present conditions outside the city. The insurgency remains a threat in rural areas. Dr Gubio stated plainly: 'If you are not able to make it to Maiduguri, you are a dead person.'[124] This assessment calls into question the government's frequent proclamations that the military's efforts to secure the north-east are proving successful, and casts doubt on the ability of Borno State to close all the IDP camps in Maiduguri as soon as possible. According to Governor Shettima, the closure of IDP camps is an attempt 'to restore the dignity of our people by rebuilding their homes, rebuilding their schools, engaging them in gender empowerment initiatives so as to enable them to return back to their homes'.[125]

A shoddy tool box: rehabilitating the north-east

The strain that caring for IDPs has placed on the government and host communities alike has made planning the return and reintegration of IDPs a priority across all levels of government. Although plans for returning the displaced to their communities have broad political support, they have little tangible economic support. The programmes that do exist to help returnees are piecemeal and frequently delayed.

In 2014, then-President Goodluck Jonathan established an NGO dedicated to providing relief and helping to rebuild the north-east, called the Victims Support Fund (VSF). The management team of the VSF was replete with successful Nigerian businesspeople. Funds for the programme were raised at a glitzy fundraising dinner, where Nigeria's well-heeled elites pledged more than 58 billion naira to the cause – exceeding President Jonathan's goal of 50 billion naira.[126] Aliko Dangote, a titan of industry in Nigeria, pledged 1 billion naira himself, while representatives from the oil sector contributed 17 billion naira, and government ministers contributed a total of 50 million naira.[127] In press statements released immediately after the fundraiser, the government's spokespeople lauded the generosity of the attendees, saying that 'it shows that the public is genuinely concerned about the threat of terrorism to our common humanity and stands ready to support worthy causes and pro-people policies'.[128]

Yet, nearly two years after the fundraising dinner was held, only 24 billion naira of the pledged total had been received by the VSF.[129] It appears that the 'genuine concern' of attendees was more elusive when the lights came up and the media faded away. Tellingly, even the federal government had not yet released the 5 billion naira that President Jonathan pledged on its behalf.[130] The NGO, and many of its members, are based in Abuja, with a limited presence in the country's most affected areas. The lack of a consistent presence within the communities they are tasked with helping has made it difficult for the organisation to carry out its mandate. Certainly, part of the delay in programming and the limited geographic scope of the VSF's interventions can be attributed to the difficulties of accessing certain parts of the north-east. Despite the challenges the group faces, the VSF has begun programmes in earnest, generally focusing on rebuilding roads and public buildings. The group announced in July 2016 that it had partnered with the state government to rebuild nearly 40 buildings in Dikwa, Borno State, 35 of which were homes for IDPs.[131] Given that there will be tens of thousands of people returning to this town, the question of allocating access to these buildings is critical – but unaddressed. It is easier to build a house than to provide social support to its intended residents.

The VSF's delayed programming could be justified if it appeared to be the result of long-term strategic planning that included extensive consultations with the affected communities. However, the lead-footed character and the patchwork programming of the VSF reflect a widespread lack of coordination and strategy for rebuilding the north, extending from the government up to the international community and all the way down to local NGOs. Further, it is unclear why the government would funnel money and resources to an NGO to rebuild the north, rather than use government agencies tasked for this purpose. The fracturing of the effort to rebuild the north is replicated in a number of initiatives. This lack of coordination threatens to make this effort amount to less than the sum of its parts.

Also illustrating the shortcomings of the existing strategy to revitalise the north are the 2,000 tractors purchased by the Borno State government in October 2015.[132] The machinery was purchased with the intention of kick-starting the agricultural production of resettled farmers.[133] However, the mechanisms for resettlement have never been clear. Even after the military was able to successfully dislodge the militants from territory they had taken through its renewed 2014 campaign, it was widely recognised that the security sector was having difficulty holding that territory. In IDP camps and informal settlements, residents recount apocryphal stories of people trying to return to their communities only to be slaughtered by the insurgents. Purchasing the tractors was, at best, overly optimistic government expenditure. At worst, it was a waste of money to purchase machinery that is ill-suited to the smallholder agriculture that characterises the region; the tractors would likely have been useless after a few years due to lack of maintenance. These sort of half-baked, never enacted schemes seem to dominate the post-conflict redevelopment agenda across the north-east.[134]

The international community is complicit in this slapdash approach to the reconstruction and rehabilitation of communities. In 2015, the World Bank, after sending a delegation to assess the situation, agreed to invest $2.1 billion in low-interest loans through the International Development Agency; these loans were aimed at improving physical infrastructure across the region. The following year, the World Bank also pledged to provide an additional $800 million for 'recovery, rehabilitation, de-mining, waste management, and debris processing' in the north-east.[135] The general reaction among politicians in the north-east was that this amount was 'grossly inadequate' given the pre-existing poverty in the region and the extent of the crisis.[136] Governor Shettima, reacting to the World

Bank's announcement, observed that 'the developed world gave Turkey $2 billion to resettle refugees from Syria. There are about two million IDPs from Borno and 20 local government areas were overran [sic] by Boko Haram and there is [a] food crisis now in the state', but Nigeria was receiving significantly fewer resources, despite being poorer than Turkey while facing a greater existential threat.[137]

Although the reconstruction of the city's physical infrastructure is certainly necessary and the support that has been offered is heartening, the current plan of doing *anything* to do *something* is a disservice to communities across the north. Further, the notion of physically rebuilding the region's infrastructure implies that the objective is a return to the status quo prior to the crisis. Not only is such a return not possible, it is not necessarily desirable. The demographics and political economy of the region have been indelibly altered by the Boko Haram insurgency. Reflecting these changes, the reconstruction effort must be ambitious enough to imagine a new future for the troubled region.

Tragic politics: the international community's failures

Given the immensity of the humanitarian situation, the international community's reluctance to engage is alarming. In fact, despite the Lake Chad Basin having a greater number of displaced people than South Sudan, the crisis in the region has yet to receive the same sort of press coverage and international support. The delayed and contested designation of the situation in the Lake Chad Basin as an 'L3' humanitarian crisis – the highest, most pressing category in the humanitarian system – illustrates the marginalisation of this disaster. Deliberations regarding L3 designation are 'based on five criteria: the scale, urgency, and complexity of the needs, as well as the lack of domestic capacity to respond, and the reputational risk for the humanitarian system'.[138] The designation of a conflict as an L3 crisis is a signal to the humanitarian community that it should 'mobilize the resources, leadership, and capacity of the humanitarian system to respond to exceptional circumstances'.[139] A review of the impacts of L3 designation by the International Council of Voluntary Agencies (ICVA) network revealed that designation was not a mere symbolic overture – there are operational consequences. The group observed that, following such a declaration, there was 'an increase in the prioritization of material assistance' and a clearer division of responsibilities between actors. IVCA found that, following an L3 designation, NGOs' increased activities 'mainly focused on operational support, [while] the UN's main focus has been on coordination support'.[140] Designation thus means more resources, coordinated more efficiently, helping to avoid duplication of efforts and operational gaps. The failure to designate the crisis in the Lake Chad Basin as an L3 in a timely fashion is bureaucratic dithering that undoubtedly cost lives.

The ongoing hostilities and insecurity in Borno State, outside a handful of urban outposts, certainly complicate the provision of humanitarian support and will continue to be problematic for a number of years. Some of the UNHCR support that is already on the ground noted that the ongoing conflict made it difficult to engage in the sorts of humanitarian relief they were trained to provide. One employee asserted that 'the north-east in general is quite different from other programmes. You are dealing with an insurgency, a faceless insurgency. In other situations you have people with an objective that you can negotiate with. People here are killing for the sake of killing.'[141] His co-worker noted with exasperation: 'We are working in a practical war zone.'[142] They both agreed: 'Protection here is a huge issue, because the insurgents kill, the soldiers kill, there is massive displacement.'[143] Humanitarian intervention outside a few urban pockets is next to impossible, given the extent to which the insurgents still control territory and maintain the capacity to engage in raids and attacks, despite the reported military gains.

Yet, if the security situation were the primary constraining factor, the humanitarian presence in the secured urban centres would still be much more robust. Additionally, the UN humanitarian system has security protocols to follow when confronted with an active conflict – UN agencies are not unaccustomed to operating in violent contexts.[144] In fact, at the time of writing, all three of the L3 designations (Iraq, Syria and Yemen) are active conflict zones.[145]

The situation that the international community finds itself in, with record numbers of displaced people and a variety of crises demanding humanitarian aid, has stretched the international humanitarian budget to breaking point. In 2016, the UN's humanitarian coordinator requested $20 billion to respond to crises in 37 countries. Stephen O'Brien, the UN Under-Secretary-General for Humanitarian Affairs and Emergency Relief Coordinator, observed that 'this amount is five times the level of funding we needed a decade ago, and it is the largest appeal we have ever launched'.[146] In July 2016, only one-third of the necessary funds had been allocated for the year.[147] The scarcity of funds has forced the UN to triage crises – non-L3 situations receive scant resources.

The budget shortfall is tangible in Nigeria, where the humanitarian efforts have been chronically underfunded. A mere 12 per cent of the annual budget necessary for the protection programmes the UN intended to run in the country had been provided as of July 2016. As of April 2017, only 17 per cent of the annual budget request for the year had been provided – with few signs of increased funding in the near future.[148] Food aid and nutritional support have been among the best-funded humanitarian endeavours – yet even in this field, in July 2016 less than 25 per cent of the budget for nutritional support was furnished.[149] Overall, roughly a quarter of the budgetary needs were met that year. This paucity of funds reflects a longer-running trend in Nigerian humanitarian funding: between 2011 and 2012, funding fell from $516 million to just $16 million.[150] Despite the escalating violence of Boko Haram's attacks, funding remained low, rising to only $158 million in 2015 after remaining below $50 million from 2012 to 2014.[151] The lack of financial support has had tangible effects on communities all across the region. A former OCHA employee noted with dismay that the international humanitarian community was not only having trouble delivering rape kits to conflict-affected areas, but was also struggling to produce them at the rate necessary to keep up with the pace of assaults.[152]

Clearly, although the demands placed on the international humanitarian community have increased, support for the expanding budget is elusive, straining the UN's capacity to respond to global insecurity. The scarcity of funds does not, however, explain the international community's silence on the militarisation of the humanitarian intervention and the flagrant human rights abuses (including refoulement, dispossession and gender-based violence) that have been committed by security forces in the Lake Chad Basin. On the issue of refoulement from Cameroon, UNHCR released a statement in August 2015, following an influx of returnees, that was so mildly worded as to be useless. This claimed that:

> UNHCR is unaware at this time if they include refugees who may have gone back involuntarily, but we have been in close and regular contact with the relevant governments and have expressed our concern at the way these returns were conducted. UNHCR fears that such deportations lead to shrinking of the protection and humanitarian space and the agency reminds governments of their duty to protect asylum-seekers fleeing human rights violations and to respect the principle of non-refoulement (non-return). We have reiterated in our talks with government counterparts that certain principles and international standards should be respected, even in the face of serious security concerns.[153]

The militarisation of aid presents the most egregious violation of the principle to 'provide aid but take no sides'.[154] There is ample research about the issue of aid politicisation and the role that it plays in fomenting grievances and harming the reputation of neutral humanitarian bodies. The tacit approval of the Nigerian security sector's dominant role in the provision of humanitarian aid runs the risk of undermining the international humanitarian system's principles and reputation.

The failure to designate the crisis in the Lake Chad Basin as an L3 in a timely fashion and the lack of political pressure the international community places on the government demonstrate the serious discrepancy between the situation on the ground and the international humanitarian system's posture. 'This is not the sort of crisis that the international community knows how to deal with,' Dr Gubio opined. 'This is a devil you don't know.'[155] While there are certainly challenges unique to the context of northern Nigeria that complicate the humanitarian response, Dr Gubio gives undue credit to the will and capacity of the international humanitarian community. An array of factors limits the extent of the humanitarian intervention in the Lake Chad Basin: safety concerns, an overstretched budget, and the politics of intervention are all to blame for the relative lack of international action in the crisis. However, it is also undeniably an exercise in privilege: the host communities absorbing those displaced by Boko Haram have no choice but to engage with this crisis. They do not have the option of turning a blind eye.

Gendering Vulnerability

> People make terrible demands of these women.
> *Father John Gideon, of St Patrick's Cathedral,*
> *discussing the challenges facing displaced women and girls*[156]

The demographics of displaced communities mean that the shortcomings of the humanitarian response to the crisis disproportionately affect women. Given the generally inadequate humanitarian response and the limited funding for programmes, it is not surprising that gender-sensitive programming in the humanitarian response to Boko Haram is lacking. 'Gender-sensitive programming', in which the needs and input of women are system-ically included in the planning and implementation process, is not only a means of elevating women's status, it has also been shown to improve the overall outcomes of humanitarian aid. In addition to the financial constraints preventing gender-sensitive program-ming, there appears to be a lack of political will in some circles to engage seriously with women's issues. Female returnees complain of restricted access to land, physical insecurity in rural areas, and harassment by security forces throughout their return journeys. Their urban counterparts also report sexual abuse from a number of sources, gender-based discrimination and insufficient food.[157] This lack of political will to engage with women's issues means not only that humanitarian aid lacks a gendered perspective, but that the gross violations of women's rights will likely continue with impunity into the post-conflict era. This is not only a moral failing, but also a priming factor for a relapse into conflict.

Thankfully, other Nigerian politicians, organisations and insti-tutions have been willing to critically examine the specific ways in which the crisis has had an impact on women and girls. Imple-menting gender-sensitive humanitarian programming requires all participants (domestic, international, secular, religious, govern-mental, civil society, and so on) to be on the same page regarding women's importance when designing programmes and policy. Implementing gender-sensitive programming is not merely a matter of mobilising more resources – though that is certainly necessary – it is also about utilising those resources in a way that avoids further victimisation of the displaced and recognises the unique vulnera-bilities and opportunities that women face in the post-conflict era.

On the surface, emergency humanitarian aid may appear gender neutral – shelter, food and clean water are certainly universal needs. However, the UN's humanitarian coordinating body has stated unequivocally that 'the needs of women, men, girls, and boys are different and distinct'.[158] Hunger may not discriminate on the basis of gender, but post-conflict demographic realities and social norms dictating who is responsible for providing and preparing food place a disproportionate burden on women and girls. Recognising the altered roles, responsibilities and needs of men and women as a result of the insurgency is crucial to responding appropriately to their needs, and so the crisis in the north-east calls for implementation of gender-sensitive humanitarian programming.

Gender-sensitive programming in the post-conflict era
The post-conflict environment presents not only an array of challenges, but also a valuable opportunity to lay the groundwork for gender equality through thoughtful, inclusive programming. A UN Women study of 'gender equality programming (GEP)' (a term here used interchangeably with gender-sensitive programming) in humanitarian situations found that a gender-sensitive orientation 'contributes to improving access to and use of services, increasing the effectiveness of humanitarian outcomes and reducing gender inequalities'.[159] In Turkana, Kenya, the study estimated that gender-sensitive programming increased the proportion of literate children by as many as 59 in every 1,000 children.[160] In the Philippines, the study found that hunger was correlated to women's disenfranchisement within household decision making. In all of the areas studied, GEP was 'significantly associated with lower proportions of women reporting emotional abuse from their husbands'.[161] Improving gender-sensitive indicators also set the stage for greater social stability – these programmes reduced the likelihood that a husband would threaten to abandon his wife by up to 73 per cent.[162] In light of this evidence, it would perhaps be more accurate to describe gender-equitable programming as effective humanitarian programming.

Not only does gender-sensitive programming improve the humanitarian response, incorporating women into post-conflict processes also leads to more durable peace. The more influence that women have in the process of brokering peace deals, the more likely it is that a peace deal will be reached and that the peace will last.[163]

The international community has touted economic development as a means of conflict prevention, arguably since the popularisation of modernisation theory in the mid-twentieth century. This paradigm, which contends that economic growth leads to democracy (and infers that democratic countries will be more stable and peaceful), has influenced post-conflict programming and development assistance through the prioritisation of economic redevelopment ahead of softer social matters. In the face of mounting evidence that increasing women's equality is more directly tied to a country's peace and stability than indicators of economic development, the paradigm must also shift – and, with it, international will and resources – towards an emphasis on women's empowerment through gender-sensitive programming.

The opportunity to advance women's status in a post-conflict atmosphere is more than a moralistic, 'soft' ideal grafted onto the security agenda by human rights activists. Studies have demonstrated that advancing women's status in society is one of the most effective ways of preventing a relapse into conflict. An overview of the existing qualitative and quantitative studies, written by Inclusive Security, concluded: 'It is evident that gender equality is a better indicator of a state's peacefulness than other factors like democracy, religion, or GDP.'[164] Gender inequality has been linked to increases in the likelihood of both inter- and intra-state conflict. Further, a relationship has been found between women's inability to influence the security sector's decision-making processes and the likelihood of war breaking out in the country.[165] Involving women in security and peacebuilding is crucial if future conflict is to be avoided. Further, and more controversially, one must ask: if women are sidelined and made more vulnerable in the post-conflict era, then who is peace *for*?

What, then, does enacting this sort of programming require? According to UN Women, it is guided by a 'contextual gender analysis' that 'examines gender relationships in the beneficiary population, including roles, access to and control of resources, and the constraints different groups face relative to each other'.[166] Truly gender-sensitive programmes would seek out and identify 'opportunities to support women and men in ways that contribute to the transformation of gendered power relations' by engaging in a 'rigorous and context-specific gender analysis of the populations they set out to support', one that is integrated into all phases of the humanitarian agenda.[167] According to Oxfam, such programming would lay 'the groundwork for gender equality and greater resilience to crises, by actively supporting women's leadership and by challenging attitudes and beliefs'.[168] Somewhat obviously, gender-sensitive programming involves consulting with women and their representative bodies as a matter of course. It also includes more subtle means of empowerment – such as targeting women as the heads of households, when possible. This is not merely about women – it is also about the development of gender norms, and thus requires an examination of the ways in which boys and men are affected by war and post-conflict redevelopment. UN Women found that excluded men 'tended to report unease and resentfulness towards the targeting of women and girls', undermining the process of social reconciliation.[169] Boys, and their socialisation in the post-conflict era, also warrant special attention. As Joshua Goldstein concludes in *War and Gender*, 'in raising boys into men, we can ask ourselves, day in and day out … Whether we are producing warriors, and if so at what cost to the boy' – and at what cost to the stability of communities.[170]

Supporting women's empowerment and gender equality should not be confused with an assertion that women are universally pacifistic, altruistic entities, predisposed to nurturing and cooperative styles of governance. This book and accounts from conflicts the world over document women's capacity to engage in horrific acts of violence and the importance of their contribution to insurgencies and other armed groups in fomenting instability. Further, gender essentialism of this sort, whether it exalts masculinity or femininity, contributes to inequality and oppression – and ultimately makes societies less stable. Rather, the incorporation of women into peace-making, security and governance makes countries more stable because it makes them more representative and inclusive.

The benefits of advancing women's status will not materialise in the absence of significant political mobilisation, advocacy and planning. These will require political will not only at the Nigerian level but also from the international community. Paradoxically, women's empowerment in unequal societies will require women themselves to advocate for their own interests despite the limitations on their ability to organise and mobilise. The obstacles to gender-sensitive programming extend beyond budgetary constraints and a lack of political will. Surveys of programme managers found that, 'in contexts of acute gender inequalities, it was difficult to find women with the required skills and self-confidence to participate in committees'.[171] Even when qualified and willing women were identified and placed on these committees, they often remained quiet and avoided asserting themselves. Social norms governing the 'proper' roles for women are often deeply entrenched and internalised.

In short, gender-sensitive humanitarian programming is not an unaffordable luxury in the Lake Chad Basin; it is a way of maximising returns on the limited resources of the international community and of laying the foundation for long-term peace.

Long-term displacement

Although a number of politicians in the north suggest, in interviews and through the characteristics of their policies, that the widespread displacement in the region is temporary, the statistical reality is that internal displacement on such a massive scale is a semi-permanent phenomenon. Recognising that displacement centres will likely host communities for more than a decade demands that the means by which aid is delivered, what services should be prioritised, and what a post-conflict economy looks like must be reconsidered. In rebuilding the region, it is critical to recognise that successfully integrating displaced populations into their host communities is as important as physically rebuilding the region's infrastructure. At present, responsibility for IDPs is scattered between international groups and their domestic counterparts, and among a number of organisations at both of these levels. Streamlining responsibility among international organisations would provide a valuable signal from the international community about prioritising the needs of IDPs.

However, it is not just the way in which aid is delivered that demands reform – the objectives and the conceptualisation of aid must be adjusted. Over time, displacement has an impact on social norms, particularly regarding women's empowerment and legal status. These effects are not predetermined. The design and implementation of aid to IDPs can be powerful tools for catalysing change and for laying the groundwork for a more peaceful society by promoting mutually beneficial integration into the local political economy and helping to establish local norms that are favourable to women's empowerment. Conversely, haphazard humanitarian programming can foster dependence on external actors, contribute to communal strife and the deterioration of inter-personal relationships, and undermine women's social, legal and political empowerment.

Across a number of conflicts, divorce is a common phenomenon in displacement centres, leaving women even more vulnerable without a male patron. As well as being deprived of a man's income, many women are left without access to benefit programmes that funnel family resources through fathers and husbands.[172] Furthermore, care for children often falls to women, making it all the more critical that women (married, widowed or divorced) be able to access resources. Nigeria must ensure that services reach women who are the heads of households, and that, when aid is distributed through men, it does not reinforce inequitable gender relations. Services for women in the post-conflict era should recognise the multiple sources of their insecurity and the psychological effects of structural and proximate violence.

In general, the global aid system often arrests development in its attempt to triage needs. The current global displacement crises should drive home the point that return in Nigeria may be impossible for decades. Consequently, the events that occur in displacement camps and host communities leave indelible marks on the social fabric of communities – and even when return is possible, life will not resume as it was before.

Chapter 7

THE WAY FORWARD

Nigeria is a male-dominated, chauvinistic country stifled by culture, tradition and social ranking that make the Indian caste system look feeble. There is simply no place in Nigeria today for a woman to head a country of 170 million including men who often see women as second-class citizens or simple objects of desire. Today, Nigeria is a man's country. Live with it.

Comment on Sarah Jubril's candidacy for president,
the only woman seeking that position in the 2015 election[1]

Even though it is true that women live in a man's world, life without women would be like that of a person without blood.

Dan Donkor, Daily Times, 23 June 1981

Although it will undoubtedly take generations for the region to recover from the crisis, plans must be made now for a more equitable and sustainable post-conflict society. Even under the best of circumstances, where there is robust international support, strong pre-existing institutions, a tradition of female activism, and adequate funding for gender-sensitive programming, post-conflict redevelopment and reconciliation are difficult undertakings. Given that none of these conditions exist in north-east Nigeria, one wonders what a post-Boko Haram world will be like for women when the conflict draws to a close.

Yet, there are reasons not to give in to cynicism or despair about the future of the region. In planning for the post-conflict era,

Nigeria can observe the successful endeavours of other countries and benefit from the recent swell in research on how crises can accelerate social change to rectify gender inequality in the country's political, economic and social systems. As Winston Churchill advised, you should 'never let a good crisis go to waste'; more specifically for post-conflict Nigeria, Elisabeth Wood observed that post-conflict 'legacies are not uniformly negative: the wartime destruction of some forms of political and social domination and the emergence of new actors may facilitate new forms of political order and participation in its wake'.[2] The obvious economic implications of war and conflict, in addition to some tentative work into the ways in which post-war behaviour trends towards altruism, suggest that the post-conflict era can be an opportunity to introduce egalitarian, stabilising social norms.[3]

This is particularly true with regard to gender. Evidence from a number of other post-conflict African states suggests that the disruption of social norms and the breakdown of the political economy – though devastating – provide an opportunity for countries to undertake sweeping, progressive reforms to improve the status of women that would have taken generations had the previous power structures remained intact. Evidence from other sub-Saharan African countries suggests that targeted legislative reforms enacted within a specific post-conflict window can produce rapid increases in female political participation and representation. Coupled with research on the importance of female inclusion for social stability and durable peace, it becomes clear that Nigeria's future must be female if it is to be peaceful.

Squandering opportunities by putting women on the sidelines in Nigeria

Although the inclusion of women would increase the durability and effectiveness of post-conflict programming, such engagement has not yet materialised in north-east Nigeria. As the discussions above have revealed, issues specific to the women affected by Boko Haram have not been given due attention by Nigerian politicians or the international community. One could even argue – given the legislative defeat of the proposed Gender and Equal Opportunities Bill in 2016 – that there is a national political climate that is hostile to women's empowerment and inclusion.[4]

Nigeria is not unique in sidelining women in the post-conflict era. According to Fionnuala Ní Aoláin, 'the absence of a gender dimension in the establishment, revision, and operation of new legal and political institutions in post-conflict societies has generally been acknowledged'.[5] Given that roughly half of all post-conflict countries relapse into war within the first ten years of peace, it is clear that the predominant approach is in need of reform.[6]

The World Bank identified in 2002 that the absence of gender-sensitive programming goes hand in hand with the top-down approach to post-conflict programming that has come under fire in recent years. This managerial style often marginalises communities during the planning period, and often leaves them vulnerable to continued violence. The World Bank report *Addressing Gender Issues in Demobilization and Reintegration Programs* concluded that:

With the absence of a bottom-up approach, vulnerable people, especially women, play a minor role in the preparation of development plans. Formal institutions, like cooperatives or village councils, are often the vehicle for most development assistance. Hence, poor, uneducated women, not fully accepted by the community (criteria which generally characterize female ex-combatants or ex-combatants' widows), do not participate in these formal institutions and therefore do not benefit from development assistance.[7]

Marginalising women undermines redevelopment efforts and in many cases further victimises women. Female-headed households are likely to become the norm in the region in the aftermath of this crisis, meaning that redevelopment and social reintegration will depend on women and their incorporation into post-conflict programming.

Conflict not only disrupts economies, it also results in social debates about gender norms. The result is often an atmosphere in which 'anxiety about what is a "good woman" or a "good man" seems pervasive'.[8] Evidence from other post-conflict countries suggests that 'so strong is the tie between men's self-worth and earning capacity that it may be difficult for men to even acknowledge their dependence on women's incomes'.[9] In a number of countries, the stigma and shame surrounding a woman engaging in work outside the home remain potent.

This stigma makes it difficult to gauge how economically active women are and the effects of their labour market participation on their domestic lives.[10] As a report by the Wilson Center's Maame Esi Eshun observed, 'sometimes the trauma and frustration of their marriage partners are projected on them; hence rates of rape and assault may increase'.[11] The fragility of masculinity (in particular, the rigid sort of masculinity practised in Nigeria) coupled with the lack of female advocacy groups in the north-east mean that women face an uphill battle in the aftermath of this crisis.

The failure to recognise the specific manifestations of discrimination against women in the post-conflict era leaves women more vulnerable and communities less stable by undermining women's new social, economic and political positions. The cessation of hostilities does not signify a return to the status quo; societies are irrevocably shaped by conflict, forcing communities to come to terms with new gender roles and sources of authority. However, the specific ways in which women are discriminated against in the post-conflict era will be made clear only if an effort is made to consult regularly with women.

Political empowerment and legal reform can improve women's status in the aftermath of conflict and lay the groundwork for more stable, peaceful societies, but prior to discussing such reforms, it is important to highlight that women in northern Nigeria will likely require significant external assistance to advance their agenda in the post-conflict era. The lack of women's groups in the region means that they face not only a social and organisational hurdle but also a steep learning curve as they begin their campaigns and programming. A review of the human rights-oriented civil society groups in north-east Nigeria in 2013 found that fewer than 25 per cent are headed by women, suggesting that women have limited input on a variety of social issues.[12] Since that survey, there has been little to suggest a drastic change in this marginalisation.

As previously discussed, the post-conflict era presents an opportunity to reshape social norms in favour of marginalised groups, in particular through legal and institutional reform. Aili Mari Tripp observes that 'conflict had a significant and independent impact on women's political representation in sub-Saharan Africa and correlates strongly with the sharp increase in female legislative representation in sub-Saharan Africa, which tripled between 1990 and 2010'.[13] This acceleration was part of a concerted effort to increase women's political participation, often through the adoption of gender quotas. According to Tripp's research, effective women's advocacy groups that are capable of influencing domestic political change and an encouraging international environment (replete with thoughtful partnerships) in the post-conflict era are crucial components in advancing women's rights. The international community must recognise the dearth of such organisations in the north-east and compensate for this lack.

This assistance needs to bear in mind, however, that participation in NGOs can be a burden on already beleaguered women. This was evident in northern Uganda, where development initiatives that sought to empower women encouraged them to 'form groups as a pre-condition for accessing services, loans, farm inputs and grants', thus placing an additional burden on the shoulders of women.[14] 'As women struggle to stay afloat, they are bombarded with demands for paperwork before they can qualify for assistance,' one report concluded.[15] The need to be a member of a group in order to access critical benefits prompted women to join a multitude of groups, 'leading to a "burden of participation"'.[16] In northern Nigeria, where there is no long-standing culture of public female political participation, the international community should help carve out a space for these nascent groups in a manner that does not eclipse women's ability to engage in other activities. These groups' near simultaneous formation and integration into policy programming will likely be a process of trial and error – international advocacy groups should be aware of this learning curve and build in regular assessments of their effectiveness.

FOMWAN is one notable exception to the generally low-profile nature of local NGOs working on women's issues in the region – and it is all the more important and impressive because it was explicitly founded by and for women. FOMWAN is an umbrella group that connects more than 500 Muslim women's organisations in all 36 states in Nigeria. Its primary focus is advocating for girls' education and the spread of Islam.[17] FOMWAN's forward-facing religiosity helps to sidestep any of the assumptions about the incompatibility of Islam and feminism.[18] Engaging with FOMWAN and others like it will help the international community identify partners in affected communities throughout the north-east, as well as serving as a mechanism for mobilising support from around the country.[19] FOMWAN has the potential to synthesise a similarly diverse set of NGOs willing to prioritise women's empowerment; however, international support in this endeavour is necessary, in terms of helping to frame a unified agenda and helping to mobilise additional resources. There is no better time than the present to start a tradition; planting the seeds for female-centred civil society in the post-conflict era will require not only supporting the nascent domestic women's networks that exist, but empowering women to form new groups based on their specific post-conflict needs.

A long way home: reintegrating women

> If economic reintegration is important, social and psycholog-
> ical reintegration is crucial.
>
> It is too simplistic to argue that economic empowerment
> is sufficient to combat effectively violence against women.
> History is filled with evidence to the contrary.[20]

Despite the persistent insecurity that women returning to newly
liberated communities face, a number of women across the north
have attempted to return to their homes and restart their lives.
These women are vulnerable not only to violence from the insurgency, but also due to the attitudes of the communities that they are
returning to.

Early into the process of return, reports are already emerging of
women and girls being rejected by their communities and families
for their perceived association with Boko Haram. UNICEF and
International Alert's joint report *'Bad Blood': Perceptions of Children
Born of Conflict-related Sexual Violence and Women and Girls Associated with Boko Haram in Northeast Nigeria* concluded that 'all
women and girls who have experienced sexual violence during the
conflict face stigmatization from communities at large'.[21] They
observed, however, that 'the stigma and potential rejection from
families and community members has been much more acute
for those who are perceived to have been associated with [Boko
Haram] – as abductees, those living in [Boko Haram] strongholds,
or those who were "wives" of [Boko Haram] combatants either by
choice or force'.[22]

There is widespread fear of and disdain for women thought
to be Boko Haram wives – including those who were brought
into the sect unwillingly. Community leaders expressed concern
that the 'ideas and ways of life' of women who had lived under the
insurgents would negatively affect their communities.[23] Even the
immediate families of many of the women are refusing to take them

in, rendering these women vulnerable and isolated. Any association with the insurgency, real or imagined, leaves women 'tainted' and untrusted. International Alert and UNICEF reported that female IDPs arriving in communities were often considered to be 'hyenas among dogs', making it difficult for them to integrate into their host communities.[24] There is a troublingly widespread belief that the women deserve the marginalisation and brutality directed against them. When asked about the women who had joined Boko Haram willingly, now being held by the government in Giwa Barracks and a handful of other detention centres or camps, a vigilante said very simply: 'If they are released, they should release them with a body bag because we will kill them.'[25]

Even those who are tasked with providing care and protection to women sometimes express distaste for the girls. A CJTF soldier leaning back in a flimsy plastic garden chair outside Safe House reported that he 'would only marry one of these girls if she came attached to millions of naira and a house'.[26] Fatima a social worker, laughed with the guard at Safe House about the prospect of anyone marrying these girls. With an emphatic shake of her head, she told me: 'I would not allow my sons to marry these women or their children. They are just from a different dimension.' Fatima's opinion reflects a widely held fear that the girls will convert their sons to Boko Haram if they are married. She concluded that the women and girls who had married insurgents willingly 'are not real IDPs', and that they are not worthy of the very services she is paid to provide them with.[27]

The difficulty in determining which women joined voluntarily and which were forced to join – and the lack of programming directed at the specific needs of both of these categories of women – has resulted in mistrust and fear of many of the women who have come into contact with the insurgents. While it is certainly possible that communities will be able to distinguish between abducted women and those who joined willingly, many women who cannot prove their non-participation in atrocities or who are suspected of sympathising with Boko Haram face intense stigmatisation.

Women who are made pregnant (willingly or unwillingly) by insurgents face an additional burden. The children of Boko Haram face violent rejection and discrimination. They are often considered to have Boko Haram's ideology ingrained in them at birth. The discrimination against this generation of children will present a significant hurdle to social stability for years to come. Women who have been forcibly impregnated generally do not have access to abortion. The country's abortion regulations are strict, prescribing narrow conditions under which abortion can be conducted legally, while sentencing for illegal abortion can entail up to 14 years in prison and a fine.[28] The UN has urged the country to ease its anti-abortion laws for women raped by the insurgents. However, no such reform has been undertaken at the time of writing.[29] Even if such reforms were enacted, the issues of access to medical care and the stigma surrounding abortion would remain.

The fragility of masculinity

One cannot think about women in a vacuum. Conflict affects all of society; men, too, have faced a sea change as a result of the Boko Haram insurgency. As elsewhere, changes in men's status have ramifications for women in the region. Thus, another critical issue in the post-conflict period is the need to address the damaged masculinity of displaced men. Formal employment is often difficult for displaced men to come by, and women often replace men as the primary economic provider. This uncertainty and frustration helps explain why domestic violence often increases in the aftermath of conflict. As Eshun notes, the loss of this social marker can lead to stress that manifests itself in violent ways.[30] Further, ignoring the gender norms during social change overlooks the very real possibility that men will consider women to be a threat to their masculinity, generating tension and potential violence.

Although shifting gender norms can generate insecurity, these changes also present an opportunity to accelerate gender equality.

As previously discussed, much of the assistance in post-conflict contexts is service-oriented, rather than focused on fostering egalitarian social change. With regard to promoting women's rights, this is especially problematic. Within the context of the Boko Haram crisis, there is a particularly significant role for the international community to play in helping establish gender equity through post-conflict assistance that advances women's ability to organise and advocate for themselves. Peace must be secured for women both in the public sphere and within their own homes.

Chapter 8

LESSONS LEARNED: APPLYING BEST PRACTICES TO BOKO HARAM

If someone says there is a military solution only to Boko Haram, they are being economical with the truth.

*Governor Kashim Shettima, on the need for robust
post-conflict social programming in Borno State*[1]

As Nigeria and other affected countries grapple with the Boko Haram insurgency, there is an opportunity to apply the lessons learned from other conflicts in Africa and around the world to advance women's position within society. This chapter focuses on the application of these principles in Nigeria, although many of the lessons are applicable throughout the region. Although the post-conflict era is not a *tabula rasa* in which history, cultural practices and political economies are erased, reforms made in this period can provide the foundation for more stable, less oppressive societies. Disarmament, demobilisation and reintegration (DDR) programmes, legislative reform and transitional justice programmes provide valuable venues for these reforms to be implemented.

Reconciliatory road maps: considering what works for post-conflict demobilisation and reintegration

At its core, DDR is a process of socialisation and rehabilitation; it is 'not simply about coming home, but about defining new guiding social values and establishing corresponding relationships and insti-tutions'.[2] Although DDR programmes often focus on how to entice fighters to participate in these programmes, they must also consider how these former fighters will be received by their communities. As such, these programmes need to 'integrate ex-combatants by dispelling gender stereotypes, building respect for all, and breaking destructive cycles'.[3]

DDR is a difficult process, but there are successful case studies to draw from and a set of internationally recognised best prac-tices. The 2006 UN report *Women, Gender and DDR* noted that, when 'those who do not fit the category of a "male, able-bodied combatant" are overlooked', not only are programmes less efficient, they also 'run the risk of reinforcing existing gender inequalities in local communities and making economic hardship worse for women and girls in armed groups and forces, some of whom may have unresolved trauma and reduced physical capacity as a result of violence experienced during the conflict'.[4]

Gendering demobilisation and reintegration

Across regions and countries, governments have also struggled to reintegrate female combatants and captives. A World Bank report by Nathalie de Watteville, *Addressing Gender Issues in Demobiliza-tion and Reintegration Programs*, concluded that 'despite their varied roles, female ex-combatants seem to share one unfortunate charac-teristic: limited access to benefits when peace and demobilization come. This is also true for girls abducted for sexual services and the families of ex-combatants in the receiving community.'[5] A particu-larly difficult issue involves how to resettle insurgent 'families' in the post-conflict era. While some women may choose to stay with their insurgent husbands following a ceasefire, other girls (particu-larly young abductees who were forced into marriage) may not want to be resettled with their partner.[6] Verifying abduction, conscrip-tion and voluntary recruitment is difficult for both male and female insurgents, and becomes all the more complicated when attempting to provide services to the children of insurgents (which are typically channelled through the mothers) and to persuade women to engage in the reintegration process (which often centre on the traditional household breadwinner). Boko Haram's mixture of enticement and abduction into the sect will make it extremely difficult to design and implement DDR programmes.

Demobilisation programmes frequently provide livelihood assistance and aid as a benefit for those who disarm (often by physically presenting a weapon), which generally end up benefiting men. Women are frequently excluded from these programmes because they lack weapons to exchange for aid. In addition, such demobilisation programmes overlook the centrality of women's reproductive labour to insurgencies and thus fail to demobilise a significant contingent of insurgents. In instances where rehabilitative programmes are targeted at the household level, there is a healthy debate over how to provide benefits to insurgent families – there are advantages and hurdles to targeting both male and female combatants, with no clear-cut conclusion about which approach is the most useful. Clearly, identifying the factors that encouraged women to support insurgencies is critical to preventing a relapse into conflict; however, there is a reticence to engage critically with the multiple, often obscure, ways in which women contribute to insurrection.

Advancing women's status without provoking a backlash is difficult – a number of reports find that improving women's status within the home (or when men are displaced from their 'breadwinner status') can lead to increased domestic violence and household tension.[7] The UN has released guidelines for incorporating both women and the broader community into DDR programming in a meaningful way, emphasising not only that female combatants should be given gender-specific opportunities, but also that the response of the community (which includes men and women of different social classes and status) to such programmes should be assessed.[8] In addition to the UN's guidelines, Nigeria can reflect on individual countries' efforts to reintegrate fighters and promote social cohesion in the aftermath of conflict.

Lessons learned for demobilisation and reconciliation: Niger Delta and the FARC

There are a number of examples and cautionary tales from around the world that Nigeria can draw from as it designs its DDR programme. In particular, Nigeria's own experience with amnesty approaches in the Niger Delta and the emerging demobilisation programme in Colombia provide particularly helpful examples, demonstrating the importance of considering the broader social context in which DDR occurs.

The Delta amnesty programme was initiated in 2009 by then-President Yar'Adua. The programme's mandate was extremely limited, focusing mainly on demobilising combatants through a weapons exchange. The programme eventually extended into jobs training and livelihood development, and it was successful in its very narrow objective of putting an end to the bloody and economically disruptive insurgency. By 2016, however, new militant groups had emerged, bombing oil pipelines and criticising the government for not improving the livelihood opportunities for communities in the Delta and not protecting the environment from the devastating effects of drilling and spills.[9]

The programme also fell short in terms of addressing the needs of women and girls. To be included in the programme, people had to present a weapon to the government as proof of participation in the insurgency. Women were thus frequently excluded from the amnesty programme because their roles within the groups were largely unarmed positions.[10] More than 20,000 people registered for the amnesty programme, but only 133 of them were women.[11] Although women certainly did not constitute the majority of the Niger Delta militants, their contributions definitely amounted to more than 1 per cent of the effort.

There are undoubtedly a number of reasons why the Niger Delta amnesty programme did not produce a durable peace (including underdeveloped and impractical job training and flawed negotiation targets), but the systemic exclusion of women from the negotiating table and their overwhelming omission from the benefit programmes are certainly among them. The Delta militias, like so many other political and social phenomena, require the support (tacit or overt) of women – the resumption of violence in the Delta probably would have been more difficult if women were stridently opposed to it. Further, the marginalisation of women in the Delta is linked to the continued underdevelopment of the region. Given that the process of demobilising combatants in the north-east will also require de-radicalising them (a problem that the Niger Delta amnesty programme did not have to contend with), it is all the more important that women be brought into the fold – not just as mothers, sisters, daughters and wives, but also as fighters and ideologically committed members.

One possible model for a more effective incorporation of women into the DDR programme may exist in the innovative approach taken by the Colombian government in its fight against the Revolutionary Armed Forces of Colombia (FARC). This effort, although nascent and undermined by the failure of a popular referendum on an agreement that would have brought about an end to the conflict between FARC and the government, has been lauded as a potential model for other countries. One of the most famous – and effective – aspects of this campaign was Operation Christmas. The campaign set up motion-sensor Christmas trees in the bush, so that when rebels passed by, the trees lit up with the message: 'If Christmas can come to the jungle, you too can come home. Demobilise. At Christmas, everything is possible.' Following this campaign, more than 300 fighters defected, an increase of more than 30 per cent from the previous year.[12] The campaign also relied on the appeals of mothers telling their children to come home.

Important to the potential success of the Colombian DDR is the inclusion of women in the process. Not only are women critical to demobilising insurgents, they are also consultants on the construction of the programme. Stella Duque, the executive director of Taller de Vida, notes that female peace activists set the stage for the Colombian peace process to advance, organising in their communities and anticipating the looming questions of how to disarm and reintegrate the combatants. She observes that women's 'years of aiding and protecting communities on the frontlines of war gave them a distinct vantage point', so that, even more than the representatives of the government and the rebel groups, 'these women could speak of the needs and demands of their communities'.[13] The inclusion of women in the negotiations between FARC and the government is a hard-fought victory for Colombian women. The proposed DDR programme recognises that women have played a variety of roles in the FARC, including as fighters. Although only time will tell whether the peace deal will eventually be accepted and how durable the Colombian peace will be, the process has already been ground-breaking and innovative, recognising the unique contributions of women to both conflict and peacebuilding.[14]

Drawing from the lessons learned from the Niger Delta amnesty programme and the ongoing process of demobilisation in Colombia, the DDR approach for northern Nigeria should emphasise the humanity of combatants, strive to include women as often as possible, and earnestly endeavour to differentiate between the motivations of participants. Further, the DDR programme must account for the attitudes of the population receiving these former fighters. As the referendum in Columbia illustrates, the resentment that civilian populations harbour can be a significant impediment to DDR programmes. Although the lack of incorporation of women and girls in the Niger Delta amnesty programme is not the only reason for its ineffectiveness, it is certainly a contributing factor. DDR programming in the north-east should acknowledge the importance of women in the insurgency and design initiatives that

recognise the forms of support that women provided to the insurgents. Participation in the DDR programme should not depend on
a woman's relationship to a man, nor on her ability to present proof
that she was a supporter in the form of a weapon.

What works for post-conflict female political empowerment

Scholar Aili Mari Tripp powerfully observes that 'after the end of
major conflicts from Uganda to Namibia, South Africa, Mozambique, Rwanda, Burundi, and Liberia women's organizations
vigorously pressed for increased representation, often in the form
of quotas', with great success.[15] At the time of writing, 25 of the 48
sub-Saharan African countries have some form of gender quotas, a
significant shift since 1995, when only six countries had such legislation.[16] While international norms, such as the 1995 UN Conference
on Women in Beijing, helped in raising awareness about women's
issues, it is clear that domestic features, such as activist constitu-
encies and conflicts, were more directly responsible for egalitarian
legislative reform after armed struggle. In fact, post-conflict countries in Africa have twice as many women in their legislatures than
those countries on the continent without conflict. The demand for
increased political power was often codified in peace agreements
and legislative initiatives. A review of such agreements found that
'women's rights language was included in 78 percent of the peace
agreements in Africa between 2000 and 2011 – more than any
other region of the world'.[17] This was possible, according to Tripp,
because 'women demanded seats at the peace talks, on electoral
commissions, on constitutional commissions that drafted new
constitutions, and in interim and newly formed governments'.[18]

Much of this space to advocate for women's rights came from
the social disruptions associated with conflict. Prior to conflict,
women's interests and groups were often marginalised or nascent.
Tripp's work found that, during conflicts, women are pushed into

traditionally masculine roles, and their new positions as bread-winners, fighters and (eventually) peace-makers can serve as a catalyst for their broader empowerment in post-conflict socie-ties. These societies enter into a virtuous cycle, in which women's empowerment is normalised (both within society generally and within women's self-conceptions) and social gains are institution-alised and built upon. Stephanie Burchard and Tiffany Barnes found evidence of female political representation catalysing attitu-dinal change; their research observed that increasing the number of women in parliament can increase women's political engagement across society.[19] These gains are not indefinite, nor are they linear. Susan Faludi has written powerfully about the 'backlash' against women's empowerment in the United States, in which women's progress has been met with strong social and political resistance – a phenomenon that has been observed in a number of countries.[20] Institutionalising women's empowerment through codification and legislation is critical to reducing the amount by which backlash can reverse the gains made by women.

The post-conflict environment appears to be especially receptive to political reform that incorporates women. Although legislative change is not necessarily accompanied by enforcement or changes in practice, the gap in the adoption of legislative pro-women reforms between post-conflict and non-post-conflict countries is suggestive. Consider that 75 per cent of post-conflict countries in the region have adopted legislation prohibiting violence against women, compared with only 50 per cent of countries that have not gone through conflict. Further, a review by Erik Melander found that female representation in the legislative branch leads to fewer rights abuses by the state's security forces; he concludes that 'these results hold when controlling for the most important factors known or suspected to influence human rights behavior: democracy, leftist regime, military regime, British colonial experience, civil war, inter-national war, wealth, population, ethnic heterogeneity, and regime transition and collapse', suggesting that women's presence in the legislature is not merely cosmetic but has a tangible impact on the security and stability of states.[21]

Although 'change between gender regimes can be uneven', it seems that inroads in the political sphere can have ripple effects in other gender regimes.[22] It is worth observing that increasing the number of women in political office does not necessarily translate to female-friendly policies. With regard to the situation in South Africa, Tina Sideris notes that: 'Although increasing numbers of women have taken up positions in the political decision-making structures, and although the constitution protects the rights of women, it has nevertheless been difficult to transform those relations of power that sustain violence against women.'[23] Similarly, although Rwanda has impressive levels of women in its parliament, the legislative branch itself exercises little power, making it difficult for women to enact change.

This is not to say that conflict itself is a transformative force that advances women's rights. Rather, the shifts in social mores interact with pre-existing political institutions during conflict, creating in some instances conditions conducive for mobilising and supporting women's empowerment. Multi-party democracies exhibit more 'political space' for women's advocacy than autocracies – explaining why autocratic Angola, despite a brutal civil war, has not seen a rapid advancement in women's rights.[24]

Gender quotas, Tripp provocatively argues, are an effective way of increasing women's political representation and shifting social norms. Legislation for quotas helps to shift the gender regime in the political sphere. Nigeria currently has no quota system in place at the legislative or party level; however, post-conflict legislative reforms to encourage women's participation at the local, state and national levels of the political system would benefit the country generally, and facilitate the stabilisation and redevelopment of the north-east.

Some types of quota have been seen to be more effective than others; if Nigeria decides to institute a gender quota system, it must decide which approach is best suited to the Nigerian political system.

Tripp identifies three types of gender quota systems, the first two of which have been instituted frequently in sub-Saharan Africa:

1) Reserved seats, mandated by constitutions or legislation or both, set aside seats for which only women can compete, guaranteeing from the outset that a predetermined percentage of seats would be held by women. 2) Voluntary quotas adopted by parties, regardless of whether there is a legal mandate. 3) Compulsory quotas, which legally require all parties to include a certain percentage of women on their candidate lists.[25]

Some argue that, even in the case of gender quotas, women's empowerment is not compatible with Islam. This suggestion has implications for north-east Nigeria, as the majority of the population is Muslim. However, Tripp's work with Alice Kang found that 'many of the countries that have adopted quotas in Africa have significant Muslim populations, including Tanzania, Mauritania, Senegal, Eritrea, Sudan, Niger, and most recently Somalia. This trend has now continued in all the countries in the Maghreb, including Libya, Algeria, Tunisia, Mauritania and Morocco.'[26] More important than the religion of the country is the political system in place – proportional representation systems are more conducive to women's inclusion than majoritarian systems, and countries with term limits are also generally more inclusive of women.[27] Thus, arguments against women's political inclusion in Nigeria based on the large Muslim population are unfounded.

Unfortunately, the implementation of these changes requires that women be empowered and well-organised enough to advocate for themselves. This presents an obstacle to gender-sensitive programming and women's political integration. Scholar Miki Caul found that political parties are more likely to adopt gender quotas when women are already in positions of power within the party.[28] In many contexts, such as north-east Nigeria, this can create a negative feedback loop that is difficult to disrupt: women's rights are not a priority because there are few groups 'at the table' advocating for them, which means that women are marginalised all the more. Although international support can be of some use, Tripp's work found that international norms supporting women's empowerment are insufficient to ensure post-conflict pro-women policies. There must be a significant domestic constituency to make demands of their politicians. She observes that 'it was rarely, if ever, donor influences alone that made a difference. It was a combination of their efforts together with local women's rights activists that were critical in bringing about change.'[29]

In Nigeria, there are cultural and structural hurdles to women's political participation. Although women have been pushed into traditionally masculine roles, most notably acting as heads of households, as a result of the Boko Haram conflict, it is unclear whether the backlash against these changes will wash away the opportunity for social change. Additionally, the female franchise is still relatively new in northern Nigeria – recall that only in 1976 were women in the region given the right to vote.[30] Lawyer and gender rights activist Oby Nwanko notes that, despite having the right to participate in politics, women are 'discouraged from seeking political offices by discriminatory attitudes and practices, family and child care responsibilities, and the high cost of seeking and holding public office, socialization and negative stereotype, reinforcing the tendency for political decision making to remain the domain of men'.[31]

The problems of northern Nigeria's nascent civil society and lack of female political representation are not insurmountable. In Sierra Leone, Sudan and South Sudan, international influence over ceasefire and peace agreements carved out spaces for women's groups, despite the fact that 'there was a weak history of women's activism prior to the conflict'.[32] Tripp observed in an interview that the drawing down of a conflict was often an opportunity for women's movements to emerge and advocate for more egalitarian and peaceful societies. Uganda, which has shown a remarkable increase in women's status, saw the emergence of women's activism only following conflict.[33]

However, some existing legal barriers make it difficult for Nigeria to advance women's political participation. Structurally, the Nigerian legislature is elected through a majoritarian, 'first past the post' system that has been found to be resistant to female inclusion.[34] During the most recent general election, in 2015, women's performance in the Nigerian political system declined. According to data collected by the national electoral commission, women's representation in both the House of Representatives and the Senate in the Fourth Republic has been on the decline since the 2007 peak of 7.2 per cent and 8.3 per cent respectively.[35] In the 2015 elections, only 87 women ran for the offices of Governor and Deputy out of the 380 seats available in those positions.[36] Even in a regional context, this level of representation is dismal. In 2016, roughly 10 per cent of Ghana's parliament was female and, in Niger, just under 15 per cent of parliamentarians were female.[37]

Furthermore, Nigerian political parties are still largely 'boys' clubs'. The prominence of 'godfatherism' (described as 'the practice of having rich male political sponsors who control political party nominations')[38] in the Nigerian political system disadvantages women by subverting meritocracy.[39] The parties that have featured female inclusion, such as the KOWA party, which fielded the only female presidential candidate in the 2015 election, are typically new and lack influence in the political system. KOWA's candidate received fewer than 0.1 per cent of the votes cast.[40] These characteristics of the Nigerian electoral and political system limit women's ability to stand for office, with some proposing gender quotas as a solution to this system. A paper published by the country's electoral commission observed that 'legislation on quota may guarantee the initial boost that women need to break the long-time barriers against their political empowerment', and ultimately advocated for a temporary quota system to be paired with affirmative action and inclusive legislation to advance women's status.[41] The identification of sympathetic legislators and the prioritisation of women's political inclusion by major political parties are crucial steps for Nigerian women to take in the post-conflict era.

In addition to the obstacles to female political inclusion presented by the structural factors of the Nigerian electoral system, the geographically limited scope of the conflict may prevent nation-wide reform. Nigeria is the largest country in sub-Saharan Africa, by population and economic influence. Although Boko Haram has devastated the country's north-east, those in the south have been largely unaffected by the crisis.

These barriers are formidable, but, if they are recognised in a timely fashion, the international community can intervene in the process of recovering from Boko Haram in a gender-progressive fashion. UN agencies and bilateral partnerships can provide support for women's civil society groups, press for women's inclusion in peace deals, advocate for the incorporation of egalitarian terms within peace agreements, and facilitate the expansion of these norms and legislative advances throughout the country. Although female participation in politics in the north is rare, figures such as Hajia Sawaba, an active member of various political parties in the north from pre-independence through to her death in 2001, can be used to inspire confidence in northern women's ability to advance their interests through the party system. Using Hajia and other strong female figures in the history of the region as a way of normalising female empowerment may be a way of circumventing culturally justified objections to women's empowerment.

Using transitional justice and legal reform to address sexual assault and land tenure

Transitional justice is the process through which 'countries emerging from periods of conflict and repression address large scale or systemic human rights violations so numerous and so serious that the normal justice system will not be able to provide an adequate response'.[42] It will be critical to resolve two particular issues in post-conflict legal reform and transitional justice, largely because of their effects on social norms and development in post-conflict Nigeria: sexual violence and land rights. The scope and scale of the abuses that have been committed during the course of this insurgency demand redress in the post-conflict era. Transitional justice, in all its forms, is an increasingly popular way to address instances of mass violence. It is particularly useful in instances where the formal legal system is overburdened, as is the case in Nigeria. As with all other post-conflict interventions and programming, transitional justice provides a valuable opportunity to reshape social mores. The natural desire to revert to 'how things were before' is tempting, but is likely to replicate the marginalisation and oppression that gave rise to conflict in the first place. Gender-sensitive transitional justice provides an opportunity to reconcile communities to the atrocities they perpetrated, suffered and witnessed, while also laying the groundwork for a more egalitarian and peaceful society. Although it is a daunting task, addressing the scope and scale of sexual violence in Nigeria is not impossible; initiatives undertaken in the aftermath of conflict throughout sub-Saharan Africa offer models worthy of consideration.

Addressing gender-based violence

Given the ubiquity of gender-based violence in the north-east, both during the Boko Haram crisis and predating it, the lessons learned from legal reform and transitional justice programming in the Democratic Republic of the Congo (DRC) may be applicable. The DRC, particularly in the east, has been (controversially) dubbed the 'rape capital of the world' because of the prevalence of sexual violence during the region's multi-decade conflict.[43] The transitional justice programme in the country, unfortunately, has not brought about the end of conflict. However, it has resulted in convictions in sexual violence cases and helped to reduce the stigma associated with sexual abuse. Valuable lessons learned and cautionary tales can be gleaned for other countries from the DRC's experience. Despite different colonial traditions and cultural backgrounds, both the DRC and northern Nigeria have suffered from armed groups that engage in sexual violence; the way in which the DRC altered its legislative framework to address these violations may guide Nigeria as it examines its own legal system and considers how to address sexual and gender-based violence.

Like the Nigerian system, 'the Congolese legal system is severely under-resourced and underfunded', in addition to being 'plagued by both petty corruption and political manipulation on a grand scale'.[44] Despite these limitations, a coalition of domestic and international advocates has been able to lobby for the adoption and application of laws against sexual abuse. For example, in 2006, the country amended its penal code to criminalise 'insertion of an object into a woman's vagina, sexual mutilation, and sexual slavery' and defined 'any sexual relation with a minor as statutory rape'.[45] The government even draws a distinction between rape and systemic rape in its legal code.[46]

According to a review by Milli Lake, the conviction of officers in rebel groups and the national army can be traced to the efforts of this coalition. She notes that 'many NGOs have pioneered programs to ensure that hard copies of relevant DRC laws are distributed among lawyers and magistrates', to raise awareness about the existence, scope and language of pertinent legislation.[47] This coalition has been so successful that in 2012 an estimated 70 per cent of inmates in Goma's main prison 'were alleged SGBV [sexual and gender-based violence] perpetrators, and that SGBV offenses formed the bulk of offenses tried by the courts'.[48] Clearly, partnerships between international advocates and domestic groups can result in legislative reforms and successful education campaigns that reduce impunity for wartime crimes. Given the number of forced marriages and assaults in camps during the Boko Haram crisis, this sort of distinction and reform could be helpful in punishing those who have sexually assaulted women.

Within the Nigerian context, the legislative framework already exists to engage in prosecutorial transitional justice focused on gender-based violence, though how readily it will be enforced is questionable. The country signed and ratified the Convention on the Elimination of All Forms of Discrimination against Women (CEDAW) in 1985; in 2015, the Nigerian Senate passed a bill approving life sentences for those convicted of rape or statutory rape of a child under 11 years old.[49] The legislative commitment also extends to the sub-national level. Section 282 of the penal code in northern Nigeria prohibits rape in the following language:

> A man is said to commit rape who ... has sexual intercourse with a woman in any of the following circumstances:- (a) against her will; (b) without her consent; (c) with her consent, when her consent has been obtained by putting her in fear of death or of hurt; (d) with her consent, when the man knows that he is not her husband and that her consent is given because she believes that he is the man to whom she is or believes herself to be lawfully married; (e) with or without her consent when she is under fourteen years of age or of unsound mind.

What remains to be done is to educate women about their legal rights, endow them with the resources to make claims, and perhaps establish special forums to cope with the widespread sexual violence associated with the Boko Haram crisis. Important throughout this process is ensuring that the incentives for bringing a claim are not misaligned and that incidences of sexual violence unrelated to Boko Haram are not overlooked.

Experiences in Zambia suggest that gender sensitisation programmes could be useful for shifting social norms without straining the legal system. Certainly, such programming (which includes 'workshops for parliamentarians on gender-based violence, training for community leaders in low-income areas, peer education in schools, radio discussion programmes, as well as school lessons on gender equality') would be a valuable complement to prosecutions.[50] In Zambia, the civics curriculum in secondary schools includes discussions of the 'social construction of gender roles and responsibilities, as well as the laws and customs that discriminate against women'.[51] An alternative model also emerges from Uganda's adoption of 'gender-responsive reparations' in 2014 for those impacted by the LRA's violence in the north.[52] While this model comes with a number of problems and the potential for manipulation, reparations could be a way not only of recognising the effects of the violence, but also of helping kickstart economic recovery.

As Milli Lake concluded in her review of the interaction between the International Criminal Court and domestic legal institutions in the DRC, 'although good laws may be passed, if the political will or institutional foundations to support that legislation are lacking, then laws will, at best, go unused and, at worst, be manipulated for political ends'.[53] Although Lake raises an important point, it is also worth observing that where there is legislation that 'specifically addresses domestic violence', mortality rates for both women and children under five are lower, suggesting that gender-sensitive legislation has ripple effects, improving women's lives in at-times unexpected ways.[54] Laws can be manipulated, but they can also have wide-reaching effects on social norms and behaviour. Further, inaction is action in its own right. The failure to pass any legislative reforms relating to sexual violence and assault would have serious implications. In post-war Sierra Leone, 'a complicated constellation of rape laws in the statutory system ensures minimal prosecution of rape'; the laws governing the prosecution of rape still place more weight on the virginity of the girl and the 'injury to family honor' rather than on the violation against the woman as an individual.[55] Laws, while imperfect and subject to manipulation, are a valuable step towards a more gender-equitable society.

Land tenure reform

Women's access to land is particularly important because of the 'direct relationship between accessing land resources, having secured land rights, achieving food security and overcoming poverty'.[56] In conflict and post-conflict situations, women's land-lessness becomes an especially critical issue – a report prepared for the World Bank documented widespread landlessness among women in post-conflict Sierra Leone, Sudan and Libya, and even following the 2007–08 electoral violence in Kenya.[57] This is not only an entrenching of discrimination against women, but also an issue for economic growth, since there are rarely enough men to return agricultural production to pre-conflict levels. Several cautionary tales emerge.[58]

In these contexts and others, one of the most common problems is that legislation ensures women's access to land but not control over land. This shortcoming is manifest in Rwanda's post-conflict legislative reform. As Marie E. Berry notes, 'despite the world's highest percentage of women in parliament, some of the strongest state-led efforts to promote women, and an entire government apparatus designed with gender equality in mind, profound imped-iments to women's equality are deeply entrenched and appear unlikely to dissipate any time soon'.[59] Berry continues, observing that, although 'as a purely legal matter', women have access to land and a number of legal rights and resources, 'they can only fully access these rights if they are granted permission to do so by husbands, fathers, community members, and others, or if they possess the necessary tools or resources to do so on their own'.[60] Circumventing women's de facto marginalisation in contexts of de jure gender parity 'requires women's participation at policy formu-lation and at level of implementation on an equal footing with men in order to ensure [a] gender-equitable land tenure system'.[61] It also requires socialisation and education initiatives so that women know their rights relating to land access and so that communities do not ostracise women for exercising those rights.[62]

The goal of post-conflict land tenure reform should be to overcome oppressive historical legacies that have prevented marginalised groups from reaping the benefits of control over land. Doing so, particularly in agrarian contexts, sets the stage for the sort of broad-based economic growth typically assumed to be a bulwark against violent instability.

The current land tenure regime in northern Nigeria is, in theory, conducive to egalitarian land access and ownership. Thus, the process of drafting and adopting more equitable secular laws is not necessarily the most pressing concern in the region. Ensuring that women know their rights, have access to forums to exercise them, and feel comfortable asserting their ownership rights is the larger challenge. Although relatively gender-neutral land laws exist in Nigeria, the formal land tenure regime is not well known across the north (and women are even less aware than men of their rights under the current legal system). Customary land tenure systems, which frequently disadvantage women, are likely to continue to dominate the region for the foreseeable future. Thus, the process of improving women's access to land in the post-conflict atmosphere must engage traditional leaders. Some high-profile leaders, such as the Sultan of Sokoto and the Emir of Kano, have been public advocates for women's empowerment.[63] However, many of the lower-ranking traditional leaders, and the customary traditions they govern over, are less receptive to women's rights. A rapid assessment of the gender politics of traditional leaders in Nigeria concluded that: 'Religious and traditional structures in Nigeria (and in many other contexts) are male-dominated, and often actively discourage the involvement of women in decision-making.'[64] Further, even the women who work in the same political space as traditional rulers 'are mostly excluded from religious hierarchies and decision-making structures and processes'.[65] These organisations, ideally, would become more than just advocates for social change, but also venues by allowing women to rise through their ranks.

The powerfully entrenched, largely male traditional systems and repressive gender norms in the region are compounded by the lack of dedicated women's organisations. This means that the international community will likely have to play a more intentional role in the process of promoting women's advocacy and empowerment than in other contexts. Groups such as Voices 4 Change, run by the UK government, are a testament to the international community's willingness to engage with such issues; however, as discussed previously, the dearth of grassroots, domestic movements promoting women's rights is a disadvantage. Women have expressed their political preferences through activism on the issue of sharia law in largely peaceful groups such as the 'Yan Izala, and through their contribution to destructive groups such as Boko Haram and its predecessors; it is important for social stability to cultivate forums for women to advocate on political issues more directly.

The issues of prosecuting sexual and gender-based violence and increasing women's access to and control over land through transitional justice programmes demonstrate that gender-equitable legislation is a necessary but insufficient step towards empowering women in the aftermath of conflict. Even following the passage of such legislation, powerful coalitions of women (and their international and domestic partners) are necessary to ensure proper implementation and to help shift oppressive gender norms. One of the most critical – and historically, most feasible – means of facilitating both of these objectives is to increase women's representation in the political system. Women's marginalisation was a key factor in enabling Boko Haram to become such a destructive force; the post-conflict era must recognise that women's security is integral to national security.

CONCLUSION: NIGERIA AT A CROSSROADS

This book has attempted to convey the myriad ways in which women have shaped the development and course of the Boko Haram insurgency. Not only did Boko Haram's founder, Mohammed Yusuf, use women's issues and place in society to attract female members, this was also a means of differentiating his movement from other Salafist groups. Women within the insurgency play various roles. As in a number of modern conflicts, women have served as porters, cooks and sexual slaves. However, Boko Haram has also incorporated women into new roles in the insurgency, relying on female suicide bombers to advance their campaign of terror in the face of an increasing military presence. It should not come as a surprise that women have not merely been acted upon over the course of the insurgency – although women's political activity is often shrouded or quiet, throughout the region's history women have contributed to social, political and economic developments.

The act that launched the insurgency into the global spotlight – the infamous abduction of 276 schoolgirls from their dormitory in Chibok in April 2014 – was obviously a deeply gendered human rights violation. Throughout the insurgency, both the insurgents and the Nigerian government have used women as powerful symbols. The quest to #BringBackOurGirls has become a global rallying cry, mobilising military, financial and political support around the world. While this support was certainly necessary to improve the government's response to the crisis and raise global consciousness, it has also contributed to the dehumanisation and fetishization of the girls who were abducted. The single-minded focus on the plight of the Chibok girls overlooks the wider patterns of abuse and recruitment of women and girls by Boko Haram. It also marginalises the grievances lodged against the Nigerian government by both Boko Haram and communities in the north-east in response to the military's heavy-handed response and arbitrary detention and abuse of women and girls thought to have ties to the insurgency.

The focus on the Chibok abductions also sidelines important conversations about women who join the sect voluntarily. Although it is difficult to grapple with the question of how structural violence against women contributed to the insurgency, it is necessary to do so. Gender inequality has been convincingly linked not only to economic underdevelopment, but also to social volatility and both inter- and intra-state conflict. The oppression of women and girls was a priming factor for violence and instability in the country. The lack of autonomy, the dearth of educational and vocational opportunities, and the scarcity of health services for women, combined with their overt physical abuse, incentivised female sympathy for the sect. This sympathy was expressed in a number of ways – from passive cooperation following Boko Haram's invasion, to providing emotional and reproductive support to male members in the sect, to identifying as members of the insurgency, and to participating in military endeavours.

While the extent of women's participation in the insurgency requires further investigation, the displacement crisis in the north-east is undeniably feminised. The crisis, despite being objectively one of the worst humanitarian situations in the world, has not been treated as such. Although the number of the displaced continues to rise and the region is experiencing pockets of famine conditions, international support has been slow to materialise. The result of the global community's reticence has been the militarisation of the aid process under the direction of the Nigerian security sector. This entrenches the vulnerability of women and has furthered a culture of impunity for human rights abuses. Humanitarian programmes and even the nascent post-conflict reconciliation initiatives suffer from myopia and a lack of gender inclusion. Oppressive customary legal systems and traditional leadership have prevented women from accessing resources – particularly land – that they depend upon for their survival. The social stigma displaced women face from communities who associate them with the insurgents compounds the psychological trauma they have experienced at the hands of Boko Haram. Unfortunately, support for women's mental health is of secondary concern to providing food and shelter to the displaced – which remains difficult, underfunded, and woefully inadequate.

Despite the devastating consequences of the insurgency, which is the most lethal conflict in the turbulent history of the Nigerian Fourth Republic, the crisis also represents an opportunity to implement egalitarian legal reforms and to shift social mores towards gender equality. Although there are no hard-and-fast rules as to how to facilitate gender equity in the post-conflict era, cross-national research and the experiences of other African countries provide a number of potential programmes and policies. Such gender-equitable reform is an investment in peace. Not only has research demonstrated the security imperative behind gender-equitable societies, it has also illustrated pathways to cultivate gender inclusivity. Inclusion of women during the peace process makes it more likely not only that the negotiating parties will come to an agreement, but also that the peace deal will be more durable. There is no single set of gender-sensitive post-conflict reforms universally applicable; however, the institution of quotas for women's participation in politics is one particularly effective means of accelerating the process of women's empowerment and has been linked to overall improvements in the quality of governance.

Facilitating the sort of widespread, normative social change necessary to advance women's rights in the aftermath of Boko Haram requires international support. However, for this support to reach its potential, the international community must revise its shallow conceptualisation of women. Similar to the 'madonna–whore complex' identified in psychoanalysis, programmes and initiatives relating to women suffer from a false dichotomy in which women are either a helpless, vulnerable population completely lacking in autonomy, or they are an unadulterated altruistic force for change. Consider the ubiquity of 'women and children' programming, a category that is as much a product of women's typical responsibility for children as it is of the view that women have as much autonomy as minors. On the other hand, an increasingly common refrain is that women are the world's 'greatest untapped resource', transforming gender-equitable programming into a process of mining for women.

Clearly, neither conceptualisation does women justice. It is uncomfortable, especially for those seeking to advance women's rights, to acknowledge that women can engage in violence just as men do. Female ambition, translated through various cultural lenses and opportunities, is a source of discomfort globally. Some countries have been more successful than others in providing channels for female ambition. Some contexts, perhaps well-illustrated by the case of north-east Nigeria, lack channels for all but the most elite to achieve a sense of self and a sustainable livelihood. The crises that inevitably result from widespread marginalisation and social stagnation, though devastating, provide an opportunity to renegotiate the social contract. The (admittedly imperfect) processes of post-war redevelopment and female empowerment in the aftermath of conflicts in Liberia, Uganda and Rwanda suggest that Nigeria is at a crossroads. In my conversations with female Boko Haram members, it was clear that they joined for many reasons, but a common theme was that participation gave them a sense of identity. Many said that membership was one of the few ways in which they could exercise autonomy and feel powerful. This pattern is not uncommon – a review of women in Al Qaeda by Katharina von Knop concluded that 'female subordination is linked to female participation in terrorism'.[1] Mats Utas, considering conflict in Liberia, observes that, 'precarious and treacherous as it may be, the war zone is thus not merely a wasteland for young women, but at times may also be a field ripe with possibilities for upwards social and economic mobility, even as it may also contain unforeseen pitfalls that lead to increased marginalization'.[2] The challenge is to find a way for women to use their power to take a more peaceful place.

Unfortunately, the wave of populism and xenophobic nationalism that swept through a number of important Western donor countries, including the United States and United Kingdom, in 2016 reduced the likelihood of a nuanced, well-financed and gender-sensitive response to the situation in the Lake Chad Basin. In fact, it appears that the United States may reverse its foreign policy of promoting women's rights. At the time of writing, the Trump administration had not released a coherent foreign policy platform, but there are troubling signs. Officials at the State Department were asked in December 2016 to provide information to the Trump transition team about 'existing programs and activities to promote gender equality, such as ending gender-based violence, promoting women's participation in economic and political spheres, entrepreneurship, etc.'[3] This is an unprecedented request; although it may be a ham-fisted way of getting information, many advocates and civil servants fear that this request signifies an intention to curtail or eliminate these programmes.

The choice between rebuilding the oppressive, unstable order or reconfiguring societies in the north-east to be more inclusive, peaceable and stable is an easy one. The actual process of building such a society is infinitely more difficult and will require the inclusion of women in decision making early and often. Ensuring that women and their needs are recognised during the demobilisation and reintegration of fighters, in the planning of how to care for the long-term displaced, in the post-conflict land tenure deliberations, during the process of legislative reform, and, finally, through their concerted incorporation in the political system requires identifying and cultivating women's advocacy groups. Amplifying these women's voices and needs is a necessity for the international community.

Women's inclusion in post-conflict programmes is a necessity, not only because women will be the dominant able-bodied demographic when the guns are silenced, but also because non-inclusive societies have proven to be prone to violence. The oppression of women both drove women into the insurgency's ranks, as they sought autonomy, and also incentivised the use of gendered violence by the insurgents. Peace in northern Nigeria will not be durable if it is peace made by and for men. Women's struggles in northern Nigeria are waged on a number of fronts, not just in the fight against Boko Haram, but also in domestic, political and private domains. These fights for autonomy, equality and security must also be resolved if the peace after Boko Haram is to be legitimate, inclusive and durable.

NOTES

Introduction

1 Interview with Governor Kashim Shettima, Maiduguri, Borno State, June 2016.
2 It is worth noting that the bags conveniently bore the pictures of Governor Shettima and President Buhari, both members of the All Progressives Congress (APC) political party.
3 Pseudonyms have been used where anonymity was requested.
4 Interviews, 2016.
5 Interviews, Safe House, Maiduguri, Borno State, June 2016.
6 'Nigeria Social Violence Database', School of Advanced International Studies, Johns Hopkins University.

Chapter 1

1 Lubeck 1985.
2 Moodley 2014.
3 Walker 2012.
4 *Ibid.*
5 Anonymous 2012.
6 Brigaglia 2012.
7 Interviews with residents, Railway neighbourhood, Maiduguri, Borno State, June 2016.
8 Tijaniyya is a popular Sufi brotherhood. Salafists condemn Sufis for not abiding strictly by the Qur'an and integrating local practices.
9 Interviews with residents, Railway neighbourhood, Maiduguri, Borno State, June 2016.
10 Fieldwork interview, Maiduguri, Borno State, 2016.
11 Anonymous 2012.
12 Berman 2009.
13 Berman's case studies draw heavily on jihadist groups in the Middle East, but he asserts that the logic can be found among radical religious communities around the world, observing that 'an example familiar to Americans is a communal barn raising, where an entire Amish or Mennonite community turns out to donate labor for a day or two' (*ibid.*).

14 Harnischfeger 2014.
15 *Nigerian Gazette* 2014.
16 Smith 2015.
17 Walker 2016.
18 *Ibid.*
19 *Ibid.*
20 Interview with Adam Higazi, Maiduguri, Borno State, June 2016.
21 Interviews, Safe House, Maiduguri, Borno State, June 2016.
22 Opejobe 2016a. Although this is a controversial claim, it is widely held throughout northern Nigeria.
23 Governor Ali Modu Sheriff of Borno State, Nigeria Governors' Forum 2011.
24 Walker 2016.
25 The role of marital assistance in promoting recruitment and loyalty will be discussed later, but it is worth noting that marriage is a crucial marker of social status and identity in the region and had become increasingly difficult since the 1990s. I discuss this in an article with Valerie Hudson pending publication in *International Security*.
26 Brigaglia 2012.
27 Thurston 2015.
28 *Ibid.*
29 Interviews with residents, Railway neighbourhood, Maiduguri, Borno State, June 2016.
30 Walker 2016.
31 Interviews with residents, Railway neighbourhood, Maiduguri, Borno State, June 2016.
32 *Ibid.*
33 Walker 2016.
34 Interviews with residents, Railway neighbourhood, Maiduguri, Borno State June 2016.
35 *Ibid.*
36 *Ibid.*
37 *Ibid.*
38 *Ibid.*
39 Mshelizza 2009.
40 BBC 2009.
41 Fieldwork interview, 2016.
42 BBC 2014c.
43 Mercy Corps 2016.
44 *Ibid.*
45 Interview, Adam Higazi, Maiduguri, Borno State, June 2016.
46 Nigeria Social Violence Project 2015.
47 'Nigeria Social Violence Database', School of Advanced International Studies, Johns Hopkins University.

48 Eloka n.d.
49 Matfess 2016a.
50 Interviews, Safe House, Maiduguri, Borno State, June 2016.
51 *Ibid.*
52 *Ibid.*
53 *Ibid.*
54 *Ibid.*
55 Interviews with resident of Madina mosque settlement, Maiduguri, Borno State, 2016.
56 *Ibid.*
57 *Ibid.*; fieldwork interview, Adamawa State, December 2015 – January 2016.
58 Fieldwork interview with displaced man in Maiduguri, Borno State, June 2016.
59 Interview with elder, leader of the CJTF, Maiduguri, Borno State, March 2016.
60 Interview with social workers, Maiduguri, Borno State, June 2016.
61 Interviews, Safe House, Maiduguri, Borno State, June 2016.
62 *Ibid.*
63 *Ibid.*
64 Amnesty International 2015b.
65 Interview with Mohammed Kyari, Yola, Adamawa State, December 2015
66 Interviews, Safe House, Maiduguri, Borno State, June 2016.
67 Interview with displaced woman, Mubi, Adamawa State, December 2015.
68 Mercy Corps 2016.
69 Pérouse de Montclos 2014.
70 Hirose *et al.* 2016.
71 Faul 2016.
72 Interviews, Safe House, Maiduguri, Borno State, June 2016.
73 *Ibid.*
74 *Ibid.*
75 Interview with UNICEF field staff, Maiduguri, Borno State, June 2016.
76 Interviews with residents, Railway neighbourhood, Maiduguri, Borno State, June 2016.
77 *Ibid.*
78 Zenn and Pearson 2014.
79 *Ibid.*
80 *Ibid.*

Chapter 2

1 While other analyses of the Boko Haram insurgency have traced the group's roots all the way back to the caliphates and conquests of the nineteenth century (raising interesting points for discussion while doing so), this text will confine itself to the twentieth and twenty-first centuries. For a more thorough discussion of these historical roots, see Walker (2016).

2   Under the tenure of Lord Frederick Lugard, who subdued the north through a brutal military campaign against the Sokoto caliphate and subsequently served as the High Commissioner of the Northern Protectorate from 1900 to 1906, the British relied on 'indirect rule'. In practice, this meant that the British colonial administrators relied on the emirs they defeated to adopt and implement the British colonial policy. Over time, this raised the Hausa-Fulani ethnic coalition to a position of prominence.

3   International Organization for Migration 2016.

4   Harnischfeger quoted in Pérouse de Montclos 2014.

5   Sahara Reporters 2016a.

6   Pérouse de Montclos 2014.

7   *Ibid.*

8   Kendhammer 2016.

9   *Ibid.*

10   *Ibid.*

11   *Ibid.*

12   *Ibid.*

13   Harnischfeger quoted in Pérouse de Montclos 2014.

14   Lubeck 1985.

15   *Ibid.*

16   Anonymous 2012.

17   Lubeck and Britts 2001.

18   Pérouse de Montclos 2014.

19   For a more comprehensive discussion of the emergence and significance of the 'Yan Izala, see Kane (2003).

20   *Ibid.*

21   Masquelier 2009.

22   Kane 2003.

23   Gregoire 1994.

24   Kane 2003.

25   *Ibid.*

26   *Ibid.*

27   Pérouse de Montclos 2014.

28   Bala-Gbogbo 2015.

29   *The Economist* 2010.

30   UNESCO 2012.

31   Hoechner forthcoming.

32   *Ibid.*

33   Interview with anonymous NGO director, Yola, Adamawa State, December 2015 – January 2016.

34   Hoechner forthcoming.

35   *Ibid.*

Chapter 3

1   Interview with anonymous State Department official, Washington DC, 2015.
2   Interview with Mfoniso Akanamos, Yola, Adamawa State, December 2015.
3   UNDP 2015.
4   NPC and ICF International 2014.
5   Adeniran 2007.
6   *Ibid.*; NPC and ICF International 2014.
7   UK AID 2012.
8   Creative Associates International 2009.
9   Okeke 2013.
10 Voices 4 Change 2015.
11 Okeke 2013.
12 Correspondence with Khalifa Aliyu Ahmed Abulfathi of Madina mosque, via email, 2016.
13 Hudson and Matfess forthcoming.
14 *Ibid.*
15 UK AID 2012.
16 *Ibid.*
17 *Ibid.*
18 *Ibid.*; Hudson and Matfess forthcoming.
19 NPC and ICF International 2014.
20 Nigerian CEDAW NGO Coalition 2008.
21 UK AID 2012.
22 *Ibid.*
23 *Ibid.*
24 Interview with Dr Bulama Gubio, Maiduguri, Borno State, June 2016.
25 Immigration and Refugee Board of Canada 2000; Renne 2013.
26 Kane 2003.
27 Hugo 2012.
28 *Ibid.*
29 Zakaria 2001.
30 Adeniran 2007.
31 UK AID 2012.
32 *Ibid.*
33 *Ibid.*
34 *Ibid.*
35 Enwelu *et al.* 2014.
36 Falobi 2015.
37 *Ibid.*
38 *Ibid.*
39 Hudson *et al.* 2012.
40 *Ibid.*

41 *Ibid.*

42 Oyelere 2007.

43 Cockburn 2013.

44 Tripp *et al.* 2013.

45 Tripp 2015.

46 Interview with Hamsatu Allamin, Maiduguri, Borno State, June 2016.

47 Kendhammer 2016.

48 Ahmed-Ghosh 2004.

49 *Ibid.*

50 Religious credentials generally serve as markers of social status across the north. The *hajj*, in particular, is a religious credential that serves to elevate social standing. Cooper observes that the completion of the *hajj* serves to advance the social standing of both men and women in the north; recollections of the *hajj* and the completion of the pilgrimage bestow authority and respect on those who attend (Cooper 1999).

51 Interviews, Safe House, Maiduguri, Borno State, June 2016.

52 *Ibid.*

53 Interviews with residents, Railway neighbourhood, Maiduguri, Borno State, June 2016.

54 *Ibid.*

55 *Ibid.*

56 Interviews, Safe House, Maiduguri, Borno State, June 2016.

57 *Ibid.*

58 *Ibid.*

59 Interview with Hamsatu Allamin, Maiduguri, Borno State, June 2016.

60 *Ibid.*

61 Interviews, Safe House, Maiduguri, Borno State, June 2016.

62 *Ibid.*

63 *Ibid.*

64 *Ibid.*

65 *Ibid.*

66 Müller-Kosack quoted in Walker 2016.

67 *Ibid.*

68 Ahmed-Ghosh 2009.

69 Vaughn and Banu 2014.

70 US Department of State 2015.

71 *Ibid.*

72 *Ibid.*

73 Kendhammer 2016.

74 Interviews with residents, Railway neighbourhood, Maiduguri, Borno State, June 2016.

75 *Ibid.*

76 *Ibid.*
77 *Ibid.*
78 *Ibid.*
79 *Ibid.*
80 *Ibid.*

Chapter 4

1   Meintjes *et al.* 2002.
2   Human Rights Watch 2014.
3   *Ibid.*
4   *Ibid.*
5   *Ibid.*
6   *Ibid.*
7   *Ibid.*
8   BBC 2014b.
9   *Ibid.*
10 Interviews in Maiduguri, Borno State, March and June 2016.
11 Abubakar 2015; *Today Nigeria* 2016.
12 Abubakar 2015.
13 *Ibid.*
14 Information Nigeria 2014.
15 Collins 2014.
16 Dorell 2014.
17 BBC 2014a.
18 *The Economist* 2014a.
19 Reuters 2014a.
20 *Ibid.*
21 Reuters 2014b.
22 BBC 2014a.
23 Freeman 2014.
24 *Nigerian Sun* 2014.
25 *Ibid.*
26 *Ibid.*
27 Al Jazeera 2015.
28 Olokor *et al.* 2016.
29 BBC 2016.
30 Amina Ali and her mother were reunited in their village (Mbala), before being taken back to a military camp to be debriefed.
31 Sahara Reporters 2016b.
32 Al Jazeera 2014.
33 Burke 2016.

34 Sahara Reporters 2017.
35 For more on the kidnapping of the Chibok girls, see Habila (2016).
36 Smith 2014.
37 Interview with anonymous journalist, Maiduguri, Borno State, March 2016.
38 *Premium Times* 2016a.
39 Haruna 2016.
40 *Ibid.*
41 *Ibid.*
42 Stein 2015.
43 Kumar 2004.
44 *Ibid.*
45 Chappell 2014.
46 Freeman 2016.
47 Wolfe 2014.
48 *Ibid.*
49 Adesulu 2016.
50 Mazumdar 2015.
51 Interviews, Safe House, Maiduguri, Borno State, June 2016.
52 Interviews in IDP camps and informal settlements in Maiduguri, Borno State, March and June 2016.
53 Interviews, Safe House, Maiduguri, Borno State, June 2016.
54 Interview with anonymous vigilante, Maiduguri, Borno State, June 2016.
55 Amnesty International 2015a.
56 Human Rights Watch 2014.
57 *Ibid.*
58 *Ibid.*
59 Zenn and Pearson 2014.
60 *Ibid.*
61 *Ibid.*
62 *Ibid.*
63 *Ibid.*
64 *Ibid.*
65 Smith 2010.
66 See http://afrobarometer.org/online-data-analysis (accessed 2016).
67 Abiodun 2000.
68 *Ibid.*
69 *Ibid.*
70 *Ibid.*
71 *Ibid.*
72 Open Society Justice Initiative and the Network on Police Reform in Nigeria 2010.
73 *Ibid.*

74   Campbell 2014.
75   Amnesty International 2014.
76   *The Economist* 2012.
77   Human Rights Watch 2014.
78   *Ibid.*
79   *Ibid.*
80   *Ibid.*
81   *Ibid.*
82   *Ibid.*
83   Interview with Halima, Dalori I IDP camp, Maiduguri, Borno State, June 2016.
84   Human Rights Watch 2014.
85   Human Rights Watch 2014.
86   Cockburn 2013.
87   Bergsmo *et al.* 2012.
88   Cohen 2016.
89   Human Rights Watch 2014.
90   *Ibid.*
91   *Ibid.*
92   Interview with Umma, Madina mosque settlement, Maiduguri, Borno State, March 2016.
93   *Ibid.*
94   *Ibid.*
95   Interview with Amina, Madina mosque settlement, Maiduguri, Borno State, March 2016.
96   Interview with a displaced woman in Maikohi IDP camp in Yola, Adamawa State, December 2015.
97   Interview with Amina, Madina mosque settlement, Maiduguri, Borno State, March 2016.
98   *Ibid.*
99   Interview with Kaka in Maikohi IDP camp in Yola, Adamawa State, December 2015.
100 *Ibid.*
101 Human Rights Watch 2014.
102 Interviews with resident of Madina mosque settlement, Maiduguri, Borno State, June 2016.
103 Duru n.d.
104 Interviews with resident of Madina mosque settlement, Maiduguri, Borno State, March 2016.
105 *Ibid.*
106 Interview with Hamsatu Allamin, Maiduguri, Borno State, June 2016.
107 *Ibid.*
108 *Ibid.*

109 Interview with Governor Kashim Shettima, Maiduguri, Borno State, June 2016.

110 *Ibid.*

111 *Ibid.*

112 Interview with Shettima's neighbours, Maiduguri, Borno State, June 2016.

113 Interview with man in IDP camp in Yola, Adamawa State, December 2015.

114 Duru n.d.

115 UNICEF and International Alert 2016.

116 *Ibid.*

117 Warner 2014.

118 *Ibid.*

119 *Ibid.*

120 *Ibid.*

121 *Ibid.*

122 *Ibid.*

123 Rachele 2000.

124 Warner 2014.

125 See the Concerned Parents Association of Uganda for more information on advocacy on this issue.

126 Grover 2012.

Chapter 5

1 Ahmed-Ghosh 2004.

2 *Ibid.*

3 Mahmood 2001.

4 *Ibid.*

5 *Ibid.*

6 Pastner 1974.

7 McKay 2005.

8 *Ibid.*

9 Interviews, Safe House, Maiduguri, Borno State, June 2016.

10 Interview with anonymous girl in Dalori I IDP camp, Maiduguri, Borno State, June 2016.

11 Interviews with resident of Madina mosque settlement, Maiduguri, Borno State, 2016.

12 Busari and Jones 2016.

13 Interviews, Safe House, Maiduguri, Borno State, June 2016.

14 *Ibid.*

15 *Ibid.*; ICG 2016.

16 Interviews, Safe House, Maiduguri, Borno State, June 2016.

17 *Ibid.*

18   *Ibid.*
19   *Ibid.*
20   Nossiter 2015.
21   Human Rights Watch 2014.
22   *Ibid.*
23   Interviews, Safe House, Maiduguri, Borno State, June 2016.
24   *Ibid.*
25   Zakaria 2001.
26   Pastner 1974.
27   Interviews, Safe House, Maiduguri, Borno State, June 2016.
28   *Ibid.*
29   *Ibid.*
30   *Ibid.*
31   *Ibid.*
32   Mahdi 2009.
33   *Ibid.*
34   *Ibid.*
35   Renne 2013.
36   Mahdi 2009.
37   Renne 2013.
38   Mahdi 2009.
39   Fieldwork interviews.
40   Interviews, Safe House, Maiduguri, Borno State, June 2016.
41   *Ibid.*
42   *Ibid.*
43   *Ibid.*
44   *Ibid.*
45   *Ibid.*
46   *Ibid.*
47   *Ibid.*
48   *Ibid.*
49   Rusyana n.d.
50   Interview with displaced woman living in Yola, Adamawa State, December 2015.
51   Interviews, Safe House, Maiduguri, Borno State, June 2016.
52   *Ibid.*
53   *Ibid.*
54   Amnesty International 2015a.
55   Interviews, Safe House, Maiduguri, Borno State, June 2016.
56   *Ibid.*
57   Fieldwork interviews, Adamawa State.
58   *Ibid.*

59 Interviews with displaced women in Malkohi IDP camp, Yola, Adamawa State, December 2015.
60 Bloom and Matfess 2016.
61 Nossiter 2015.
62 Sieff 2016.
63 Interview with Governor Kashim Shettima, Maiduguri, Borno State, June 2016.
64 USAID n.d.
65 Interviews, Safe House, Maiduguri, Borno State, June 2016.
66 *Ibid.*
67 Interviews with resident of Madina mosque settlement, Maiduguri, Borno State, 2016.
68 Interview with Dr Bulama Gubio, Maiduguri, Borno State, June 2016.
69 Interview with Hamsatu Allamin, Maiduguri, Borno State, June 2016.
70 Interviews, Safe House, Maiduguri, Borno State, June 2016.
71 *Ibid.*
72 *Ibid.*
73 *Ibid.*
74 *Ibid.*
75 *Ibid.*
76 Interview with Governor Kashim Shettima, Maiduguri, Borno State, June 2016.
77 Interviews, Safe House, Maiduguri, Borno State, June 2016.
78 *Ibid.*
79 *Ibid.*
80 *Ibid.*
81 *Ibid.*
82 *Ibid.*
83 *Ibid.*
84 *Ibid.*
85 *Ibid.*
86 *Ibid.*
87 Amnesty International 2015a.
88 Interview with anonymous soldiers, 7th Division Garrison, Maiduguri, Borno State, March 2016.
89 *Ibid.*
90 Interview with vigilante Bulus Mungopark, Maiduguri, Borno State, March 2016.
91 Interview with Alhassan, anonymous security sector official, Maiduguri, Borno State, June 2016.
92 Fillion 2011.
93 *Ibid.*

94 *Ibid.*
95 Dalton and Asal 2011; Bloom and Matfess 2016.
96 Bloom and Matfess 2016.
97 Walker 2016.
98 Bloom and Matfess 2016.
99 *Ibid.*
100 Interview with displaced woman, Abuja, Nigeria, March 2016.
101 Quoted in Riley 2013.
102 Interviews, Safe House, Maiduguri, Borno State, June 2016.
103 Conversations with Adam Higazi during fieldwork.
104 Interview with Dionne Searcey, Maiduguri, Borno State, June 2016.
105 Fillion 2011.
106 Interviews, Safe House, Maiduguri, Borno State, June 2016.
107 *Bits of Borno* is a photojournalism project that documents life in Borno State, highlighting not only the devastating effects of the insurgency, but also residents' remarkable resilience. Work is featured on the @Bits_of_Borno instagram.
108 Cohen 1961.
109 *Ibid.*
110 *Ibid.*
111 This was predicted by Louis Brenner, who asked: 'Will their religious ideologies better equip the Islamists to resolve the crises which have contributed to their ascendancy, or have they simply contributed to the substitution of one dominant class by another?' (Brenner 1994).
112 Fieldwork interview, 2016.
113 *Ibid.*; correspondence with Khalifa Aliyu Ahmed Abulfathi of Madina mosque, via email, 2016.
114 Interviews, Safe House, Maiduguri, Borno State, June 2016.
115 *Ibid.*
116 *Ibid.*
117 *Ibid.*
118 *Ibid.*
119 *Ibid.*
120 *Ibid.*
121 Utas 2005.
122 *The Denver Post* 2013.
123 Annan *et al.* 2010.
124 *Ibid.*
125 *Ibid.*
126 *Ibid.*
127 *Ibid.*
128 *Ibid.*

129   Interviews, Safe House, Maiduguri, Borno State, June 2016.
130   McKay 2005.
131   *Ibid.*
132   *Ibid.*
133   *Ibid.*
134   *Ibid.*
135   Cohen 2016.
136   McKay 2005.
137   *Ibid.*

Chapter 6

1   Interview with Dr Bulama Gubio, Maiduguri, Borno State, June 2016.
2   Interview with UNHCR field staff, Maiduguri, Borno State, June 2016.
3   UN News Centre 2017.
4   OCHA 2016a.
5   OCHA 2016b.
6   Human Rights Watch 2016.
7   MSF 2016.
8   *Ibid.*
9   Anonymous interviews with activists in Maiduguri, Borno State, June 2016 and February 2017.
10   Anonymous interviews with activists in Maiduguri, Borno State, June 2016 .
11   Umoru 2016.
12   OCHA 2015.
13   Interview with IDPs in transit camp, Mubi, Adamawa State, December 2016.
14   UNHCR 2007.
15   Organisation of African Unity 1969.
16   *Ibid.*
17   Interview with IDP in Fufore IDP camp, Yola, Adamawa State, December 2015.
18   *Ibid.*
19   Interviews with journalists, Maiduguri, Borno State, June 2016 and Abuja, May 2017; interviews with displaced people, Fufore IDP camp, Mubi transit camp, and Malkohi IDP camp, Adamawa State, December 2015 – January 2016; interviews with security personnel, Maiduguri, Borno State, March 2016, July 2016 and March 2017.
20   Interviews, Safe House, Maiduguri, Borno State, June 2016.
21   Interviews with security personnel in Maiduguri, Borno State, March 2016, July 2016 and March 2017.
22   Interview with UNICEF field staff, Yola, Adamawa State, December 2015.
23   *Ibid.*

24 Amnesty International 2015c.
25 *Ibid.*
26 *Ibid.*
27 *Ibid.*
28 *Ibid.*
29 Interview with anonymous resident of Maiduguri, Maiduguri, Borno State, March 2016.
30 Amnesty International 2015c.
31 Interview with anonymous resident of Maiduguri, Maiduguri, Borno State, March 2016.
32 Opejobe 2016b.
33 *Ibid.*
34 Iroegbu 2016.
35 Kumar 2004.
36 Handrahan 2004.
37 Interviews with resident of Madina mosque settlement, Maiduguri, Borno State, March 2016.
38 *Ibid.*
39 *Ibid.*
40 Interview with Hamsatu Allamin, Maiduguri, Borno State, June 2016.
41 UN 2016.
42 Interview with UNHCR field staff, Maiduguri, Borno State, June 2016.
43 UN 2016.
44 This is a by-product of the military's centralisation at the federal level. I have addressed other constitutional issues that prime the country for conflict in Matfess (2016a).
45 Interviews with security personnel, Maiduguri, Borno State, March 2016.
46 *Ibid.*
47 *Ibid.*
48 *Ibid.*
49 Amnesty International 2016.
50 *Ibid.*
51 Interviews with security personnel, Maiduguri, Borno State, March 2016.
52 Amnesty International 2016.
53 *Ibid.*
54 *Ibid.*
55 *Ibid.*
56 *Ibid.*
57 *Ibid.*
58 *Ibid.*
59 *Ibid.*
60 Interview with anonymous girl, Maiduguri, Borno State, June 2016.

61 *Ibid.*
62 *Ibid.* The closing of the programme was widely considered to be crass politics, rather than a judgement on its value.
63 Jammai 2016.
64 *Ibid.*
65 Osborne 2016.
66 *Premium Times* 2016b.
67 Interviews with security personnel, 7th Division Headquarters, Maiduguri, Borno State in March 2016.
68 *Ibid.*
69 *Ibid.*
70 *Ibid.*
71 *Ibid.*
72 Amnesty International 2016.
73 All Things Considered 2016.
74 Interview with Governor Kashim Shettima, Maiduguri, Borno State, June 2016.
75 *Ibid.* It is worth noting that Kenya later rescinded its pledge to close Dabaab and that many believe that Kenya uses Dabaab as leverage in its negotiations with the international community.
76 OHCHR n.d.
77 Audu 2015.
78 MSF 2015.
79 *Leadership* 2016.
80 *Ibid.*
81 *Ibid.*
82 Fieldwork interview, 2016.
83 Interview with anonymous girl in Dalori I IDP camp, Maiduguri, Borno State, June 2016.
84 *Ibid.*
85 *Ibid.*
86 *Ibid.*
87 *Ibid.*
88 NOI Polls 2016.
89 Interview with UNHCR field staff, Maiduguri, Borno State, June 2016.
90 Interview with anonymous NGO staff, Maiduguri, Borno State, June 2016.
91 *Ibid.*
92 Visit to Dalori I IDP camp, March 2016.
93 Brookings and University of Bern 2008.
94 Matfess 2016b.
95 *Ibid.*
96 Interview with anonymous activist, Maiduguri, Borno State, June 2016.

97   Interview with anonymous UN staff, Maiduguri, Borno State, June 2016.
98   Interview with anonymous UN field staff posted at Dalori I, Maiduguri, Borno State, June 2016.
99   Interview with anonymous UN staff, Maiduguri, Borno State, June 2016.
100 Nigeria Social Violence Project 2016.
101 *Ibid.*
102 Krähenbühl 2011.
103 *Ibid.*
104 Interview with OCHA staff, Yola, Adamawa State, December 2015 – January 2016.
105 Hamman *et al.* 2014.
106 Interview with Governor Kashim Shettima, Maiduguri, Borno State, June 2016.
107 Interview with Dr Bulama Gubio, Maiduguri, Borno State, June 2016.
108 Interviews with resident of Madina mosque settlement, Maiduguri, Borno State, June 2016.
109 *Ibid.*
110 *Ibid.*
111 *Ibid.*
112 *Ibid.*
113 Interview with Dr Bulama Gubio, Maiduguri, Borno State, June 2016.
114 *Ibid.*
115 *Ibid.*
116 Interviews with resident of Madina mosque settlement, Maiduguri, Borno State, June 2016.
117 *Ibid.*
118 *Ibid.*
119 *Ibid.*
120 *Ibid.*
121 Interview with NGO staff and displaced people in Kuchigoro IDP camp, Abuja, 2015.
122 Interview with UN and SEMA staff, Maiduguri, Borno State, June 2016 and February 2017.
123 Interview with Dr Bulama Gubio, Maiduguri, Borno State, June 2016.
124 *Ibid.*
125 *Punch Nigeria* 2016.
126 *Premium Times* 2014.
127 *Ibid.*
128 *Ibid.*
129 Ibukun and Olukayode 2015.
130 Wakili 2015.
131 Olanreqaju 2016.

132 Collyer 2016.

133 Abubaker 2015.

134 New Internationalist 1999. One of the most critical, but least discussed, preconditions for rebuilding the country's north-east is the removal of landmines planted by Boko Haram. De-mining is a notoriously difficult aspect of post-conflict redevelopment; although landmines can be purchased for between $3 and $30, it can cost more than 50 times that to remove one safely.

135 Francis 2016.

136 *Ibid.*

137 *Ibid.*

138 Although an L3 designation mobilises support, it is worth observing that it is not a panacea for the humanitarian crisis in the Lake Chad Basin. ICVA notes that 'where leadership and coordination structures were considered effective prior to L3 designation, the L3 has been able to positively strengthen these existing systems'. Where these systems were weak, however, 'surge capacity was reported to remain mainly in the capital, leaving little effective subnational coordination'. The need for solid domestic relief infrastructure makes it all the more critical for the international community to scrutinise Nigeria's policies. There is more information in the documents and reports of the UN's 'Education Cluster' (see http://educationcluster.net/).

139 Global Nutrition Cluster n.d.

140 ICVA 2015.

141 Interview with UNHCR field staff, Maiduguri, Borno State, June 2016.

142 *Ibid.*

143 *Ibid.*

144 UN 2014.

145 Education Cluster n.d.

146 Cumming-Bruce 2015.

147 OCHA 2016b.

148 OCHA 2017.

149 OCHA 2016b.

150 *Ibid.*

151 *Ibid.*

152 Personal correspondence with OCHA employee via email 2016.

153 UN Refugee Agency 2015.

154 Spang 2009.

155 Interview with Dr Bulama Gubio, Maiduguri, Borno State, June 2016.

156 Interview with Father John Gideon, Maiduguri, Borno State, June 2016.

157 Interview with OCHA staff, Maiduguri, Borno State, June 2016.

158 OCHA 2012.

159 UN Women 2015.

160 *Ibid.*

161 *Ibid.*

162 *Ibid.*

163 See the work done for the Center for Complex Operations' journal *PRISM*'s 'Women, Peace, and Inclusive Security' edition (vol. 6, no. 1, 2016; see http://cco.ndu.edu/Portals/96/Documents/prism/prism_6-1/Prism%20Vol%206%20No%201%20-%20Final.pdf).

164 O'Reilly 2015.

165 See the work done for *PRISM*'s 'Women, Peace, and Inclusive Security' edition.

166 UN Women 2015.

167 Oxfam 2013.

168 *Ibid.*

169 UN Women 2015.

170 Goldstein 2001.

171 UN Women 2015.

172 Benjamin and Fancy 1998.

Chapter 7

1   Wader *et al.* 2015.

2   Wood 2015.

3   *Ibid.*

4   Abiola 2016.

5   Aoláin 2013.

6   Collier 2004.

7   Watteville 2002.

8   Narayan 2000.

9   *Ibid.*

10 *Ibid.*

11 Eshun 2016.

12 Fink *et al.* 2016.

13 Tripp 2015.

14 International Alert 2010.

15 *Ibid.*

16 *Ibid.*

17 Berkley Center for Religion Peace and World Affairs n.d.

18 Uganda provides a valuable example of how women's organisations can partner with each other, leveraging the comparative advantages of each group to enact change. Following conflict in that country, the Uganda Women's Network and the Uganda Association of Women Lawyers Action for Development partnered with the Uganda Land Alliance to undermine discriminatory customary land practices and increase women's access to and control over resources.

19 Odeny (2013) summarises: 'women have been at the forefront through organizations such as the Uganda Land Alliance (ULA) and Uganda Women's Network (UWONET) in the struggle for approval of the co-ownership clause by the legislative body. The ULA coordinated efforts of lobbying legislators and campaigned for co-ownership, by producing information, education and communication (IEC) materials, used to raise awareness of the general public on the need for such a clause. The Uganda Association of Women Lawyers Action for Development conducted legal education in collaboration with the Uganda Land Alliance, and female journalists used the media to present the case.'

20 Meintjes *et al.* 2002.

21 UNICEF and International Alert 2016.

22 *Ibid.*

23 *Ibid.*

24 *Ibid.*

25 Interviews, Safe House, Maiduguri, Borno State, June 2016.

26 *Ibid.*

27 *Ibid.*

28 Iaccino 2015.

29 *Ibid.*

30 Eshun 2016.

Chapter 8

1 Interview with Governor Kashim Shettima, Maiduguri, Borno State, June 2016.

2 Greenberg and Zuckerman 2009.

3 *Ibid.* In addition to demobilising insurgents, another significant security issue relating to the issue of reintegration is the future of the vigilantes who have contributed to the fight against Boko Haram. It is difficult to estimate how many vigilantes there are across the north-east. In Borno State, the ranks of just one vigilante group (the CJTF) are thought to include between 26,000 and 50,000 people – most of whom are young men who have few employment prospects once the conflict subsides. Already, frustrations are mounting within the ranks of the vigilantes. A commander of the CJTF in Maiduguri argued that: 'Since we have lost men like the military, the CJTF should be treated like the military with training with foreign partners and benefits.' While reintegration is critical, if the process overlooks the issue of the abuses committed against civilians in the course of the insurgency, it could be seen as sanctioning violence as a means of venting grievances. Additionally, if these programmes rely on binary models of men as soldiers and women as victims, they will be inadequate.

4 UN DDR Resource Center 2006.

5 Watteville 2002.

6   *Ibid.*
7   UN DDR Resource Center 2006.
8   *Ibid.*
9   Anthony 2014.
10 *Ibid.*
11 *Ibid.*
12 Ricks 2016.
13 Susskind and Duque 2016.
14 *Ibid.*
15 Tripp 2015.
16 *Ibid.*
17 *Ibid.*
18 *Ibid.*
19 Barnes and Burchard 2012.
20 Faludi 1991.
21 Melander 2005.
22 Tripp 2015.
23 Meintjes *et al.* 2002.
24 Tripp 2015.
25 Tripp 2013.
26 *Ibid.*
27 Yoon 2004.
28 Caul quoted in Tripp and Kang 2008.
29 Tripp 2012.
30 As cited in Wader *et al.* 2015.
31 *Ibid.*
32 Tripp 2012.
33 Tripp 2013.
34 Tripp 2015.
35 Quadri 2015.
36 *Ibid.*
37 Data accessed through the World Bank's online analysis portal (see http://data. worldbank.org/indicator/SG.GEN.PARL.ZS).
38 Egwurube 2016.
39 Quadri 2015.
40 *Ibid.*
41 *Ibid.*
42 See https://www.ictj.org/about/transitional-justice. There is not sufficient space here to address the totality of the transitional justice issue in northern Nigeria; a volume could be dedicated to just the issue of how to bring about justice for the civilians abused during this conflict by the military, the vigilantes and the insurgents.

43 Laache 2015.
44 Lake 2014.
45 Human Rights Watch 2009.
46 Zongwe 2012.
47 Lake (2013) describes one such programme: 'For example, an American Bar Association Rule of Law Initiative (ABA ROLI) project, which operates in partnership with local NGOs, such as HEAL Africa, has disseminated thousands of copies of the country's 2006 law on sexual violence across eastern provinces of DRC.'
48 Lake 2013.
49 *Premium Times* 2015.
50 Evans 2014.
51 *Ibid.*
52 ICTJ 2015.
53 Lake 2014.
54 Sakhonchik *et al.* 2015.
55 Jefferson 2004.
56 Odeny 2013.
57 *Ibid.*
58 In Sierra Leone, in particular, a large proportion of the land has been transferred to foreign investors under long-term leases. Rwandan women have fared better in their endeavour to get access to land in the post-conflict era – in large part because of post-conflict legal reforms that elevated women's status.
59 Berry 2015.
60 *Ibid.*
61 Odeny 2013.
62 Berry 2015.
63 Sokoto 2016
64 Voices 4 Change 2014.
65 *Ibid.*

Conclusion

1 Knop 2007.
2 Utas 2005.
3 Elizabeth 2016.

REFERENCES

Abiodun, Alao (2000) *Security Reform in Democratic Nigeria*. Conflict, Security and Development Group Working Paper. London: Centre for Defence Studies, Kings College, University of London.

Abiola, Saratu (2016) 'How We Make Sure Nigeria's Gender Equality Bill Passes Next Time', *Quartz Africa*, 18 March.

Abubakar, Aminu (2015) *How Many Schoolgirls Did Boko Haram Abduct and How Many Are Still Missing*. Factsheet. Johannesburg: Africa Check.

Abubaker, Shehu (2015) 'How Borno Plans to Revive Agriculture', *Daily Trust*, 14 October.

Adeniran, Isaac Adebusuyi (2007) *Nigeria: Educational Inequalities and Women's Disempowerment in Nigeria*. New York NY: Women's UN Report Network.

Adesulu, Day (2016) 'Two Years After: Will the 219 Chibok Girls Ever Return?', *Vanguard*, 14 April.

Ahmed-Ghosh, Huma (2004) 'Portraits of Believers: Ahmadi Women Performing Faith in the Diaspora', *Journal of International Women's Studies* 6 (1): 73–92.

— (2009) *The Hijab in Nigeria: The Woman's Body and the Feminist Private/Public Discourse*. Working Paper. Evanston IL: Institute for the Study of Islamic Thought in Africa, Northwestern University.

Al Jazeera (2014) 'Chibok Girls: Nigeria Denies Boko Haram Prisoner Swap', *Al Jazeera*, 14 October.

— (2015) 'Nigeria Ready to Talk to Boko Haram about Missing Girls', *Al Jazeera*, 31 December.

All Things Considered (2016) 'The World's Largest Refugee Camp Looks Like a Slum/Star Wars Mashup', National Public Radio (NPR). http://www.npr.org/sections/goatsandsoda/2016/01/11/462698276/the-worlds-largest-refugee-camp-looks-like-a-slum-from-star-wars.

Amnesty International (2014) *Nigeria: More than 1,500 Killed in North-eastern Nigeria in Early 2014*. London: Amnesty International.

— (2015a) *'Our Job is to Shoot, Slaughter, and Kill': Boko Haram's Reign of Terror in North East Nigeria*. London: Amnesty International.

— (2015b) 'Nigeria: Abducted Women and Girls Forced to Join Boko Haram Attacks', Amnesty International, 14 April.

— (2015c) *Stars on their Shoulders, Blood on their Hands: War Crimes Committed by the Nigerian Military*. Washington DC: Amnesty International.

— (2016) *'If You See It You Will Cry': Life and Death in Giwa Barracks.* Washington DC: Amnesty International.

Annan, Jeannie, Christopher Blattman, Dyan Mazurana and Khristopher Carlson (2010) *Women and Girls at War: 'Wives', Mothers, and Fighters in the Lord's Resistance Army.* HiCN Working Paper 63. Brighton: Households in Conflict Network (HiCN), Institute of Development Studies, at the University of Sussex.

Anonymous (2012) 'The Popular Discourses of Salafi Radicalism and Salafi Counter-radicalism in Nigeria: A Case Study of Boko Haram', *Journal of Religion in Africa* 42 (2): 118–44.

Anthony, Agbegbedia Oghenevwoke (2014) 'Gender Mainstreaming and the Impacts of the Federal Government Amnesty Programme in the Niger Delta Region', *International Journal of Gender and Women's Studies* 2 (2): 177–95.

Aoláin, Fionnuala Ní (2013) 'What does Postconflict Security Mean for Women?' in Aili Mari Tripp, Myra Marx Ferree and Christina Ewig (eds), *Gender, Violence, and Human Security.* New York NY: NYU Press.

Audu, Ola' (2015) 'Over 70,000 IDPs to Vote in Borno Camps – INEC', *Premium Times*, 27 March.

Bala-Gbogbo, Elisha (2015) 'Nigeria to Raise 2016 Spending Even as Key Oil Price Lowered', *Bloomberg*, 7 December.

Barnes, Tiffany D. and Stephanie Burchard (2012) '"Engendering" Politics: The Impact of Descriptive Representation on Women's Political Engagement in Sub-Saharan Africa', *Comparative Political Studies* 46 (7): 767–90.

BBC (2009) 'Nigeria Row over Militant Killing', BBC News, 31 July.

— (2014a) 'Boko Haram "To Sell" Nigeria Girls Abducted from Chibok', BBC News, 5 May.

— (2014b) 'Nigeria Abductions: Chibok Raid Warnings "Ignored"', BBC News, 9 May.

— (2014c) 'Nigeria's Boko Haram Leader Abubakar Shekau in Profile', BBC News, 9 May.

— (2016) 'Chibok Girls: Amina Ali Nkeki Meets President Buhari', BBC News, 19 May.

Benjamin, Judy A. and Khadija Fancy (1998) *The Gender Dimensions of Internal Displacement.* Concept paper and annotated bibliography. New York NY: Women's Refugee Commission.

Bergsmo, Morten, Alf Butenschon Skre and Elisabeth J. Wood (2012) *Understanding and Proving International Sex Crimes.* Beijing: Torkel Opsahl Academic EPublisher.

Berkley Center for Religion Peace and World Affairs (n.d.) 'Federation of Muslim Women's Associations in Nigeria'. Washington DC: Berkley Center for Religion Peace and World Affairs, Georgetown University. https://berkley center.georgetown.edu/organizations/federation-of-muslim-women-s-associations-in-nigeria (accessed 2016).

Berman, Eli (2009) *Radical, Religious, and Violent: The New Economics of Terrorism.* Cambridge MA: MIT Press.

Berry, Marie E. (2015) 'When "Bright Futures" Fade: Paradoxes of Women's Empowerment in Rwanda', *Signs: Journal of Women in Culture and Society* 41 (1): 1–27.

Blanchfield, Luisa, Rhoda Margesson, Tiaji Salaam-Blyther, Nina M. Serafino and Liana Sun Wyler (2011) *International Violence Against Women: U.S. Response and Policy Issues.* Washington DC: Congressional Research Service.

Bloom, Mia and Hilary Matfess (2016) 'Women as Symbols and Swords in Boko Haram's Terror', *PRISM* 6 (1): 105–21.

Brenner, Louis (1994) *Muslim Identity and Social Change in Sub-Saharan Africa.* Bloomington IN: Indiana University Press.

Brigaglia, Andrea (2012) 'Ja'far Mahmoud Adam, Mohammed Yusuf and Al-Muntada Islamic Trust: Reflections on the Genesis of the Boko Haram phenomenon in Nigeria', *Annual Review of Islam in Africa* 11: 36–44.

Brookings and University of Bern (2008) *Protecting Internally Displaced Persons: A Manual for Law and Policymakers.* Washington DC: Brookings.

Burke, Jason (2016) 'Nigeria Denies Paying Ransom and Freeing Boko Haram Leaders for Chibok Girls', *The Guardian,* 14 October.

Busari, Stephanie and Bryony Jones (2016) 'Escaped Chibok Girl: I Miss My Boko Haram Husband', CNN, 17 August.

Campbell, John (2014) 'Crimes Against Humanity and Nigeria's Giwa Barracks', *CFR Blogs: Africa in Transition,* 1 April. http://blogs.cfr.org/campbell/2014/04/01/crimes-against-humanity-and-nigerias-giwa-barracks/ (accessed 2016).

Center for Complex Operations (2016) *Women, Peace, and Inclusive Security.* Washington DC: Center for Complex Operations.

Chappell, Bill (2014) 'Boko Haram Says Kidnapped Girls Are Now "Married"', National Public Radio (NPR), 1 November.

Cockburn, Cynthia (2013) 'War and Security, Women and Gender: An Overview of the Issues', *Gender and Development* 21 (3): 433–52.

Cohen, Dara Kay (2016) *Rape During Civil War.* Ithaca NY: Cornell University Press.

Cohen, Ronald (1961) 'Marriage Instability among the Kanuri of Northern Nigeria', *American Anthropologist* 63 (6): 1231–49.

Collier, Paul (2004) *Development and Conflict.* New York NY: United Nations Development Programme.

Collins, Matt (2014) '#BringBackOurGirls: The Power of a Social Media Campaign', *The Guardian,* 9 May.

Collyer, Rosie (2016) 'As Northern Nigeria Begins to Rebuild', *The Africa Report,* 30 June.

Cooper, Barbara M. (1999) 'The Strength in the Song: Muslim Personhood, Audible Capital, and Hausa Women's Performance of the Hajj', *Social Text* 60 (Autumn): 87–109.

Creative Associates International (2009) *Creative Associates's State Education Sub-Accounts: Nigeria*. Washington DC: Creative Associates International.

Cumming-Bruce, Nick (2015) 'U.N. Seeks Record Amount for Humanitarian Aid in 2016', *The New York Times*, 7 December.

Dalton, Angela and Victor Asal (2011) 'Is It Ideology or Desperation: Why Do Organizations Deploy Women in Violent Terrorist Attacks?', *Studies in Conflict and Terrorism* 34 (10): 802–19.

Dorell, Oren (2014) 'Terrorists Kidnap More Than 200 Nigerian Schoolgirls', *USA Today*, 21 April.

Douma, Nynke and Dorothea Hilhorst (2012) *Fond de commerce? Sexual violence assistance in the Democratic Republic of Congo*. Wageningen, Netherlands: Disaster Studies, Wageningen University.

Duru, Onyekachi (n.d.) 'Nigerian Legal Position on Spouse Rape'. Legal Essay Series. https://www.academia.edu/6792858/Nigerian_Legal_Position_on_Spouse_Rape.

Education Cluster (n.d.) 'L3 Emergencies and High Priority Countries', Global Education Cluster. http://educationcluster.net/country-coordination/high-priority-countries/ (accessed 2016).

Egwurube, Joseph (2016) 'Challenges Facing Women Empowerment in Contemporary Nigeria', *Revue Miroirs* 2 (8): 134–67.

Elizabeth, De (2016) 'People Are Suspicious of Trump's Team's Request for Women's Rights Data', *Teen Vogue*, 16 December.

Eloka, Jonathan (n.d.) 'Terrorist Bombing in Nigeria: A Critical Analysis of its Socio-political Roots from 2000–2011'. Thesis, University of Nigeria, Nsukka.

Enwelu, I. A., U. L. Morah, M. U. Dimelu and C. I. Ezeano (2014) 'Women Farmers' Access and Use of Land for Agriculture in Selected Communities of Anambra State, Nigeria', *Mediterranean Journal of Social Sciences* 5 (26): 37–43.

Eshun, Maame Esi (2016) 'Peacebuilding in Africa: What Comes After?', Africa Up Close blog. Washington DC: Africa Program, The Wilson Center.

Evans, Alice (2014) 'Does Gender Sensitisation Work?', *Open Democracy*, 28 July.

Falobi, Funmi (2015) 'Nigeria: Marginalisation of Nigerian Women in Politics', *Daily Independent*, 25 January.

Faludi, Susan (1991) *Backlash: The Undeclared War against American Women*. New York NY: Crown Publishing Group.

Faul, Michelle (2016) 'Some Officers Selling Weapons to Boko Haram, Nigeria Military Says', *Associated Press*, 4 September.

Fillion, Kate (2011) 'In Conversation with Mia Bloom', *Maclean's*, 14 January.

Fink, Naureen Chowdhury, Sara Zeiger and Rafia Bhulai (2016) *A Man's World? Exploring the Roles of Women in Countering Terrorism and Violent Extremism*. Abu Dhabi and Washington DC: Hedayah and Global Center on Cooperative Security.

Fischer, Martina (2004) *Recovering from Violent Conflict: Regeneration and*

(Re-)Integration as Elements of Peacebuilding. Berlin: Berghof Research Center for Constructive Conflict Management.

Francis, Ndubuisi (2016) 'World Bank to Spend U.S.$800 Million in Rebuilding N'East', *This Day*, 1 April.

Freeman, Colin (2014) 'Red Cross Involved in Secret Boko Haram Prisoner Swap to Bring Back Kidnapped Girls', *The Telegraph*, 14 September.

— (2016) 'Boko Haram Demands "$50m Ransom" for Release of Kidnapped Chibok Schoolgirls', *The Telegraph*, 9 April.

Georgetown Institute for Women, Peace and Security (2016) *Women's Economic Participation in Conflict-affected and Fragile Settings.* Occasional Paper Series. Washington DC: Georgetown Institute for Women, Peace and Security.

Global Nutrition Cluster (n.d.) 'L3 and High Priority Countries', Global Nutrition Cluster. http://nutritioncluster.net/nutrition-clusters-working-groups/.

Goldstein, Joshua S. (2001) *War and Gender.* Cambridge: Cambridge University Press.

Greenberg, Marcia E. and Elaine Zuckerman (2009) 'The Gender Dimensions of Post-conflict Reconstruction: The Challenges in Development Aid' in Tony Addison and Tilman Bruck (eds), *Making Peace Work: The Challenges of Social and Economic Reconstruction.* New York NY: Palgrave Macmillan and UNU-WIDER.

Gregoire, Emmanuel (1994) 'Islam and Identity in Maradi (Niger)' in Louis Brenner (ed.), *Muslim Identity and Social Change in Sub-Saharan Africa.* Bloomington IN: Indiana University Press.

Gross, Rita (1996) *Feminism and Religion: An Introduction.* Boston MA: Beacon Press.

Grover, S. C. (2012) *Child Soldier Victims of Genocidal Forcible Transfer.* Berlin: Springer Verlag.

Habila, Helon (2016) *The Chibok Girls: The Boko Haram Kidnappings and Islamist Militancy in Nigeria.* New York NY: Columbia Global Reports.

Hamman, Suleiman, Ibrahim Khalid Mustafa and Kayode Omojuwa (2014) 'The Role of Nigeria in Peacekeeping Operations from 1960 to 2013', *International Affairs and Global Strategy* 21: 42–5.

Handrahan, Lori (2004) 'Conflict, Gender, Ethnicity and Post-conflict Reconstruction', *Security Dialogue* 35 (4): 429–45.

Harnischfeger, Johannes (2014) 'Boko Haram and its Muslim Critics: Observations from Yobe State' in Marc-Antoine Pérouse de Montclos (ed.) *Boko Haram: Islamism, Politics, Security and the State in Nigeria.* Leiden: African Studies Centre and Institut Français de Recherche en Afrique.

Haruna, Abdulkareem (2016) 'Chibok Girls in U.S. "Used by NGOs for Money" – Minister, Parents', *Premium Times*, 9 September.

Hirose, Kentaro, Kosuke Imai and Jason Lyall (2016) 'Civilian Attitudes and Insurgent Tactics in Civil War', *SSRN*, January.

Hoechner, Hannah (forthcoming): *Qur'anic Schools in Northern Nigeria: Everyday Experiences of Youth, Faith, and Poverty.* Cambridge and New York NY: Cambridge University Press for the International African Institute.

Hudson, Valerie and Hilary Matfess (forthcoming) 'In Plain Sight: The Neglected Linkage Between Brideprice, Raiding, and Rebellion', *International Security.*

Hudson, Valerie, Bonnie Ballif-Spanvill, Mary Caprioli and Chad F. Emmett (2012) *Sex and World Peace.* New York NY: Columbia University Press.

Hugo, Nicola (2012) 'Purdah: Separation of the Sexes in Northern Nigeria', *Arcana Intellego*, 13 June.

Human Rights Watch (2009) *Soldiers who Rape, Commanders who Condone.* Washington DC: Human Rights Watch.

— (2014) *'Those Terrible Weeks in Their Camp': Boko Haram Violence against Women and Girls in Northeast Nigeria.* New York NY: Human Rights Watch.

— (2016) 'Northeast Children Robbed of Education', Human Rights Watch, 11 April.

Iaccino, Ludovica (2015) 'Boko Haram: Nigeria Urged to Ease Abortion Laws for Girls Raped by Terrorists', *International Business Times*, 2 July.

Ibukun, Yinka and Michael Olukayode (2015) 'Boko Haram Destruction in Northeast to Cost Nigeria over $1 Billion; 27% of Population Displaced', *Mail & Guardian Africa*, 9 September.

ICG (2016) *Nigeria: Women and the Boko Haram Insurgency.* Africa Report 242. Brussels: International Crisis Group (ICG).

ICTJ (2015) '"My Healing Has Begun:" Uganda Votes to Provide Gender-Sensitive Reparations Fund', International Center for Transitional Justice (ICTJ) blog, 23 April.

ICVA (2015) *NGO Perspective on Humanitarian Response in Level 3 Crises.* Geneva: International Council of Voluntary Agencies (ICVA).

Immigration and Refugee Board of Canada (2000) *Nigeria: The Practice of Purdah in Nigeria and Current Government Attitude Towards It.* Ottawa: Immigration and Refugee Board of Canada.

Information Nigeria (2014) 'Patience Jonathan Orders Arrest of #BringBackOurGirls Abuja Protest Leaders, You Won't Believe Why', *Information Nigeria*, 5 May.

International Alert (2010) *Changing Fortunes: Women's Economic Opportunities in Post-war Northern Uganda.* London: International Alert.

International Organization for Migration (2016) 'Nigeria'. http://nigeria.iom.int/media/news/npc-we-lack-accurate-figures-nigeria%E2%80%99s-population.

Iroegbu, Senator (2016) 'Nigerian Military "Rescues 11,595 Boko Haram Hostages" in March', *This Day*, 6 April.

Jammai, Abdul (2016) 'Amnesty: Nigerian Military Launches "Operation Safe Corridor" for Boko Haram Terrorists', *The Trent Online*, 6 April.

Jefferson, LaShawn R. (2004) *In War as in Peace: Sexual Violence and Women's Status.* Washington DC: Human Rights Watch.

Kane, Ousmane (2003) *Muslim Modernity in Postcolonial Nigeria*. Leiden: E. J. Brill.

Kendhammer, Brandon (2016) *Muslims Talking Politics: Framing Islam, Democracy, and Law in Northern Nigeria*. Chicago IL: University of Chicago.

Knop, Katharina von (2007) 'The Female Jihad: Al Qaeda's Women', *Studies in Conflict and Terrorism* 30 (5): 397–414.

Krähenbühl, Pierre (2011) 'The Militarization of Aid and its Perils', International Committee of the Red Cross, 22 February.

Kuch, Amelia (2016) 'Naturalisation of Burundian Refugees in Tanzania. Thinking Ahead: Displacement, Transition, Solutions', *Forced Migration Review* 52.

Kumar, Deepa (2004) 'War Propaganda and the (Ab)uses of Women: Media Constructions of the Jessica Lynch Story', *Feminist Media Studies* 4 (3): 297–313.

Laache, Fredrik Brogeland (2015) 'Scars of Rape in the DR Congo', *Al Jazeera*, 14 September.

Lake, Milli (2013) 'Organizing Hypocrisy: External Actors and Building Rule of Law in Fragile States'. Paper presented at the American Political Science Association Annual Conference, 29 August–1 September.

— (2014) 'Ending Impunity for Sexual and Gender-based Crimes: The International Criminal Court and Complementarity in the Democratic Republic of Congo'. *African Conflict and Peacebuilding Review* 4 (1): 1–32.

Lake, Milli, Ilot Muthaka and Gabriella Walker (2016) 'Gendering Justice: Opportunity and (Dis)empowerment through Legal Development Aid in the Eastern Democratic Republic of Congo', *Law and Society Review* 50 (3): 539–74.

Laurie, Melissa and Rosalind P. Petchesky (2008) 'Gender, Health, and Human Rights in Sites of Political Exclusion', *Global Public Health* 3 (suppl. 1): 25–41.

Leadership (2016) 'Nigeria: Borno IDPs Decry Poor Living Condition in Camp', *Leadership*, 21 February.

Lubeck, Paul (1985) 'Islamic Protest Under Semi-industrial Capitalism: 'Yan Tatsine Explained', *Africa* 55 (4): 369–89.

Lubeck, Paul and Bryana Britts (2001) 'Muslim Civil Society in Urban Public Spaces: Globalization, Discursive Shifts, and Social Movements' in J. Eade and C Mele (eds), *Understanding the City: Contemporary and Future Perspectives*. Oxford: Blackwell.

Mahdi, Hauwa (2009) *The Hijab in Nigeria, the Woman's Body and the Feminist Private/Public Discourse*. Working Paper. Evanston IL: Institute for the Study of Islamic Thought in Africa, Northwestern University.

Mahmood, Saba (2001) 'Feminist Theory, Embodiment, and the Docile Agent: Some Reflections on the Egyptian Islamic Revival', *Cultural Anthropology* 16 (2): 202–36.

Masquelier, Adeline (2009) *Women and Islamic Revival in a West African Town*. Bloomington IN: Indiana University Press.

Matfess, Hilary (2016a) 'Institutionalizing Instability: The Constitutional Roots of Insecurity in Nigeria's Fourth Republic', *Stability* 5 (1): 1–19.

— (2016b) 'Why Nigeria's Military Make Bad Aid Workers', *IRIN*, 5 July.

Mazumdar, Tulip (2015) 'Chibok Girls "Forced to Join Nigeria's Boko Haram"', BBC News, 29 June.

McKay, Susan (2005) 'Girls as "Weapons of Terror" in Northern Uganda and Sierra Leonean Rebel Fighting Forces', *Studies in Conflict and Terrorism* 28 (5): 385–97.

Meintjes, Sheila, Anu Pillay and Meredeth Turshen (2002) *The Aftermath: Women in Post-conflict Transformation*. London and Chicago IL: Zed Books.

Melander, Erik (2005) 'Political Gender Equality and State Human Rights Abuse', *Journal of Peace Research* 42 (2): 149–66.

Mercy Corps (2016) *'Motivations and Empty Promises': Voices of Former Boko Haram Combatants and Nigerian Youth*. Washington DC: Mercy Corps.

Mitchell, Neil J., Sabine C. Carey and Christopher K. Butler (2014) 'The Impact of Pro-government Militias on Human Rights Violations', *International Interactions* 40 (5): 812–36.

Moodley, Kiran (2014) 'This Is What it Looks Like When Boko Haram Comes to Town', *The Independent*, 11 November.

MSF (2015) 'Nigeria: Cholera Spreads in Camps for Displaced People in Borno State', Médecins Sans Frontières (MSF), 17 September.

— (2016) 'Doctors Without Borders Warns of Humanitarian Crisis in Nigeria's Bama', *AfricaNews*, 23 June.

Mshelizza, Ibrahim (2009) 'More Than 700 Killed in Nigeria Clashes: Red Cross', Reuters, 2 August.

Narayan, Deepa with Raj Patel, Kai Schafft, Anne Rademacher and Sarah Koch-Schulte (2000) *Voices of the Poor: Can Anyone Hear Us?* Washington DC: World Bank.

New Internationalist (1999) *Landmines Fact Sheet*. Oxford: New Internationalist.

Nigeria Social Violence Project (2015) 'The Boko Haram Insurgency: a Mixed Methods Approach'. Paper presented at the American Political Science Association Annual Conference, 5 September. https://convention2.allacademic.com/one/apsa/apsa15/index.php?cmd=Online+Program+View+Paper&selected_paper_id=1000886&PHPSESSID=5sdsa2kqbsnbkakm99h32opt6o.

— (2016) 'Datatset'. Washington DC: Paul H. Nitze School of Advanced International Studies, Johns Hopkins University.

Nigerian Gazette (2014) 'Photos from the Legaçy Housing Project (Phase 1)', *Nigerian Gazette*, 1 June.

Nigerian NGO CEDAW Coalition (2008) 'The Nigeria CEDAW NGO Coalition Shadow Report Submitted to the 41st Session of the United Nations Committee on the Elimination of All Forms of Discrimination Against Women Holding at the United Nations Plaza New York between June 30 – July 18, 2008'. https://www.fidh.org/IMG/pdf/Nigeria-report.pdf.

Nigerian Sun (2014) 'Nigerian Government "Called Off Deal" to Free Kidnapped Girls', *Nigerian Sun*, 27 May.

NOI Polls (2016) 'Most IDPs Suffer from Lack of Food, Potable Water and Healthcare', NOI Polls, 20 September. http://www.noi-polls.com/root/index.php?pid=403&parentid=14&ptid=1.

Nossiter, Adam (2015) 'Boko Haram Militants Raped Hundreds of Female Captives in Nigeria', *The New York Times*, 18 May.

NPC and ICF International (2014) *Nigeria Demographic and Health Survey 2013*. Abuja, Nigeria, and Rockville MD: National Population Commission (NPC) and ICF International. https://dhsprogram.com/pubs/pdf/FR293/FR293.pdf.

OCHA (2012) *What is Gender Equality in Humanitarian Action?* New York NY: United Nations Office for the Coordination of Humanitarian Affairs (OCHA).

— (2015) *Humanitarian Bulletin: Nigeria*. Issue 8, November. New York NY: United Nations Office for the Coordination of Humanitarian Affairs (OCHA).

— (2016a) *Lake Chad Basin Emergency: Humanitarian Needs and Response Overview 2016 (January 2016)*. New York NY: United Nations Office for the Coordination of Humanitarian Affairs (OCHA).

— (2016b) *Nigeria: Humanitarian Funding Overview (as of 29 June 2016)*. New York NY: United Nations Office for the Coordination of Humanitarian Affairs (OCHA).

— (2016c) *Nigeria: Humanitarian Funding Overview (as of July 2016)*. New York NY: United Nations Office for the Coordination of Humanitarian Affairs (OCHA).

— (2017) 'Nigeria – North-east: Humanitarian Emergency'. Situation Report 12. New York NY: United Nations Office for the Coordination of Humanitarian Affairs (OCHA).

Odeny, Millicent (2013) *Improving Access to Land and Strengthening Women's Land Rights in Africa*. Washington DC: World Bank Conference on Land and Poverty.

Ogunkolade, Olutosin O. (2011) *Great Words for Great Living*. Bloomington IN: AuthorHouse.

OHCHR (n.d.) 'Questions and Answers About IDPs'. Office of the United Nations High Commissioner for Human Rights (OHCHR). http://www.ohchr.org/EN/Issues/IDPersons/Pages/Issues.aspx#4 (accessed 2016).

Okeke, Uju Peace (2013) 'Child Marriage: A Breach of Human Rights', Women's UN Report Network, 12 August.

Olanreqaju, Timothy (2016) 'Borno Govt, VSF to Rebuild Dikwa with N500m', *The Sun*, 9 May.

Olokor, Friday, Adelani Adepegba, Leke Baiyewu and Ramon Oladimeji (2016) 'Chibok Girls: Rights Groups Attack FG as Police Halt BBOG Protest', *Punch Nigeria*, 7 September.

Olson, Mancur (1993) 'Dictatorship, Democracy, and Development', *American Political Science Review* 87: 567–76.

Opejobe, Seun (2016a) 'PDP Leadership Crises: Sheriff Created Boko Haram', *Daily Post*, 24 June.

— (2016b) 'Army Rescue 5, 000 Boko Haram Captives', *Premium Times*, 26 June.

Open Society Justice Initiative and the Network on Police Reform in Nigeria (2010) *Criminal Force: Torture, Abuse, and Extrajudicial Killings by the Nigeria Police Force*. New York NY: Open Society Justice Initiative.

O'Reilly, Marie (2015) *Why Women? Inclusive Security and Peaceful Societies*. Washington DC: Inclusive Security.

Organisation of African Unity (1969) *OAU Convention Governing the Specific Aspects of Refugee Problems in Africa*. Addis Ababa: Organisation of African Unity (OAU).

Osborne, Samuel (2016) '800 Boko Haram Militants Surrender to Nigerian Military, General Claims', *The Independent*, 7 April.

Oxfam (2013) 'Gender Issues in Conflict and Humanitarian Action'. Oxfam Humanitarian Policy Note. Oxford: Oxfam.

Oyelere, Ruth Uwaifo (2007) *Within and Between Gender Disparities in Income and Education Benefits from Democracy*. Discussion paper. Bonn: Institute for the Study of Labor (IZA).

Pastner, Carroll McC. (1974) 'Accommodations to Purdah: The Female Perspective', *Journal of Marriage and Family* 36 (2): 408–14.

Pérouse de Montclos, Marc-Antoine (ed.) (2014) *Boko Haram: Islamism, Politics, Security and the State in Nigeria*. Leiden: African Studies Centre and Institut Français de Recherche en Afrique.

Premium Times (2014) 'Boko Haram: Victims Support Fund Target Overshot by N8.79 Billion – Jonathan', *Premium Times*, 2 August.

— (2015) 'Senate Approves Life Sentence for Rape, Underage Sex', *Premium Times*, 4 June.

— (2016a) 'Nigeria Sacks Guardian of Escaped Chibok Girls in U.S., Hands Girls to Embassy', *Premium Times*, 31 May.

— (2016b) 'Insurgency: This is What Army Plans to Do to Repentant Boko Haram Members', *Premium Times*, 16 June.

Punch Nigeria (2016) 'Borno to Close IDP Camps in May 2017 – Shettima', *Punch Nigeria*, 25 November.

Quadri, Aryam Omolara (2015) *Women and Political Participation in the 2015 General Elections: Fault Lines and Mainstreaming Exclusion*. Lagos: INEC Nigeria.

Rachele, Sister, interview by Paulo Brenna (2000) *Sister the Rebels are Here*. Brest Inc.

Renne, Elisha (2013) *Veiling in Africa*. Bloomington IN: Indiana University Press.

Reuters (2014a) 'Nigeria Police Arrest Protest Leader for Abducted Girls', *Reuters*, 5 May.

— (2014b) 'Boko Haram Offers to Swap Kidnapped Nigerian Girls for Prisoners', *Reuters*, 12 May.

Ricks, Thomas (2016) 'The Lesson of Colombia's Demobilization of FARC Can Help Us Work against ISIS', *Foreign Policy*, 28 January.

Riley, Robin Lee (2013) *Depicting the Veil: Transnational Sexism and the War on Terror*. London: Zed Books.

Rusyana, Ayi Yunus (n.d.) 'Poverty from Islam Perspective'. Ayi Yunus blog. https:// punayi.wordpress.com/2011/01/20/poverty-from-islam-perspective/.

Sahara Reporters (2016a) 'ICPC Arraigns Former "Sharia Governor" Senator Ahmed Sani Yerima Over Corruption', Sahara Reporters, 20 January.

— (2016b) 'How High Stakes Negotiations Led to Release of 21 Chibok Girls', Sahara Reporters, 13 October.

— (2017) 'Boko Haram Commanders Released in Swap Deal for 82 Chibok Girls Issue Threat to Bomb Abuja', Sahara Reporters, 12 May.

Sakhonchik, Alena, Isabel Santagostino Recavarren and Paula Tavares (2015) *Closing the Gap: Improving Laws Protecting Women from Violence*. Washington DC: Women, Business, and the Law, World Bank.

Sieff, Kevin (2016) 'They Were Freed from Boko Haram's Rape Camps. But Their Nightmare Isn't Over', *The Washington Post*, 3 April.

Smith, David (2010) 'More than 700 Inmates Escape During Attack on Nigerian Prison', *The Guardian*, 8 September.

Smith, Mike (2015) *Boko Haram: Inside Nigeria's Unholy War*. London: I. B. Tauris & Co.

Smith, Mikey (2014) '"We See Our Own Daughters in Missing Nigeria Girls": Michelle Obama's Emotional White House Address to the World', *Mirror*, 10 May.

Sokoto, Sultan (2016) *A Conversation with the Sultan of Sokoto: Peace and Development Initiatives, Challenges, and Potential Prospects in Nigeria*. Washington DC: Africa Program, Wilson Center.

Spang, Lyra (2009) 'The Humanitarian Faction: The Politicization and Targeting of Aid Organizations in War Zones', *International Affairs Review* 18 (1). http:// www.iar-gwu.org/node/63.

Stein, Chris (2015) 'Hope Returns for Some Chibok Girls, a New Life at University', *Voice of America*, 5 February.

Susskind, Yifat and Stella Duque (2016) 'Women Are on the Frontline of Making Peace in Colombia Last', *The Guardian*, 18 July.

The Denver Post (2013) 'Kony's LRA Has Killed More Than 100,000: UN', *The Denver Post*, 20 May.

The Economist (2010) 'Stagnation Stirs Everything Up', *The Economist*, 28 January.

— (2012) 'Violence in Nigeria: The Worst Yet', *The Economist*, 23 January.

— (2014a) 'A Clueless Government', *The Economist*, 10 May.

— (2014b) 'Education in Northern Nigeria Mixing the Modern and the Traditional', *The Economist*, 26 July.

Thurston, Alex (2015) 'Nigeria's Mainstream Salafis between Boko Haram and the State', *Islam in Africa* 6 (1–2): 109–34.

Today Nigeria (2016) 'Salkida Freed after Boko Haram Questioning', *Today Nigeria*, 7 September.

Tripp, Aili Mari (2012) *Women's Political Empowerment in Statebuilding and Peacebuilding: A Baseline Study.* Ottawa and London: International Development Research Centre and Department for International Development.

— (2013) 'Women and Politics in Africa Today', Democracy in Africa blog. http://democracyinafrica.org/women-politics-africa-today/.

— (2015) *Women and Power in Postconflict Africa.* Cambridge: Cambridge University Press.

Tripp, Aili Mari and Alice Kang (2008) *The Global Impact of Quotas: On the Fast Track to Increased Female Legislative Representation.* Lincoln NE: University of Nebraska.

Tripp, Aili Mari, Myra Marx Ferree and Christina Ewig (2013) *Gender, Violence, and Human Security: Critical Feminist Perspectives.* New York NY: NYU Press.

True, Jacqui (2016) 'Post-conflict Economic Reform is a Women, Peace and Security Issue', Progress in Political Economy blog. http://wilpf.org/post-conflict-economic-reform-is-a-women-peace-and-security-issue/.

UK AID (2012) *Gender in Nigeria Report 2012: Improving the Lives of Girls and Women in Nigeria.* London: UK AID.

— (2015) *Nigeria Men and Gender Equality Survey: NiMAGES.* London: UK AID and ProMundo Global.

Umoru, Henry (2016) 'SGF, Babachir Lawal Awarded N220m Grass Removal to his Firm', *Vanguard Nigeria*, 18 December.

UN (2014) 'Security Council, Adopting Resolution 2175 (2014), Sets Out Steps to Halt "Increasingly Common" Attacks on Humanitarian Workers'. New York NY: United Nations.

— (2016) 'Banki: Inter-agency Assessment Report', United Nations, 28 June.

Unah, Linus (2017) '#IStandWithNigeria Protests: "We Can Change Nigeria and We Are Coming Together To Do Just That"', *African Arguments*, 18 February.

UN DDR Resource Center (2006) *Women, Gender and DDR.* New York NY: United Nations.

UNDP (2015) *Gender Equality Index 2015.* New York NY: United Nations Development Programme (UNDP).

UNESCO (2012) 'Reaching the 2015 Literacy Target: Delivering on the Promise! High-level International Round Table on Literacy'. Symposium, UNESCO, Paris, 6–7 September. http://www.unesco.org/new/en/unesco/events/education-events/?tx_browser_pi1%5BshowUid%5D=6871&cHash=46f69dccc7.

UNHCR (2007) 'Advisory Opinion on the Extraterritorial Application of *Non-Refoulement* Obligations under the 1951 Convention relating to the Status of Refugees and its 1967 Protocol'. Geneva: Office of the United Nations High Commissioner for Refugees (UNHCR).

UNICEF and International Alert (2016) *'Bad Blood': Perceptions of Children Born of Conflict-related Sexual Violence and Women and Girls Associated with Boko Haram in Northeast Nigeria.* Washington DC: UNICEF and International Alert.

UN News Centre (2017) 'Security Council Wraps Up Lake Chad Basin Visit; Stops in "Epicentre" of Boko Haram Violence', UN News Centre, 6 March. http://www.un.org/apps/news/story.asp?NewsID=56298#.WTofOcbTWUk.

UN Refugee Agency (2015) *UNHCR Concern about Return of Nigerians, Shrinking Humanitarian Space.* Geneva: Office of the United Nations High Commissioner for Refugees (UNHCR).

UN Women (2015) *The Effect of Gender Equity Programming on Humanitarian Outcomes.* New York NY: United Nations.

USAID (n.d.) *Demographic and Health Survey.* Washington DC: USAID.

US Department of State (2013) 'Leahy Vetting: Law, Policy, Process'. Washington DC: US Department of State.

— (2015) *2014 Human Rights Reports: Nigeria.* Washington DC: US Department of State.

Utas, Mats (2005) 'Victimacy, Girlfriending, Soldiering: Tactic Agency in a Young Woman's Social Navigation of the Liberian War Zone', *Anthropological Quarterly* 78 (2): 403–30.

Vaughn, Olufemi and Suraiya Zubair Banu (2014) *Muslim Women's Rights in Northern Nigeria.* Occasional paper. Washington DC: Woodrow Wilson Center.

Voices 4 Change (2014) *Strategy on Working with Religious and Traditional Institutions and Leaders.* Abuja: Voices 4 Change.

— (2015) *Being a Man in Nigeria: Perceptions and Realities.* Abuja: Voices 4 Change. http://www.v4c-nigeria.com/wp-content/uploads/2014/09/BeingaManInNigeria_Perceptions_and_Realities_25_09_20152.pdf.

Wader, Mohamed M., Tanko Yusuf Dahiru and Mukhtar Imam (2015) 'The Myth and Reality of Women's Political Marginalization in Nigeria', *International Journal of Humanities and Social Sciences Invention* 4 (12): 1–15.

Wakili, Isiaka (2015) 'Nigeria: Boko Haram: Buhari Releases N5bn for Victims Support Fund', *Daily Trust*, 1 August.

Walker, Andrew (2012) *What is Boko Haram?* Washington DC: United States Institute of Peace.

— (2016) *'Eat the Heart of the Infidel': The Harrowing of Nigeria and the Rise of Boko Haram.* London: Hurst.

Warner, Gregory (2014) 'Nigerian Abductions Part of a Terrible Pattern in African Conflicts', KPBS, 17 May.

Watteville, Nathalie de (2002) *Addressing Gender Issues in Demobilization and Reintegration Programs.* Washington DC: World Bank.

Wolfe, Lauren (2014) 'The Lost Girls', *Foreign Policy*, 5 May.

Wood, Elisabeth Jean (2015) 'Social Mobilization and Violence in Civil War and their Social Legacies' in Donatella della Porta and Mario Diani (eds), *The Oxford Handbook of Social Movements.* Oxford: Oxford University Press.

World Bank (n.d.) *Changing Gender Relations in the Household.* Washington DC: World Bank.

Yoon, Mi Yung (2004) 'Explaining Women's Legislative Representation in Sub-Saharan Africa', *Legislative Studies Quarterly* 29 (3): 447–68.

Zakaria, Yakabu (2001) 'Entrepreneurs at Home: Secluded Muslim Women and Hidden Economic Activities in Northern Nigeria', *Nordic Journal of African Studies* 10 (1): 107–23.

Zenn, Jacob and Elizabeth Pearson (2014) 'Women, Gender and the Evolving Tactics of Boko Haram', *Journal of Terrorism Research* 5 (1). http://jtr.st-andrews.ac.uk/article/10.15664/jtr.828/.

Zongwe, Dunia Prince (2012) 'The New Sexual Violence Legislation in the Congo: Dressing Indelible Scars on Human Dignity', *African Studies Review* 55 (2): 37–57.

INDEX